KANGAROO

YUZ ALESHKOVSKY

KANGAROO

Translated by Tamara Glenny

FARRAR, STRAUS & GIROUX
NEW YORK

To my son

KANGAROO

*L*ET'S BEGIN at the beginning, Kolya, though I really have no idea whether this ridiculous story can have a beginning or an end at all . . .

That year—1949—I was the unhappiest man on earth. Maybe in the whole solar system. Of course I was the only one who knew this, but then personal unhappiness isn't like being world famous—you don't need the recognition of all mankind for it.

So here goes. It was Monday and I was on my way over to the workshop with a bunch of veils I'd finished, when the phone rang. I fooled around with the veils to show I was still some use to society even if I was disabled—that's what those workshops are all about, anyway—and I kind of liked dripping those little black drops of India ink on the cotton net. It's peaceful; you sit, you drip, you remember the good times— drinking that great White Horse scotch with the chief of customs in Singapore, for instance.

So the phone rings, long distance. I pick it up. "Gulyaev speaking," I say cheerfully. "Alias Sidorov, alias Katzenelenbogen, von Patoff, Ekrantz, Petyan-chikov, alias Etcetera!"

"Forget the jokes, you reactionary jerk," a voice replies. I turn quietly toward the window. I won't be seeing freedom much longer, I can tell, so I'd better get a good look at it now.

"Be here in exactly one hour. There'll be a pass waiting for you. Twenty-four hours in the cooler for every minute you're late. And no faking temporary insanity this time, either. That theory of yours about the two Gauguins and a Repin disappearing from that actress's bedroom by centrifugal force from the earth's rotation won't work. It won't work! Capito, Citizen Etcetera?"

"I have to bring my things?" I ask.

"Right," says this KGB louse, after a pause. "And bring some Indian tea, grade A. I don't have time to shop. We'll brew some chifir."

The asshole slams down the receiver, and I stand there listening to the mournful beeping: beep-beep-beep, sharp little splinters piercing your heart. Then I yanked the receiver out by its roots—believe it or not, it went on beeping by itself on the floor for a whole minute. Like it was breathing its last. And why not? Our nails and beards go on growing after we die, right? Hey, Kolya, if I croak before you do—please God—you put an Era electric shaver and a pair of nail clippers in my coffin, okay?

But you know as well as I do—if we reacted to these official screwups like big executives or certain Jews, we'd both have had twenty heart attacks and strokes and colon cancers by now. I kicked the dead receiver under the couch. I have to rejoice in the moments left to me before I give myself up for Christ knows what—or how long. God, Kolya, I can still remember every second of those two hours it took me to get to the Lubyanka. They were some seconds—even the *fractions* of the seconds and the fractions of the fractions. I had to say goodbye to all those dear faces in my family album, didn't I? And I had to get a last look at those free sparrows hopping around outside the window. I wiped the poplar-blossom fluff off the Van Gogh. I decided where to stash the gold and the dough. But fuck the utility bills, if you'll excuse the expression. Academician Nesmeyanov, that great chemist, can pay for the gas and let Einstein himself pay for the electricity—that's his specialty.

After that, I got everything ready for my return to freedom—set the table for two with the cognac bottle a bit closer to my place. It crossed my mind that there'd be a few more stars on the label after I'd done my stretch. One year, one star, hey, this brandy's going to be Special, Extra Special—but even if it gets to be Napoleon I'll get out to drink it. I'll be drinking to my lifeblood with that sweet young thing in the white pinafore down there on the street, skipping out of school—she went into the bakery for something.

I didn't bother making the bed. Why waste precious minutes, like pennies stuck in a piggybank? If things go right, someday I'll have another chance to make it. Then I sat down for a moment like you're supposed to before a long trip. Only fifteen minutes since the phone call. I said a little prayer. Switched off the refrigerator. Then I saw a bedbug. You know, I was going to squash it, Kolya? Then I felt kind of sorry for it. Excuse me, I said. I'm going off to Horror Country—there won't be anyone around to bite for a while. You have my pity, you little living creature, for you were meant to live five hundred years and now you're going to kick off prematurely. No blood ration, see? So I scooped up the little sucker and carefully pushed it under my neighbor Zoya's door. That took another half a minute at least. Then I took the geranium out to the kitchen, packed my suitcase, and left the house.

Well, get this. I leave the house, I stand at the entrance, and I can't *mcve*. I mean, my legs aren't weak, they just won't move. Why should they, when you think about it? They can't choose which way they're going. The route's been mapped out by Lieutenant Colonel Kidalla, and who wants to go anywhere when there's no choice about it. I know, Kidalla said one hour, plus twenty-four in the cooler for every minute you're late. But what the hell. No problem. My soul's as peaceful as my legs. Lieutenant Colonel Kidalla has mapped the route for my soul, too—the way, the path, the highway, it doesn't matter. You might say my destiny.

I went, in the end, but kind of without noticing it. Life had given me such a kick in the nuts, Kolya, I swear to God I couldn't tell if I existed or not. Then some old bag jumps out at me on the street. Thinks I'm giving the Karpo Marx portrait in a grocery-store window a funny look.

"I've had my eye on you," this snake says. "If you're not one of us, you should go right along and report yourself to the authorities. Maybe," this four-eyed cootie goes on, "you don't care for the way the world's changed? Then you'd better say so! Here and now! I've seen your type before—gutless know-it-alls, giving us the finger behind our backs, besmirching your enemy with impotent spit and thinking you're such big shots!"

Then this old douchebag called me "a worthless good-for-nothing." But the really terrible part, Kolya, was that she wouldn't stop. She had to know whose side I was on. So I talked through my nose like I had the clap and told her my side was where the furniture was older and softer. I was headed for the VD clinic for a Wassermann test subsequent to fornication with an attractive descendant of native remnants of capitalism. I purposely spat all over her face; it occurred to me it wouldn't be a bad idea to get busted for something ordinary like hooliganism—Article 74. But if the Cheka's after you they'll poke through every nook and cranny in the gulag, peek up the asshole of every town in the boonies if they have to. They find whoever they're looking for.

About the furniture. I pulled this dressing table here out of one of the Kiev street barricades in 1916. It's worth as much as a Volga sedan on the black market. But I haven't sold it, buddy, and I'm never going to. Marie-Antoinette in person used to sit behind it when she combed her hair.

So tell me, Kolya, what's happening to our planet? Why are they chopping the heads off queens? Why? What for? And some old bag doesn't like the way I eye-balled Karpo's picture! Don't tell me to keep cool. I'm not an epileptic. My nerves are stronger than the armature on the Stalingrad hydroelectric plant. Here's looking at you, kid. Down the hatch! Thank God you and I are normal. Just remember, the normal guys are the patient ones, the ones who carefully dismantle the barricades when all the hellish racket's over,

7

so that not even one leg of a simple, battered old Viennese chair gets knocked off. And the abnormal ones are the other way around: those scumbags who think they know just what they want out of life. But what can they want, those guys who drag chairs out of houses onto the cobblestones? People relax on those chairs! They drag out *tables* as well, Kolya—the same tables our fellow human beings eat, nosh, feed, munch, gobble, in a word, nourish themselves at! And then finally they drag beds out on the muddy streets: divans and ottomans and couches and inner-spring mattresses and straw pallets, the stuff we spend a third—some of us a half, even—of our lives on, what we use for the wedding night, the deathbed, for sick people, for hurt people to weep on, for mothers to give birth on, for lovers to screw on. I tell you, they're abnormal. Plus they're always squabbling about who should be on which side of the barricades.

But that's enough about them.

I got rid of the old bag and hit the road again. Marching along in a farewell bid to freedom and liberty. Breathing in that good old carbon monoxide. Sipping at a glass of seltzer. Smoking Herzegovina Flor, just like Big Brother up there in the Kremlin, who loves it so much. Checking out the chicks. Bye! So I mosey along, not wasting a second of the time I've got left, like I said, not even a fraction of those seconds. As I got nearer the Lubyanka I started to feel like that guy on Death Row who'd been given a crust and told it's his last piece of bread on earth. This guy was a physicist—a sly old fox. He divided the crust into pieces, and the pieces into pellets, and the pellets into crumbs. The executioner's begging him to finish.

"Hey, quicker, asshole. I should have settled your hash hours ago—it's quitting time, for chrissake."

But the guy says, "The law says I can chew my last crumb. Leave me alone, goddamn it, or I'll call the public prosecutor. You got any water to go with this?"

So what could the executioner do? He brings him a mug of water. The guy pops a crumb in his mouth, rolls it around with his tongue, sucks it, smacks his lips, weeps with the pleasure of his hunger for life. The executioner's really steamed, he's bitching about missing the Spartacus v. Army hockey game and how he has guests coming over from the Irkutsk jail. But the guy's threatened not to sign his death warrant if he stops him from munching his bread and drinking his water. You know, not even Beria himself, in person, had the right to prevent a condemned man from consuming his food. He *liked* pretty rules, was what it was. For instance, before looking up a zek's ass, the inspector had to say, "Excuse me, Citizen or Citizeness So-and-so." Unfortunately, this rule doesn't get observed too often in our country. In practice, they only used it for Tupolev, Korolyov, and Voznesensky, the chairman of State Planning.

Anyway, the executioner waits one hour, two, four—he's threatening to shoot the guy some special way they only showed him at the continuing-education classes—he calls the authorities, but no way they'd give permission to shoot until the condemned man's eaten his last crumb and swallowed the last drop of water. Finally, he doesn't have a single crumb left. But get this, Kolya. This physicist announces, "Now I'll start on the molecules, and then the atoms." And he threatened the executioner again that he'd let the bosses know that the executioner had actually denied the existence of matter—that he'd objectively shown himself to be a Trojan horse of subjective idealism in our model top-security jail, by demonstrating criminal doubt about the officially recognized structure of the material world. The fucking executioner turned yellow and his eyes overflowed with green pus. He said to the guy, "Let's see you gobble when there isn't an atom left, you bastard. You're as good as dead."

So the guy says, "Then, with your permission, I'll start on the electron, which is, in Lenin's own words, practically inexhaustible. You may disagree, and then let's see how the Ministry of State Security's department of theoretical physics reacts to this kind of provocation. Looks like we have an entrenched case of obscurantism here," he adds. "See how slyly it's established itself and is shooting the most committed materialists in the head!"

You better believe it, Kolya, twenty hours went by like this. Twenty hours of life from 300 grams of stale bread and a mug of water! Then—zap—they commuted the condemned man's sentence to twenty-five years and took him away to a "research institution." Alive. And why? Because you should never be in too much of a hurry for anything.

Well, there I was, like the condemned physicist, sucking on my last precious seconds like caramels, and I suddenly understood, man, I *knew* that my time on the outside had run out. Goodbye, Freedom Time, I said, and I'll tell you, I was shaking with fear. I was shaking because it's pretty scary crossing over into Jail Time just like that. But when I'd done it—asking for my pass at the window, walking up the steps, shaking some general's hand (he stared at me for the longest time, I guess trying to decide which industry I was minister of), putting a smile on my face so I'd look good, knocking on the door with the yellow sign saying KIDALLA, I. I. lettered in red—when I'd done it I guess my fear just melted away. I was even a little curious—what did this red jack stand for in my deck? I go in. "Greetings," I say, "to a cool head and a warm heart!"

"Come in, come in, Citizen Etcetera. Remember I promised you twenty-four hours in the cooler for every minute's delay, faggot?"

"Sure I remember, Citizen Prosecutor for Special Cases," I say. "But I regret to inform you that you can't pull that number on me today. You told me to pick up a package of Indian tea, and the stores are closed for lunch from one till two. Hence the delay. *Excusez-moi.*"

"What do you mean, lunch?" He was just a baby when it came to the ordinary details of living, Kolya. But what do you expect from a guy who spent his whole life interrogating, nothing but interrogations around the clock until he was due for a vacation. Guys like us count our lives by days and nights—they count theirs by vacations. Which was why I had to explain to Kidalla what "lunch break" meant, while inside I was rejoicing about grabbing a whole extra hour for myself. I'm no sucker—I brought the tea from my apartment. Then we stared at each other for the longest time. We were remembering the first time we met, long before the war, when Kidalla caught me and my buddy red-handed at the Kievsky train station.

It was a dumb job, but it called for Comrade Cutthroat. Some little speculator's wife had been begging me to rub out her husband—for a lot of dough. I have

ing taxes. They killed him and fed him to the lions, tigers, panthers, and leopards a little piece at a time. Last night. This index finger's all that's left. His wife and some local party colleagues identified it. Binezon wagged it at them more than once when he caught them negotiating deals."

"Symbolic, isn't it. Comrade Binezon leaving behind an index finger, not a miserable little pinky. The enemy will never feed the party and the Central Committee to the wild beasts. We're Bolsheviks, not early Christians. The Soviet Union isn't ancient Rome. They can't have it both ways. That's the end of this New Economic Policy. Brush up on industrialization and collectivization. You've got your orders," said Stalin.

So you see, Kolya, if I hadn't fed Binezon's hand to the tiger that night, Russian history could have gone a totally different route and private enterprise would have beaten out that dumb, bloody, Stalinist socialism. It's all my fault and I'll never forgive myself. Anyway, we hightailed it out of that zoo and picked up a couple of broads. I'd just goosed this conductress I knew and given her our tickets when I hear those fatal words "Hands up!"

I put 'em up. It was Kidalla who frisked me—he was only a lieutenant in those days. Here's what happened, Kolya. That cheap hooker the speculator's wife took some stud straight home with her after *Swan Lake*. Just picture her reaction: he's on top of her, she's moaning away, going to come any second—and I'll tell you, she never came easily—when wham, in walks her husband, alive and well, three hundred stark-naked pounds of him, cock standing at attention. Well, he sees a pretty amazing tableau unfolding right there on his little old bed. The boyfriend—they found out he was a jittery left-wing deviationist—hollered "Halt! Who goes there?" and pumped some hot lead into Gulyenka on the spot. He wanted to scram, of course, but no such luck. The bitch gripped him between her thighs like a vise, and wouldn't let go till she came.

Then she made him tie her up and beat her, to complete the picture. The stud did as he was told, gave the widow what she'd been asking for, and took off. She kicked up a terrible racket, and along came the Cheka. So that's how I met Kidalla. That miserable hustler Kitty gave him me and my buddy's descriptions and cooked up an incredible story about how we'd viciously raped her, poor baby, right in front of her dear husband. Then we'd blown him to bits, swiped all the valuables, raped her again, tied her up, and beat it. They really throw the book at you for that kind of rap. All the evidence was against us. Can you imagine it? Of course, I didn't know at the time what had really happened, so I testified to Kidalla that we'd doped Gulyenka with chloroform, lifted his signet ring, and made off. Of course, we'd be glad to confess to fraud, blackmail, and purchasing a dead hairy hand from the pilferers of personal property at the morgue.

"We've got a cast-iron alibi," I told Kidalla.

"I've got a blowtorch that'll melt your cast-iron alibi," Kidalla replied.

To which I riposted, "I've got a ray gun that's bigger than your blowtorch!"

For that, I got an ashtray (once used by Stolypin) on the cranium. I wiped the blood off and stuck to my story. "We had better things to do than kill the old guy. And you want to make this a felony, but with the rape it's a political offense. What's the game?"

Just then Kogan the dentist arrived. While Gulyenka was being murdered, my pal and I were passing Kogan a little gold for his cavities. Thank the Lord that Jews have always loved to bargain! We haggled for two hours straight. And Kidalla wasn't in a position to doubt a guy who'd made false teeth for Lenin, Bukharin, Rykov, Zinoviev, and Kamenev. He's hesitating—thinking about it.

"Lay a trap for her," I suggest. "Tell her you found pubic hairs in her antique bed. They aren't Gulyenka's or mine or my buddy's, they belong to someone the agency's after for the attempted assassination of Krupskaya and Zemlyachka. And tell her if she denies it she'll be up for aiding and abetting an enemy of the people," I added.

I have to admit, Kolya, that cunt amazed me. She stuck to her story when we had the official confrontation. "They raped me, they murdered him, they stole everything!" Then, in a stroke of genius, I asked her, "Did you or did you not come during the first and second violations?"

She blushed and stammered, and said, "Yes, I did." This was taken down in evidence. Then I said, "How could you testify that the rapes lasted five minutes each and say you came both times, when according to my personal information it actually takes you at least forty-seven minutes to come? Something doesn't fit here." I demanded they conduct an experiment on Kitty and me, but she caved in before we could start and gave them the description of her stud. They picked him up the next day, watching *Raymonda* at the Bolshoi. This time Kidalla got the right guy—he really had gone there to shoot Kaganovich (a great ballet fan, so they tell us). So he threw me and my pal out and didn't press charges. But the bastard said I owed him one.

After that, he hauled me in a couple of times, at the Ethiopian embassy and a diplomat's dacha in the Crimea. Both times he let me go. "Out, dear Etcetera" —he liked this best of all my aliases—"until the time comes. I'm saving you for a very important case," he said.

γ OU TRY to imagine my life now, Kolya. A streetcar goes off the rails somewhere, the perpetrator disappears, and I wait for them to tell me to come with my things. I wait one year. Two. They bump off Kirov. This is it, I think, my very important case at last! Funny thing, though: they don't arrest me. That really got to me. What could possibly be more important than the Kirov case? And they don't want me? I couldn't figure it out. Anyway, I'm still waiting. Safety-razor blades went off the market—I'm waiting. Meat grinders disappeared—I'm waiting. Boris Goldstein the violinist got mugged in the Arcade department store—I'm waiting. The kulaks murdered Pavlik Morozov—I'm waiting. The cotton crop failed somewhere—I'm still waiting. Son of a bitch! What they can do to an ordinary guy! I wait, and wait, and wait. Maxim Gorky—I'm waiting. Dzhambul got the clap at the Hotel Metropole—I'm waiting. They found out about us in Spain—I'm waiting.

I'm quietly going bananas. Believe it or not, I started longing for my very own special case. So get on with it, pricks! What are you dragging your feet for when this is your chance to realize all your reactionary plans and plots and diversions and sabotage? What are you waiting for, you lousy creeps? Shut your mouth, Kolya. Quit telling me to cool it or you can find some other international crook to spout his memoirs—if there are any more. Put yourself in my shoes. This agonized waiting is interfering with my real work. The years fly past. I have gambling debts in Italy, Switzerland, Canada, Siam, and the Udmurt Autonomous Republic. Like a jerk I got involved in a game of gin by phone. It was organized by a Yank named Jerry. They called him Beau because he had bandy legs—get it? I walked into it like a lamb to the slaughter, Kolya. An idealist. No good anymore. When I was banker, I didn't cheat once. And Beau was stiffing me. I never dreamed he'd stoop to screwing me in a gentlemanly game of gin. Then Vasya Clemenceau hung him up with a telephone wire in Tokyo.

Go on, put yourself in my shoes, Kolya. 1936—I'm waiting. Ordzhonikidze—I'm waiting. Seventeenth Congress—I'm waiting. 1937. Lake Hassan. Manchukuo. The sinking of the *Chelyuskin*—I'm waiting. They get Levanevsky, or he disappears—I'm still waiting. Krupskaya. Chkalov. The White Finns . . . they get almost everyone *except* me. There're more paddy wagons on the streets than buses, and they're all bursting at the seams. Next stop Kolyma, citizens, get your tickets here, no exit from the last car. Maybe they forgot about me. Maybe Kidalla got pinched himself—they gobble each other up like spiders. No such luck. I waited on Dzerzhinsky Square across from the Lubyanka three days straight. Kidalla came out of the entrance, looked up at the sky suspiciously, and plopped

They didn't get their raglan coats with silver buttons for nothing. The bastards sure knew how to make up their cases.

Later, Kidalla showed me the electronic computer that helped cook these things up—mine in particular. They fed it various data about me, the all-conquering teachings of Marx–Lenin–Stalin, the Soviet era, the Iron Curtain, Socialist Realism, the struggle for peace, cosmopolitanism, the subversive activities of the CIA and the FBI, the number of workdays on collective farms, Tito the hireling of imperialism, and it brought up the very important case yours truly got involved in. More about that later. The assassination attempts on Joseph Vissarionovich I flushed right down the can, pardon my French. Ditto the ones on Kaganovich, Malenkov, Molotov, and all three together. And if I felt that way about them, would I be taking on the entire organization of an armed attack on Turkey, with the aim of capturing Mount Ararat and proclaiming a Pan-Armenian state? The case had its points, and was even kind of noble, no doubt about it, but it was a job for a gang, Kolya. I've got my principles, and one of them is never do anything you can't do on your own.

I sifted through a lot of cases. I took a closer look at a scheme for printing bank notes with portraits of Peter the Great on the hundreds, Bobrov the soccer player on the fifties, and Ilya Ehrenburg on the thirties, but I changed my mind. As for swiping one of the Mongolian prime minister's kidneys when he's under the knife, forget it. Trying to stage *The Brothers Karamazov* in the Central Theater of the Red Army—no way. Wrecking, poisoning rivers and seltzer water in areas where tank troops were stationed, sabotage, praising the theory of relativity, agitation and propaganda, infiltrating literary journals with far-reaching aims like *Novy Mir*, destroying plans and timetables, years of sabotage activity in the U.S.S.R. Meteorological Center, spying for seventy-seven countries, including Antarctica —it was all just depressing and disgusting. Immoral.

Just before Kidalla came back, I spotted it—guess what, old buddy?—I spotted "Case of the vicious rape and murder of an aged kangaroo in the Moscow Zoo on a night between July 14, 1789, and January 9, 1905." I guess that dumb computer was probably mixing up the French Revolution with collective-farm workdays, my fingerprints, Bloody Sunday, Australian reactionaries, and the dangerous creation of the State of Israel. Anyway, it had printed out the very case I'd waited all those years for, hustling and screwing around. I start reading.

I, Perdebabaev-Valois, Doctor of Philology, declare that during the night rounds of the exemplary elephant-keeper carrying an antique night watchman's rattle, I recorded sounds in which the modulus of the suffix prevailed over the semantic dominant a bulletin board of anti-Soviet anecdotes mocking the lyrical hero long live Comrade Vyshinsky who turned out to be a kangaroo set light to an oil lamp a flare a torch Bengal lights Alpha Centauri fuck your mother watchdogs anxiety of the lion's share traces of the struggle in the kangaroo's pouch Stalin's *Short Course on the History of the All-Union Communist Party (Bolsheviks)*

chapter 4 have you ever been accused of yes relatives in occupied territories no pulse zero this testimony by Perdebabaev-Valois.

What a mishmash, Kolya. But I kind of liked it. Who
in hell could ever dream of banging that poor kangaroo
and murdering it? But finally it hit me: this could *only*
be my work. Mine! Me, the moral skunk of all time and
all peoples. All through those long winter evenings,
from the very top of the skyscraper on Uprising Square
overlooking the Moscow Zoo, I followed that aging kangaroo's movements. I was a little confused about sexual
matters, and so I prepared to commit a crime that would
freeze the blood of all progressive forces.

I did it, and I was going to answer for it openly,
before the most democratic court of justice in the world.
Themis, beloved friend of international crooks, our
tryst is coming soon. Don't bother telling the judges it's
none of your business, because it is! Yours and mine!
And I waited for it so long. Seems as if my whole life
was just a preliminary to the bestial murder of an innocent animal, and a camp murder, too, a zoo's only a kind
of camp—a detention center, a closed zone, a lifetime
in the cooler for those poor little birdies and beasties
that God created to live free forever. Bottoms up,
Kolya, let's toast all of them in there! To kangaroos, blue
squirrels, and white swans!

"There's just one little case that happened to catch
my eye," I say to Kidalla when he comes in.

"Okay, you tell me," the accursed scumbag replies.
"I'll bet I know which one."

We make the bet. He scribbles something on a scrap
of paper. I say, "The kangaroo." He hands me the note

and he's won, the creep! You said it, Kolya. I had goat's crap dipped in powdered sugar for brains in those days. And I lost. But how could I guess Kidalla kept me on ice for twenty years not for Article 58—terror, sabotage, treachery—but for a case about a kangaroo dreamed up by a fucked-up computer?

"You see, Citizen Etcetera," says Kidalla. "I wanted to get hold of you especially. You have a 96 percent coefficient of useful performance corresponding to the crime under investigation. It's an absolute record for our ministry. Up to now, the highest was only 1.9 percent. Congratulations. You were worried about that messed-up statement by Perdebabaev-Valois, right? It's the computer that garbled it. I'm going to interrogate the inventor, Kooler, personally, and get at the real reasons for these defects. Just remember, you can't play me for a sucker. Sometimes I can even get an enemy to remember details of his former life a couple of centuries ago, before the dawn of the workers' movement. Let alone the details of passing the blueprints for a new battleship to that Jap Yakitofu. Capito?"

"Yep," I said. Then I asked him straight out: "But what the hell are you doing with that machine, when any of your Sholokhovs could turn out this kind of thing without your having to change a word?"

"You're no dope, Etcetera, but you're like all the enemies. You're just congenitally incapable of understanding that we have to move with the times. The struggle of the new with the old is going on all around us. The alignment of forces in the world arena is largely dependent on the agency's technical equipment. Imperialism isn't asleep, you know. It's introducing computers into production, into everyday life, government, defense, aggression, every sphere of life. We've decided to play the game by their rules and put the science of cybernetics—though, objectively speaking, it's reactionary—to work in the cause of peace. We've got to neutralize the enemy within before he really makes trouble. So we've got to help him see exactly which case corresponds to his world view, political temperament, IQ, and all his baser instincts. We have to exclude any possibility of a potential necrophiliac exhumer of tsarist ladies-in-waiting and old Bolsheviks turning into a parachute wrecker, for instance. And vice versa. But the biggest plus, the most revolutionary one—we can say it fearlessly now—is that we can jump straight from the enemy's sometimes unconscious criminal intent to the right punishment, bypassing the actual crime altogether, with its blood, horrors, cynicism, information leaks, pain, tears of the relatives of those who've suffered, and damage to our military might. We've totally eliminated investigation's indifference to the evolution of a crime, and we've thrown the notorious assumption of innocence on the garbage heap of history, along with the productions of that White Guardist whore Akhmatova and that faggot Zoshchenko."

So let's drink to venomous snakes, Kolya, because there isn't an insect, a snake, a little worm, a wild beast on earth that doesn't deserve freedom! Let's curse the jails and the camps and the zoos, although they're very different. I just want to say that some people are worse than cobras and stinking polecats, because those assholes know what they're doing. But it's all a big mess, Kolya, and as you so rightly put it, we don't know who fucks who or why, and I guess we're not meant to untangle the skein of world history. We didn't pull it off the knees of that old granny, Life, and tangle it up, it was some little kitten. So let the kitten untangle it, while we get back to Kidalla.

So he told me about his plans for a revolutionary approach to crime and said not to worry about the electronic mix-ups in the statements. One of our great Socialist Realist prose writers would fix them. We had dinner. Smoked. I looked out the window—they hadn't even thought of the Children's World department store on the block just across from the Lubyanka then. Where it stands now was the Irtysh luncheonette and a great bar, the String.

"Okay, Comrade Kidalla," I say, "let's get down to our very important unsolved business. I'm going along with this, so I've got a right to some conditions. First of all," I say, "the cell has to be on the sunny side of the building. Newspapers: *The New York Times*, the *Moscow Evening News, Le Figaro*, the railroad workers' paper the *Whistle*, and *Pioneers' Pravda*. Catering by the Irtysh—crayfish and beer. And a powerful shortwave radio. I want objective information about life in our country. Don't let's forget about sex either, Comrade Kidalla. A guy should never forget about sex, even during a prolonged preliminary inquiry, and my guess is this one's going to be a biggie. Plenty of time to turn a girls' high school into the Lepeshinskaya women's clinic. Change the girls every night. No virgins. Also no daughters or relatives of enemies of the people. I'm not the kind of guy who takes advantage of an official position and then dumps on the unfortunate. That's just not my style, Comrade Kidalla."

The guy's turned pale, his eyes are pouring green pus, his hand's reaching for the ashtray. I turn so I'll receive the blow on the lobe that controls oral testimony. Kidalla gnashed his teeth and went out somewhere, without hitting me.

"What's gotten into you?" I said when he came back.

"It comes over me regularly," says Kidalla. "Three times a day. It's stress. I need exercise, so I lend a hand to my friends interrogating enemies. Just now I was dealing with an actress. The bitch wouldn't fuck Beria himself, oh no, but she served herself up on a platter to some Filipino. Disgusting. And Zoya Fyodorova—here's 'a musical story' for you—know what she's up to? Fell for an American! You never get to the end of a job like mine. Okay, pervert, let's have the rest of your demands."

"Movies," I say, "three times a week. Preferably neo-realism, Chaplin, and 20th Century-Fox. Buñuel, Hitchcock, Ivan Pyriev. After the court case, I want to go to a special camp reserved for very dangerous political opponents—survivors of the storming of the Winter Palace and Vladimir Ilyich's closest colleagues. I mean the *crème de la crème*. Okay. Now I've got a personal request for you, Comrade Kidalla. If it weren't for my friendly support, you wouldn't be getting the medal "For Capture of a Spy" and a badge marking your millionth arrest for introducing a computer into this investigation. So I humbly beg you to put the computer's inventor into my one-room cell, my cozy little stone nest, just for a couple of days. I'll even shorten the preliminary investigation period if I can meet the man whose bust will one day adorn the vestibule of Moscow's Butyrki prison and the foyer of the Conciergerie and the Tower of London."

"Look, quit fucking around," says Kidalla. "You're

not going home. Start getting into your role as kangaroo murderer and rapist. Make up a scenario of the case along the lines of Stanislavsky's Method, and think up some versions and variations. Be happy, scumbag: you've immortalized yourself, you'll go down in *The Secret History of the Cheka* along with me. And it shall be written someday! They *shall* write about our labors! They'll tell how we helped to change the world, not explain it!"

"Hey—who's going to deal with the kangaroo?" I asked. "Maybe we don't have to kill her at all. Couldn't we let her live? What does the agency want to mix up life and art for? Kangaroos aren't like Kirov, somebody has to pay good cash for them."

"The committee's farting around with the kangaroo problem right now. It's no business of your criminal little mind. We'll bump off a couple of dinosaurs if we have to. The end justifies the means. You can have all your conditions except one. You won't get your filthy mitts on *Pioneers' Pravda*, you little pervert!"

I asked why, naturally, but he suddenly went white again and hollered, "Silence! Guard!"

In comes the cop, with a face so huge it'd take three days' worth of shit to cover it, and even a team working in shifts would take twenty-four hours. Kidalla tells him to take me to Cell No. 3 (Deluxe), top security, three-star conditions.

Could we maybe take time out, Kolya, have a break and a smoke? No? Well, let's drink to elephants and all large predators, then, and hope that goddamn human beings will leave them in peace pronto. And you and me, too!

*T*HE COP doped me with something in the duty room, and I woke up—after snoozing I don't know how long—on clean sheets in a cute little room without a single window. But the air was gorgeous, cool as summer in the country. Geraniums in pots. Cornflowers and daisies in a vase. Can you believe it, Kolya, I don't remember if the room had a ceiling? Did it? Funny. How could I forget anything so basic? Anyway, there were cornflowers and daisies in a vase. A powerful Telefunken, photographs, pictures. The entire history of the revolutionary movement in Russia, the party struggle, and Soviet power, framed on the walls. Voltaire. "Radishchev's journey from Leningrad to Stalingrad." "Budyonny kissing his sword after the execution of the imperial family." "The villain who put the hole in the battleship *Chelyuskin* and the tuberculosis in Gorky's lungs." "Lenin's massive forehead." "Stalin singing 'Suliko' at Lenin's estate." "Plekhanov's and Stakhanov's childhood." "So-called famine in the Ukraine." "Misha Botvinnik's mommy during the solemn reception at the gynecologist's." "Collectivization makes Krupskaya's eyes bulge." "Trotsky and Bukharin committing an act of pederasty in the Museum of the Revolution." "The world listens to Lemeshev and Kozlovsky."

What didn't they have on those walls instead of wallpaper, Kolya? Of course the most visible place was reserved for a hologram of Karpo Marx. He had no beard, mustache, or curly locks at all, and Lenin, on the contrary, had a full head of hair and down on his cheekbones. What else? Books. A sideboard with crystal wineglasses. No closet, but a table and chairs. Cozy, you know. A telephone. I hopped out of bed like a little kid and dialed a chick's number. But it was Kidalla at the other end. He told me to eat breakfast quick and get started on my zoology and geography homework. The teacher was on his way already. Then I dialed another chick's number and got Kidalla again.

"If you don't stop bugging me in the middle of an important interrogation, asshole," he says, "I promise I'll put you on a totally different case. This phone's reserved for confessions, recantations, inner doubts, and rational proposals. Move your ass, jerk! Stop playing with yourself when you're talking to a counter-espionage agent!"

Naturally, I asked him how he knew what I was doing at that particular moment, but he yelled even louder that he could see my disgusting face on the screen and he was going to sling the ashtray at it again. I hung up. I lie down again. I check out the monograms on the pillowcases, sheets, and comforter covers. The whole lot are birthday gifts for Yakir, Tukhachevsky, Yegorov, and other military bigwigs from the boys they captured the Kronstadts and Perekops with, when they cauterized the bourgeois ulcer on the body of Russia with red-hot steel. The linen was confiscated from their executioners by meaner and more successful executioners. I got up. Went to the john. A dear tiny little john. On the door somebody had scratched: "Workers of the world, unite. History will sentence the internal enemy yet." You stupid jerk, I thought, history sentenced you already! You want extra time? You'll get it. Don't make waves, and you'll get it, no problem. You go to the gate, stick out your face for your release slip, and you get another five or ten in the kisser from Mother History, steaming along with the momentum you gave her yourself, before your pals caught you on the barricades. You should be enjoying in a john like this, you poor sucker, not making appeals to the workers.

Thump. A little window opens and *Le Figaro* drops on the floor. I bang on the door and ask what happened to the *Whistle*. A voice out of nowhere says, "No *Whistle* today. The printing press went on strike."

Unbelievable. I dial a third chick's number, the one at the puppet theater. "Comrade Kidalla," I say, "did the *Whistle* guys really go on strike? Where's the *Whistle*? It was the only paper I liked to read on trains! It's hard on me without it in captivity."

Kidalla patiently explained that it was the Hearst press that was on strike and the *Times* that wasn't coming out. The *Whistle*'s printing was delayed due to sabotage by one of the editors; in a front-page photograph of "Kaganovich in a birch grove" you could see a four-letter word and the name "Gosha" carved on one of the trees. "Our guys caught Gosha just now while he was attempting to cross the Finnish frontier. The rest is only technical. They'll liquidate the editor in a day or two and the *Whistle* will be out again as if nothing had happened."

Bang! The window opens again with my breakfast. I picked at it. Lit a cigarette. I couldn't tell where the smoke went but it was going out to freedom, anyway. Ring after ring. Bye-bye! And nobody knows anything about me or where I am except Kidalla and that cop with the huge ugly mug. No teacher yet either. I flip through a few books. Pretty nice books. From the private collections of enemies of the people. On the flyleaf of *The Three Musketeers* I read: "To my dear Bukharin —the Porthos of the first Five-Year Plan. Stay friendly with Richelieu's guards. J. Stalin." He didn't listen, the sucker. Walked right into the meat grinder. I pull down a pamphlet by Tolstoy, *Nonviolent Resistance to Evil*. "To my faithful friend Zinoviev, in the hope that he will dance on the bodies of the Pretorian guard of the Caucasus. Kamenev." I wonder, is our Dearly Beloved in on the case of the kangaroo? But I hear a voice.

"Your teacher's here. No discussion of irrelevancies. No whispering, no passing notes. Study hard."

The wall opened up noiselessly. "Shvernik" moved away from "Budyonny kissing his sword." An old guy was pushed in toward me, and the wall swung back again and just missed squashing him. It caught his old pants. He had to jump out of them and stand around in his long johns, which were tied around his ankles with drawstrings. I feel sorry for him, shivering like an old rooster. His little gray beard's trembling as he introduces himself: "Professor Bolensky. My field is marsupials. Detailed consultations. With whom do I have the honor . . ."

"How do you do, Professor," I say. "Don't worry about a thing. Call me Fan Fanych. Are you a zek or a free man?"

"For the time being he's a free man!" Kidalla barked over the intercom. "Get on with it, assholes!"

The professor pretended he had the sniffles, but he was crying, really. It was maybe the first time in his life anybody had insulted him. He's just terrorized. He's muttering into his handkerchief, "My goodness . . . my goodness . . . my goodness . . ."

So, to make him forget about his wounded honor, I started asking him scientific questions. What's a kangaroo got a pouch for and what kind of historical necessity thought that one up? When does a female kangaroo want a male, and do they do little mating dances before they make out? What do they nosh on? What time do they hit the sack? Do they bite? Do they have hoofs or claws, and why did Australia become an island, anyway? While I'm asking him all these questions, I'm stuffing a note in the professor's hand asking him to drag out every answer for as long as he possibly can. I added, "Don't wet your pants, granddad, we'll get out of this and sentence history ourselves, you'll see."

The professor read the note and nearly did us both in right there, shaking my hand and squeaking: "Absolutely! Without fail! You have an astounding perspective on things, my dear colleague!"

"What's up? What's going on in there, you snakes?" Kidalla snapped over the intercom.

The old guy was amazing. He came right back and said he'd been deeply struck by my intelligence and vision, he meant my powers of observation, and any great scholar would be proud of a pupil like me.

"You don't want to be proud of a guy like him, ape-face. Get on with the lesson," said Kidalla.

It turned out they'd picked up the professor that evening at the buffet in the Conservatory, and dragged him off to Kidalla, who asked the old guy what a biology ace like him knew about kangaroos. The poor bastard caved in right away, of course, squealed on his beloved kangaroos lock, stock, and barrel, saying he knew everything there was to know about them and was ready to prove it. In the end, Kidalla sent him off to teach me—they couldn't stick me in court without a script. So we chatted about this and that, and switched to science when the speaker crackled behind "Budyonny kissing his sword." For instance, the professor's explaining that kangaroos are the scourge of Australian farmers because they ravage the pastureland, and Kidalla butts in over the intercom:

"It's a good thing they do, let's hear some more of that stuff. It's all playing into the hands of the world socialist system."

"Excuse me," the old guy says, "but we'll still have to buy wheat from Australia if there's a drought. Not to mention America."

"No, we won't," Kidalla says. "We don't have kangaroos on our collective farms. Say, Bolensky, you weren't by any chance thinking about an assassination attempt on Lysenko and the other figures in the forefront of the biological sciences, were you?"

The old guy got mad. "Citizen Investigator," he said, "I wouldn't soil my pristine hands with such shit!"

"Sissy. Get on with the lesson."

So we got on with it, Kolya . . . we lived together for five days. I got to hear the whole story of his life, and they fed us like kings. Beer. Crayfish. Steak. When I found out the old guy was a virgin (his fiancée was killed by a proletarian cobblestone thrown from a barricade in 1905 and he'd never gotten within sniffing distance of another woman), I remembered a swell broad's number, dialed it, and told Kidalla to send over a couple of bimbos right away. I said we need to relax. The professor's arteries were contracting and his temperature dropping dangerously, from fright and restricted hormonal activity. He's got to have a warm body or he'll choke from hiccups.

The old guy was gobbling up jail learning like a hungry wolf, gulping it down without chewing. He hiccupped terrifically all day. When I made the announcement, Kidalla gnashed his teeth over the intercom, but he couldn't do anything about it. If there was dough for girls listed in the estimated budget for the case, you paid up and shut up. Soviet authorities insist on order in prisons, morgues, and drunk tanks.

Suddenly that evening the professor and I hear giggles and titters, and Budyonny swings away from Karpo Marx. Surprise, surprise, two stewardesses drop out of the sky into my No. 3 (Deluxe). Blue flight caps. Short skirts. Hips to make you die. The professor grabbed his pants, which had gotten stuck in the wall when he first came in.

"Hi, enemies of the people," say these heavenly creatures. Bolensky turned beet red and kept bowing and mumbling something in French. I picked the raunchier-looking one for him and said: "Jump to it, honey, I won't put up with slackers. The old guy's got nothing to lose, he killed the director of a condom factory with a fire extinguisher and they sentenced him to death. Make love to him as if you were making love for the last time and you're miserably ashamed of all the years you've wasted."

I fed the professor the same spiel about painful shame and lovemaking, and told him to try Lumumba's position (we still called it Trotsky's position in those days). We opened a bottle of champagne and switched on the little portable phonograph—a present to Rykov from Molotov. It plays "Masha and me at the samovar." I look around, Kolya, and the stewardess is already sitting on the old guy's knees. He's gasping for air, doesn't know whether he's coming or going. She's unbuttoning his fly in a professional kind of way and cooing: "And who gave us the fire extinguisher? Who gave this little old pussycat a fire extinguisher? Where did it happen, hmmm? In a diplomat's apartment or the restaurant at the Hotel National? Now where did our little gray-haired sweetie hide the radio transmitter and the codes? Tsk, tsk, tsk!"

My bitch is slobbering all over me, too, trying to find out if I kissed the kangaroo, if I gave her any little gifts, who taught me such bestiality: was it those enemies of Academician Lysenko, Shostakovich and Prokofiev and Anna Akhmatova, or was it just cosmopolites and Bandera's bandits? Primitive stuff, Kolya. I asked the bitch if she had some big examination or test today. What subject was it? She was green, and cracked pretty quickly. She burst into tears and whispered: "Please help us, honey! Nadya and I've failed Obtaining Information during Foreplay with Enemies of the People twice. They'll throw us out and send us away to do Komsomol construction work. It's no fun there . . . You only get cotton wool for your periods and not even enough of that . . . Please say something, anything . . . You're going to die anyway, but we've got all our lives ahead of us . . . Tell us something, baby!"

Well, Kolya, you know me, I'm a real soft touch. I poured out such a heap of crap she would have had enough for a Ph.D., let alone some lousy test. She tried to remember everything and scribbled it down on her thigh with a lipstick, while I faked it—I pretended to fuck her to keep Kidalla happy while he watched on the TV.

Suddenly the old guy gave an inhuman howl. He was humping his broad like crazy and yelling in Latin: "Hail, Caesar! We who are about to lose our cherries salute you!"

The intercom crackled. I hear voices over the ether and Kidalla reporting, "We're conducting observations, Comrade Beria. In connection with the kangaroo case."

Everything was quiet again except for the professor. The couch was rocking violently. He's saying something. Bellowing. Groaning. Roaring like a lion. Promising to leave her everything, even his stamp collection. Arranging an assignation on Revolution Square, and bellowing and bellowing again like a young bull tearing over a field toward a brown-and-white heifer. The coed got off on this. "Oh, wow . . . oh, wow . . . oh, what got you this way . . . my sweet little kid." Then she got totally carried away. "Fire . . . fire . . . extinguisher . . . fire . . . extinguisher . . . fire, fire, fi-i-i-re!"

Don't butt in, Kolya, I'm not getting you excited on purpose. The professor's teeth are chattering like casta-nets and he keeps saying the same word over and over, "Apogee . . . a-apogee . . . a-a-apogee!" Then the speaker crackles again and someone, probably Beria with that accent, is saying to Kidalla: "Just look at that energy, comrade. An enemy of the people has an incredible second wind. Redouble your vigilance! Where are you with the case of that group of architects who wanted to revise the architecture of Lenin's tomb?"

"We've nearly finished forming the group. We're go-ing to be starting active interrogation momentarily," said Kidalla. "In honor of Lenin's birthday."

"Carry on with the observation!" Beria ordered.

Our stewardesses took off toward morning, Kolya. Just flew away as if they'd never been. The professor went out like a light. He's smiling in his sleep, because he became a man in his seventy-eighth year, and he's drib-bling like a nursing baby onto Blücher's official pillow, given him by Stalin.

I fell asleep, too. I was pretty depressed, Kolya. I never got to fuck the broad at all, because I spent the whole night helping her study for the test. Let's drink to polar bears and brown bears and blue flamingos!

Can you believe it? I fooled around for a whole month with Professor Bolensky, an honored member of academies all over the world, a Stalin Prize laureate, a deputy of the U.S.S.R. Supreme Soviet. Soon there was nothing I didn't know about kangaroos, Kolya, and in exchange, the old guy asked me his questions about sex and female psychology. By the end he could draw for me blindfolded their greater and lesser distinguishing features, and all the rest in between. In practical matters, my pupil was like a kid in a candy store. The stewardesses must have passed their test with flying colors, because the chicks came pouring into our room every evening, each one in a different uniform and role. Waitresses—the biggest finks in the world—chess players, torch singers, milkmaids, crane operators, lab assistants, train-station whores, writers, salesgirls, Ph.D. candidates, blind ones, deaf-mutes, polio victims. Every one trained by Kidalla—he was a professor in a secret technical school—and he thought the old guy and I were great teachers. Don't wish you'd been there, Kolya. You can crush the head of my member—which you crudely call a prick—on a five-kopeck coin if I got to screw one of them even once. You can bet I would have jumped on them if they hadn't been collecting information during foreplay for their tests, and not just one of them, either. I would have dragged out my time with the professor longer, too. But I couldn't. I couldn't—that's all. Leave me alone, for chrissake! Why? Why? Because! I don't know why!

The professor—or the sex maniac, as Kidalla once called him over the intercom after his eighth fuck—fixed up the girls with some fascinating little stories. The fire-extinguisher idea that I'd launched became his favorite topic. He hid H-bomb blueprints in it, sprayed napalm with it, kept cameras, tape recorders, disorganized-energy generators, et cetera, in it. And of course agents of every secret service in the world, including Papua's, had passed fire extinguishers on to him. Along the way the professor betrayed to the girls imaginary accomplices: Churchill, dead colleagues, party secretaries, nonexistent neighbors, lovers, even

Lysenko himself. The old guy kissed me once because he was so happy, a geriatric like him, one foot in the grave, to have such a kind and wonderful teacher about life as Fan Fanych.

One day a basketball player— six foot six from head to toe—crawled into our No. 3 (Deluxe) on all fours. It was love at first sight with her and the professor. And how. Kidalla shrieked over the intercom that unless Bolensky got off her—she was code-named Little Devil —he'd transfer him to the actress case immediately. But the screwing wasn't the point. It was the fusion of twin souls, despite the differences in physique and age. They quietly swore they'd never part.

Did you ever feel that way when you were a kid? You're sleeping on the cot under the apple trees at the dacha. Suddenly you're woken up by a little kitten. After you cry like crazy and beat your head against the fence for hours, Mommy lets you take the kitten home for keeps. Now you open one eye, then the other, you tell yourself you're dreaming about the kitten and you try not to wake up—it's too terrible if this little warm gray bundle's only a dream. Then finally you realize you're not asleep, but it's still too scary to believe— pardon the expression, Kolya—in the reality of happiness. Happiness, old buddy (or freedom)—remember this always—is just a fleck of dust in a ray of sunlight, floating between the dreams of our childhood and the horrors of real life.

Anyway, the basketball player grabs our naked old professor under the arms with her big strapping paws and holds him above her just like a kitten, and he purrs something, and she looks at him strangely until

Cupid gets another arrow out of his quiver. The professor's like a little kid by now. He's not fazed by the stares of onlookers.

"They're pigs and jerk-offs," he says. "They can burn up with embarrassment, it's not my fault if I'm lucky enough to be joining the human race right here."

You'll never guess who I was fooling with just then, Kolya. A midget from the Karelian Birch Orchestra. Who are you finking on, you dirty hooker, I say.

She says, "I get a lot of diplomats. They want to take dirty pictures to sell in Paris. I've got to find out the exact date and time when they're going to drop the H-bomb on us, or pollute the Volga with Coca-Cola."

The basketball player left us on all fours carrying the midget on her back. Hey, I've just remembered there really was a ceiling in our No. 3 (Deluxe).

I don't have to tell you the professor and I parted friends. Believe it or not, the old guy cried on my bosom before they took him away. "Thanks to you, Fan Fanych," he wept, "I've lived my whole life in one week, and I don't think I've betrayed Dashenka." (If you remember, Kolya, she's the one who got beaned by a proletarian cobblestone at the barricades.) "It even seems to me that Dasha's soul is inside my glorious athlete's body in some magic way. I've never excluded the possibility of such transmogrification. In fact, I've been expecting it. Thanks, my dear Fan Fanych! I'm ready to forgive all the evil in the world for the joy of knowing you, and I'm not afraid of anything. Anything! Justice shall triumph!"

That sweet old guy had really lost his fear. He stripped off his clothes, lit a cigar, and paced from side to side, lecturing me on kangaroo life-styles. Finally I had to tell him a few things about the triumph of justice.

"The triumph already happened," I said. "It's gone. The lamps have gone out, the shabby lackeys are gobbling up the pheasants. And you and I, the hungry and the cold, we were never invited, and we never shall be . . ."

I FELT lonesome without him. Very lonesome. I told Kidalla not to send any more broads; I had to start organizing all the facts I'd collected, creating a screenplay and working up a few versions and variations. I lie on my back for days, smoking, and the smoke always vanishes Christ knows where. I stare at the sundial. Yeah, I know, Kolya, there weren't any windows in the room, but there was a sundial—sheer sadism. God knows where the shadow that told the time came from. Hell, I'm low, real low. I barely touch the chow. I don't turn on the Telefunken. The sheets stink like an army stable. The bread stinks like bloody collectivization. I read the *Whistle*, which is coming out again, the *Times*, and *Le Figaro*. I call Kidalla.

"Get me out of here to a real jail. I'm going nuts here, I'll start climbing the walls, I'll go out of my skull. Or start a fire. I'll set fire to Tukhachevsky's sheets and Ordzhonikidze's chairs and Shvernik's decrees and Trotsky's yakkety-yak and Yezhov's towel and Bukharin's copy of *The Three Musketeers* and Lenin's *State*

and Revolution! I don't give a shit, I'll burn the lot!
Why are you driving me crazy? Listen, if you want I'll
take the rap for all the hundred and eighty million
cases of treason against the motherland, I'll take the
rap for Stalin himself, you scumbag. You don't like that?
So let's fix him up with Article 109, 'abuse of an official
position,' and Article 74, section 2, 'hooliganism accom-
panied by extreme cynicism.' You don't have anything
to say about that, do you, you trash, you fascist? I don't
give a damn about your stinking uniform. Take me away
to solitary, I don't care if there's ice on the walls and
they make you stand up all day! Get me out of here!
I'll freeze my ass off on the concrete, I'll catch consump-
tion, I'll give myself rheumatism, I'll lick your boots,
you can make my eyes go dumb and my ears go blind
and my blood turn to shit, but get me out of here! Take
me away to the land of ice and stone. Take me where it
doesn't stink of army stables or the battle of Perekop or
right-wing opposition or collectivization or North Pole
explorers or poor, surrounded soldiers, you bastard!
What does any of this have to do with me? Take me
away, please, please! You can keep the beer and crayfish, just give me a ray of daylight through prison bars!
I can play tic-tac-toe on the pattern of the bars all by
myself, and I wouldn't bother anyone. Who would I
bother?"

Screaming doesn't help. I can tell I'm pretty close to
the edge. Any moment I'm going to go nuts, climb the
walls, go out of my skull. Kidalla doesn't say a word,
just sits there patiently and takes the insults I'm hurling
at various higher echelons and the circles involved in
storming the Winter Palace. Nothing moves. Budyonny

doesn't shift away from the picture of young Karpo Marx without a beard, no sign of Ugly Mug, no fist slugging me in the teeth. My tantrum was simply for the birds. Then I suddenly passed out. Kidalla had slipped me a Mickey Finn—not that I knew anything about it then.

I come out of the dope dizzy and tied hand and foot. For some reason I'm lying on fresh straw on the floor. In front of my nose there's a raw carrot and some unfamiliar leafy twigs. I look around. The furniture in the room's the same. But somehow the portrait of Karpo Marx has started to grow a beard and he has this terrific gleam in his eye. He's staring at me. He looks like he's saying, "Quit trying to explain the world, Fan Fanych. I've had it up to here. It's time to *change* the sucker!"

I nearly forgot to tell you, Kolya, but a whole bunch of the pictures and photographs had somehow disappeared from the walls. "The wailing of the Bolsheviks is over," "The horror squeezed a groan out of iron," "At the graves of Gorky, Ostrovsky, and others," "Stalin crying bitterly over Kirov's corpse," "Karatsupa and his favorite dog, Indira Gandhi," "Kulaks on Red Square," "Marshal Zhukov on his white steed"—they'd all been replaced by others. "We say NO!!! to cybernetics, genetics, profits, profiteering, jazz, Nord cigarettes, French rolls, and the petty bourgeoisie." Next to that was "Members of the Politburo conducting self-criticism." "Zhdanov burning Anna Akhmatova's poetry," "Confiscating all the Shostakoviches' and Prokofievs' treble clefs," and, a little higher up, "Mikoyan making hotdogs at the Mikoyan meat factory." Looked like there'd been some shuffling in the upper echelons.

They'd probably vaporized someone. It turned out to be Voznesensky, the chairman of State Planning . . .

My arms had gone numb. I stretched my lips toward the carrot and crunched it up. I sniffed at the leaves and heard something rustle. I hear pleased voices somewhere: "He's eating it! He's eating it! And I was ready to kiss my wife and children goodbye. He's eating it! Well, he's sniffing it, anyway! Congratulations, Zina—I'll see you get a Red Star for this!"

I say to Kidalla, "Listen, Comrade Cool-Ears-and-Warm-Liver, you'd better untie me, or I'll get pissed and pass out again."

No answer. Finally, "We say no to French rolls" moves away from "The Judas of our music," and a pretty—no, I tell a lie, Kolya, gorgeous—but somehow very pale broad tiptoes into the cell. Young, somewhere between twenty-seven and thirty-five. Her hair sparkles. Soft. Fluffy. Light brown. She comes right up close to me. I can't look anywhere but up. I can see the dimples in her knees—I'd like to pour warm milk into them and lap it up. My heart's pounding. If I wasn't tied down with these ropes, it'd jump right out of my ribs. I can see her blue panties, Kolya, the blood's rushing to my head, it's going dark. The woman looks down at me, all tied up. She's smiling tenderly. Then she squatted down on her haunches and stroked my face. I kissed her cold fingers. She says, "There, there, little one, calm down, calm down, cutie . . . We love you . . . We're sorry for you . . . We won't let anyone hurt you."

"I'm quite calm, thanks," I say. "Who are you? Let's face it, right now Fan Fanych can't respond to a princess like you the way he'd like to. You're as beautiful as Poland before the First Partition, ha, ha!"

But it's like she's deaf, Kolya. She says to me again, "You've got eyes like plums in blue smoke. I can see myself in them, deep, deep down . . . like being at the bottom of a well, splashing . . . That's me . . . What a darling, good, nice, beautiful little animal . . . Look at those lips like chamois and those soft ears . . . and strong legs . . ."

What the fuck is this, I think, getting a little nervous. I say, "Untie me, please. I've got pins and needles in my arms and there's another little problem, too."

She takes a jar, unbuttons me, and pulls it out. But I've got a hard-on. I can't piss for the life of me.

"Listen," I say. "You could at least tell me how long I'm going to be tied up for. Then you can tell Kidalla he's an asshole and he's blown it with this kangaroo case. I'm not Rykov or Bukharin or Kamenev, you won't get to me this way. It bothers me about as much as bull's blood at the Kaganovich meat factory bothers Mikoyan."

I pissed lying down. No other way. She stroked my hair again, running her fingers through it and murmuring so kindly you couldn't believe it could be faked, Kolya.

"You funny little beast . . . You're probably homesick for your Australia, aren't you . . . That's why your eyes are sad . . . and your paws are trembling . . . and your little heart's beating tok-tok-tok. Just like us . . . just like us."

I freaked out totally and struggled, but I was tied up tight. I yelled at Kidalla, "Bastard! It was a spastic who fucked your mama, right? Or maybe it was an animal? Is your mama still alive, because if she is, then bring her on a visit to your Lubyanka! She should get to see the way her little boy sucks the blood of a poor crazy bitch and an ordinary guy like Fan Fanych! Go on, show her something! My blood isn't enough for you, maybe? Then eat shit, drink piss, taste my heart, scumbag! As for you"—I turned to the unfortunate broad, there's no doubt she's out of her gourd—"you think I'm a kangaroo?"

I'll give you our whole conversation from now on, Kolya.

"You think I'm a kangaroo?"

"I think you're trying to tell me something, aren't you, my little foreign friend?"

"Don't push me too far, you stupid cow, don't push me too far! You can't play me for that kind of sucker. I'm no kangaroo! I'm as sharp as a monkey and stubborn as a mule!"

"You mustn't bite! Ouch, ouch! Auntie booboo . . . You want to say something and you can't? You can't, can you, poor little thing. Wait, I think I understand. You don't like being tied up, do you? Humans don't like that, either—it hurts their souls. Do you have a soul?"

"No!" I say aloud. "Fan Fanych isn't as sharp as a monkey, he's a pathetic wet kitten. Nobody as sharp as a monkey could have let fate con him and screw him this way. He would have stayed in Ethiopia to face the Italian fascists, and not run away to the Soviet motherland. Fake! Moral profiteer! Shithouse! Scabby pukeface! Jerk! You could have been sipping coffee with Haile Selassie right now, not moldering in KGB dungeons!"

"I don't want to hurt you. I like you. You're ni-i-i-ce. I love to stroke you. I understand: you think you're human—you think I don't understand?"

"You dumb slut! What you need is shock treatment! Shut up, bitch, you want me to flip out too? Shut *up!*"

"Why do you keep biting your lips? Let me wipe your muzzle. There . . . Oh! What did I say—auntie *booboo!*"

"I think I'm going to gobble you up, cupcake, so I won't have to look at you anymore! Get out of my sight, witch! Get out of my sight!"

"There, there. Let me rub you behind the ears. Feel better? After all, you don't know we used optical transformers to remove all the human characteristics from the nerve endings of your hypothalamus. Poor little thing. Almost all the animals in the zoo—except birds, snakes, black panthers, and eagles—think they're human. They're totally uninterested in their reflection in the mirror. But you're not a man. You're a nice, sad, strong, naughty kangaroo. But you mustn't be naughty. Eat up! Don't spit it all up like that. You'll die if you don't eat and auntie will be so sorry! Auntie doesn't want you to die. Eat, baby, eat."

"Okay, Kidalla! Okay, you brilliant cross between a hyena and all the pus in the world. Believe me, I'm impressed, asshole. Hot stuff. But just take a look at your soul, shithead. Go on, chicken! You can't look, can you? You know why? No? Well, I won't tell you. Go on, suffer a little. Torture me if you like. I'm not going to tell you why you're too scared to look into your soul, even under torture. Get me the director of public prosecutions, jerk, I'm going on a hunger strike! I demand to see the public prosecutor!"

"Look, you haven't eaten in five days. Don't howl like that. I'll have to force-feed you. We won't let you die."

"Kill me, Kidalla! Look at me, I'm crying—kill me, for chrissake! Just do that for me and I'll pray to God to forgive you and ease you till the end of time and everyone like you! Kill me! Get rid of this woman! She's sick! Kill me, Kidalla!"

"Open your mouth . . . open up. Gently. You'll bang your head that way. That's iodine. Does it sting? Now don't struggle, don't struggle. Open your mouth, pig, will you? Eat the carrot, you goddamn beast! A tiger'd be easier to deal with than you, for chrissake. Eat, will you? Ow-w-w! Let go of my finger, you lousy bastard! Let go right now!"

"Untie me and I'll let go. I'll bite right through your finger if you won't untie me. Untie me!"

"That hurts, right? I'm warning you, every time you bite or you won't eat, I'll give you an electric shock, like that. You don't like it, do you? Then eat. You don't want to? Then I'll turn up the current. How about that? It hurts, right? You poor animal, you're making it worse for yourself."

"You bunch of creeps, get me a mirror! Give me a mirror just for one second! If I'm a kangaroo, I'll stuff myself like a pig and ask for more! Let me confront Fan Fanych! Agghh! Get me a mirror!"

Finally Fan Fanych got the message, Kolya. He was a master con artist who hadn't been caught since NEP in the twenties, for chrissake, what was he doing yelling blue murder and asking for public prosecutors? It was time to fake it with everything he had. Fake it, Kolya! How could Fan Fanych have wasted so much strength and nervous energy trying to prove to some crazy bitch from the Serbsky Institute that he was a Man, and proud of it? Fake it, Kolya, fake it! But Fan Fanych had totally forgotten the sounds a kangaroo makes when it's hungry or in pain or cold or in danger. Totally. Fan Fanych shut up, settled his head more comfortably on the fresh straw, and wept for the first time in the last Five-Year Plan. He's trying to remember, but he tries and tries and nothing happens. The shocks have wiped out Fan Fanych's memory.

The crazy woman dropped on the sofa and fell asleep, worn out. Fan Fanych stared at the pictures of "Lenin and Krupskaya by the Christmas tree," "Petersburg workers driving the nobility out of Leningrad," and fell asleep too.

He's dreaming he's sleeping in warm, dark silence. He's well fed, peaceful, nothing hurts anywhere and he has no desires. He just wants to sleep like this, sleep in the warmth, the darkness, the silence, sleep, sleep, sleep. But suddenly someone's shaking Fan Fanych, kicking him in the ribs, trying to wake him up. Get up, bastard, a voice says, get out to your post, the guards are freezing out there. Can't. Don't want to. They're kicking you in the ribs, chasing you out of the warm silent darkness into cold sunlight. But Fan Fanych can't move. His hands and feet are numb, he can't feel anything in them at all. Now they're turning him toward the dead, white, chilly light, pushing him, tearing him away like you tear a dry scab away from a wound, and he's gripping living flesh with his teeth, gripping the soft, familiar fur and shooting out of his Mama-Roo's pouch into the dead river Yauza, not far from the big shots' apartment house. Fan Fanych's heart stopped in terror, but as he was flying over the parapet into the dead stench, the same terror made him scream, "Keh-eh-eh-eh!" Then he woke up. His eyes were popping out of his head. The crazy woman comes rushing up, peers into them, looks pleased, and gives him a drink of water. Fan Fanych licked her hand. He licked her palm, which was warm because when she snoozed she kept her hands between her knees. Otherwise, they were always cold. Fan Fanych, no sucker anymore, said, "Keh-eh-eh!" again.

"Did you hear that, Comrade Kidalla? Did you hear that?"

"I heard. Carry on with the subject's conditioning."

While this was going on, that dummy Fan Fanych was chowing down on the carrot and trying the foreign twigs, tearing off the leaves with his lips and rolling his eyes to the ceiling with pleasure. Why hadn't he done it before? Who knows. A complete dummy, right? He could have missed the shocks and spared his poor little nerves.

"Eat, little one! I'll love you—I'll untie you, even, if you don't bite and kick anymore. Say your wonderful 'keh-eh-eh' one more time."

"Keh-eh-eh-eh!" said Fan Fanych. Whatever you say.

"Witness Bolensky, does the sound emitted by the subject correspond to one or several of the habitual sounds of the kangaroo in captivity?"

"Absolutely, Citizen Investigator! Absolutely! The timbre! The modulations! And a striking example of kangaroo-like articulation."

"Keh-eh-eh!" said Fan Fanych, tugging at his ropes.

"Don't struggle, dear. I'm going to untie you . . . You haven't forgotten that sharp iron thing, have you—booboo? Booboo . . . booboo . . . No, don't be afraid, just don't forget. Give me your front paws first. There. Turn around. How swollen they are! Wriggle your fingers, but don't try to scratch me, will you? Booboo? Booboo? Booboo?"

"Keh-eh-eh!" Oh, Kolya, it was so great when my hands were untied and the half-dead veins filled with blood flowing through my shriveled arteries and tiniest capillaries! And as it flowed, my one and only life bubbled up again.

"Keh-eh-eh!" I say. What I'm thinking is, Don't worry, cop lady, Fan Fanych won't bite you. He's wise to it now. Untie my hind paws, vampire. Let me stroke your shoe with my front paw, let me rub off the dust and that antipodean leaf sticking to it.

"There! I knew you were good. I'm going to call you Ken, okay? Aren't you funny, the way you puff up your lips like that! Now, don't sulk. It's your own fault you got hurt, you stubborn little Ken."

She untied my feet, too, Kolya. But Fan Fanych, still as sharp as that old monkey, didn't dance for joy. He crawled around the No. 3 (Deluxe) on all fours. His head started spinning, but it wasn't too bad, he could get around. "Keh-eh-eh!"

For days Fan Fanych dozed, stuffed himself on fruit and vegetables, and just rested. He got around exclusively on all fours, and would go and rub his muzzle against the douchebag's knees, nuzzling her earlobe, sniffing her all over and wrinkling his nose cutely. "Keh-eh-eh!"

"You're quite tame, Ken, aren't you? You lick nicely . . . Ha, ha, ha! You lick very nicely! Do I turn you on? Remember, the earlobe's an erogenous zone, Ken! Oh, you naughty little thing! Look, I'm undressing, now you stroke me with your little paw. It tickles . . . it tickles . . . Lick my breast . . . and the other one. Now under the breast, my nice, strong, tender kangaroo. Don't bite my nipple, don't bite—use your tongue, your tongue—ooh-h-h! Now lower . . . You just don't understand, do you? Lower . . . oh, please . . . here, where the twig is. Do you want a human female? Is that it? Look at me standing in front of you, look how beautiful I am. Well then, come on, jump on me! A woman wants to give herself to you . . . Jump!"

Of course, Kolya, you think Fan Fanych laid back his ears, flared his nostrils, bared his fangs, and threw himself on this nympho just as he was, fur and hoofs and all. Maybe, under other circumstances—in Australia, for example—he would have jumped right on top of the juicy farmer's wife. But right then Fan Fanych couldn't have done it with a woman if they'd been threatening to run the combined current from the Dnieper and Stalingrad hydroelectric stations right through him. You could make Fan Fanych walk on all fours, you could make him say "Keh-eh-eh," lick the erogenous zones of sex-mad whores, eat foreign leaves, but you just couldn't make him get it up for a human female. It's nothing to do with principles, Kolya, don't try to teach me how to live. I feel the same way about principles you do—fuck 'em, excuse the expression. I couldn't screw a human woman. It's as simple as that. Believe it or not, I could not get a hard-on. After everything I'd seen and been through, what I wanted was my little kangaroo, the pure, living creature I raped and viciously murdered in the Moscow Zoo on a night between

July 14, 1789, and January 9, 1905. That's what I wanted, Kolya, because I'm a normal guy, not a sicko like you. Let's drink to anteaters and armadillos, who yearn for their native jungles forever. God give their children freedom someday, or at least their grandchildren.

"Keh-eh-eh!" I say to the nympho, but I'm really thinking, You'll see my prick like you'll see the back of your head.

She hadn't even got dressed, but she said, "Permission to report, Comrade Kidalla. The experiment we've conducted over a period of seven days has confirmed irrefutably your hypothesis as to the partial, and sometimes complete, adaptation of the subject to new speech and locomotive functions, using progressive methods of active coercion. We've also confirmed your hypothesis as to the possibility of inoculation of the subject at a time of cyclical depression, in order to produce an organic self-conception as a kangaroo. We may accept as proof the absence in the subject of direct sexual attraction to human beings, and its opposite, the presence of an unconscious desire to copulate with a corresponding psychobiostructure."

I lay on the floor and listened to her droning on, glad the worst was behind me. She got dressed in the end, stupid bitch. "Could you do up my brassiere, citizen?" she asked me.

I act like I don't hear a thing. "Keh-eh-eh!"

"You can go, Zina. Leave me your bill and the chart of the subject's degeneration. Hey, Etcetera, get on with your deposition. Quit playacting. Half the world has nothing to eat, children in India are dying of protein deficiency, and U.S. reactionaries are jailing the Soviet

Union's friends right and left. Nobody screws around all expenses paid when the world's burning under imperialism. Capito?"

"Keh-eh-eh!" I say, goggling at Karpo Marx. His beard's gotten even longer and thicker these last few days. Lenin's going the other way. He's started to go bald and he's squinting.

"Comrade Lieutenant Colonel," says that creep Zina, "I think too fast a regeneration might be undesirable."

"You don't know this pig as well as I do. I don't trust him, Lieutenant. Well, forget it, we'll leave him alone for now. I'll shake him up tomorrow. Dismissed."

The Kukryniks' painting of "Hitler taking poison" moves away from "Stalin embracing Mao." I positioned myself and caught the senior lieutenant such a kick in the ass she probably landed in Revolution Square. Then the wall moved back again.

I waited. But nobody dropped by to haul me off to solitary. I switch on the Telefunken. I hadn't heard the national news in ages. It was weird to hear that steelworker and City Soviet member Vladlen Mytishchev was enjoying the praise of his countrymen, when the Omsk province laborers had produced a surplus of 10,000 tons, since the election of the people's judges and assessors had taken place in an atmosphere of unprecedented national enthusiasm, while the party had said "It must be!" and the people answered "It shall be!" consequently Citizen Shevelyova, a carpet-factory termite exterminator protesting against the intrigues of supporters of a new Anschluss, had declared to Soviet composers that they should go "Full astern!" . . . The subscription to the development loan for the national economy minus assimilation of protected forest zones had led the Volga–Don Canal to peaks of glory ahead of schedule risen up in a special effort Frontier Guard Day a satirical article is doomed to failure Ehrenburg anxiety over falling prices of people of good will comrade personally hands off . . .

When Yuri Levitan read this newscast—there's no bigger liar or hustler or slobbermouth anywhere in the world—my brain just crumbled. You tell me, Kolya, why couldn't every Soviet radio station interrupt with a bulletin, why couldn't Yuri Levitan—with his hustling bass voice that he kissed Stalin's ass with twenty times a day while he was alive and cursed him with when he was dead—why couldn't he broadcast a Tass report about how state security agents conducted an important experiment proving the possibility of initiating the purposeful degeneration of the higher nervous system of a human being and, for the first time in his-tor-y, introducing into his brain the sensation of belonging to a different species? The experiment was conducted on Soviet citizen Martyshkin! He feels fantastic the asshole and leper an anti-Soviet bum pulse blood pressure an artillery salvo in the hero-cities! Glory to ground-breaking So-vi-et sci-ence!

Why wasn't Yuri Levitan broadcasting such an important announcement—historic, even? Steelworker Mytishchev and that fighter for peace, Ehrenburg, they ought to know how my heart froze when I saw that crazy woman in the white coat, they ought to know how it weakened, sensing it wasn't going to survive the enthusiasm for Frontier Guard Day. And the people's assessors' tongues ought to have touched the sharp metal booboos that jerked my body, my body, my body —thanks, old buddy—and the assessors and the factory termite exterminator ought to have turned into a poor little broken kangaroo, if only for a moment, meekly swallowing strange leaves and puking them up on the floor of a No. 3 (Deluxe) along with the remains of its human soul still sticking to its bronchial tubes, and then subscribing to the development loan for the national economy . . . Okay, okay. I hope that slobbering Yuri Levitan drops dead.

Suddenly, Kolya, "Karatsupa and his favorite dog, Indira Gandhi" moves away from "He who is no friend of the U.S.S.R." A funny-looking, curly-headed guy comes bursting into my cell. He bumps his head on "Morning at the dawn of the daybreak of the workers' movement in Moscow," sits down on the Telefunken, grabs his head in his hands, and says, "What have I done? What have I done? What have I done?"

I dial your number, Kolya, and say to Kidalla, "MGB Private Etcetera, alias Ken the kangaroo, reporting. Regeneration has been successfully carried out. I feel human. I observe an increased growth of beard on the face of Citizen Karpo Marx, with whom I have never conspired criminally to change the world. I've never seen him before. I'm always ready to serve. I dedicate myself to the centenary of Malenkov's birth and death. Hurrah! Hurrah!"

"I thought I told you, fascist scumbag," says Kidalla. "This phone is reserved exclusively for inner doubts and recantations. The agency doesn't need you to tell it what's happening to you. You'd do better to think about your trial. You said you wanted to meet Kooler, Norbert Wiener's stooge. Well, there he is."

"Oh, so you're Mr. Citizen Kooler, " I say to the funny curly-headed guy. He has eyes like a sheep that's been to Meat's mikoyan factory. *"Guten Morgen, sholem aleichem,* Citizen Mr. Kooler. So. Who's the accomplice who helped you forget Ivan Nobody? Eh?"

"What have I done? What have I done? What have I done?" Kooler keeps mumbling, his sheep's eyes riveted on "How do the Alsop brothers explain that one?"

"Get up," I say. "Get a chair. Stop acting like a duck-billed platypus, alias a marsupial swan-goose. You ought to be ashamed of yourself."

"What have I done? What have I done? What have I done?" Kooler drones on and on, and I say: "Listen, you never ever ask the agency questions like that. In fact, better not ask questions at all, or there'll be hell to pay. Do you belong to a credit union?" I decided Kooler had to put himself in my shoes, Kolya.

"Of course I do. Who doesn't these days?" said Kooler, a little sharper.

"When was the last time you took out a loan?"

"Just before International Women's Day."

"How much?"

"Two thousand. So what?"

"Last name?"

"Kooler."

"First name and patronymic?"

"Valery Chkalovich. Pa changed my patronymic as a token of his admiration for the great aviator."

"So, Valery Chkalovich, just before International Women's Day, dissatisfied because your entire paycheck had been ripped off for your subscription to the national economy loan, you took out a personal loan of two thousand rubles. Repayable when?"

"By Medical Workers' Day."

"I expect you know what money they had in the credit union at your secret laboratory?"

"The money the union had in circulation, obviously."

"What would you say that money smelled of?"

"I'd say nothing. What are you getting at?"

"What I'm getting at is that maybe the money you got from the credit union didn't smell of anything, but it certainly belonged to the Swiss secret service!"

"Oh, my God! My God! My God!"

"Which of your colleagues usually said on payday: 'I screwed the credit union'?"

"Taneeva the cleaning woman, Achmed Rachmaninoff the health technician, and Ravel the theoretical physicist."

"And they're still at liberty. So there are some real Soviet citizens left! Did you sign a receipt for the loan?"

"Of course. Einstein's honor! Kurchatov's honor! But what are you getting at?"

"Quit playing games, Kooler! Quit avoiding your responsibilities! It's time to drop that 1930s infantilism!"

"But what have I done? What have I done? What have I done?"

"I'll tell you what, but first we have to make sure the trade unions can't see us or overhear us. Can you believe it, they think they're the school for communism, when everyone knows it's us, the agency."

"Exactly! Anyway, Pakhmutova, our trade-union organizer, works for you secretly. What do I have to do for the struggle against 1930s and 1920s infantilism?"

"Spit three times on that color photo over there and rub it in."

"On 'He who is no friend of the U.S.S.R.'?"

"Even a village idiot would spit on that one! On the other one, for chrissake, to the left. Yeah, that one."

"I categorically refuse to spit on that one. It's sacrilege. Desecration and self-slander! 'ZIS car factory workers receiving surplus value'—it's the pride of our national photography! I can't! Please, won't you let me spit on 'The inventor Edison stealing the phonograph from the genius Popov'?"

"Sorry, no way. If you don't hawk up on 'Surplus value,' we'll destroy your report on the advantages of creating a programmed apparatus that makes up severe sentences for enemies of Soviet power long before the preliminary inquiries."

"Anything but that! Oh, no! Anything but the death of my beloved baby! I guess you're right. A couple of gobs won't stop surplus value from existing or ZIS workers from receiving it. Right, comrade?"

"I'm not your comrade, asshole! I'm Citizen Fan Fanych, international crook. Your Academy of Sciences comrade is flying to the West in a latrine! Got it?"

"Absolutely. Unambiguously. I've got a feeling you know something about electronics and we have something to talk about, Citizen International Crook."

"Okay, let's hear it, Valery Chkalovich."

"What?"

"Everything!"

"But what have I done? Don't torture me with this uncertainty! What have I done?"

"Valery Chkalovich Kooler, you constructed a computer that became indispensable to the agency and freed many employees from having to work on preliminary inquiries. This enabled us to transfer them to executive activities, in the bloody sense of the term, and to surveillance work. What led you to build this computer?"

"The categorical imperative to penetrate the secret of matter, the objective state of scientific thought today, various philosophical and sociolegal preconditions, the apotheosis of positivism, and the desire to accelerate the development of the aesthetics of quantity. Quantity is great! And besides—this is just between you and me, Citizen International Crook Fan Fanych—we can't expect alms from nature. Our task is to help ourselves!"

"Have you or any of your relatives ever been attacked by one or more robbers?"

"Excuse me, but what has this got to do with the business I haven't got anything to do with?"

"Silence! We ask the questions!"

"Just one question, Citizen Fan Fanych!"

"Well?"

"Have you heard the Seventh?"

"You can't hear the seventh from here. Our cell's between the second on our left and the fourth on our right."

"I'm sorry, I meant Shostakovich's Seventh. The symphony."

"Very interesting. So you were listening to Shostakovich's Seventh Symphony while the siege Comrade Zhdanov brilliantly masterminded was still going on."

"You know that too!?"

"We know everything. We read the *Whistle* and the *Times*. Go on."

"One day my grandmother, grandfather, and I, almost dead of malnutrition, were walking along Uritsky Prospect. Two men stopped us. One of them, who for some reason kept calling my grandfather Akaky Akakievich, rudely demanded our bread ration cards. My grandmother and grandfather had worked with Uritsky himself, but they didn't have the strength to resist anymore. Granddad handed over the cards to the muggers. It was freezing cold. We had to help Grandma to walk. Near the cruiser *Aurora* she collapsed and said: 'Go on without me, or you'll be late.' Granddad and I got there on time. They had to carry us into the concert hall. It was an unforgettable evening for a little kid like me! That kind of moment won't happen again! When we got back to the *Aurora*, Grandma was no longer with us. Her lips had frozen in a smile. As she died, my grandmother had sensed that we'd arrived on time."

"Your grandfather sang to your grandmother: 'Pa-ra-ram-pa . . . ra-ra-rampa'?"

"How did you know?"

"Shostakovich was composing some pretty anti-patriotic music even in those days, if it could make you and your grandfather leave your starving grandmother to freeze to death. But you're right, it won't happen again. Comrade Zhdanov broke up that whole orchestra personally. Spit on 'The Judas of our music,' Valery Chkalovich! Excellent. Again. Okay, that's enough. Was it really worth leaving your grandmother to freeze in the snow? Haven't you ever been attacked yourself?"

"I was going home recently from the Bolshoi Georgievsky Palace in the Kremlin, where Comrade, sorry, Citizen Shvernik had awarded me—I'm ashamed to say it here—the Order of Lenin. A stranger stopped me in a dark alley and asked me politely for a light. He took a little time lighting his cigarette from mine. When I got home, I discovered the order had disappeared from my lapel . . . It's hard for me to talk about it.

Well, of course I reported it to the appropriate authorities right away. What really surprised me was that when the stranger lit his cigarette, he said very pleasantly, 'Thank you!' Do you think I'll get my medal back?"

"They're going to recall everybody's medals soon, they've been devalued. They'll give you a new one. You'll get the Order of Norbert Wiener instead. But let's go back to your idea that we can't expect alms from nature. Do you know what a robber is? A robber's a lazy, impatient beggar who's fed up with waiting for alms, so he's decided he's just going to take them directly from any passing gentleman or worker or peasant or intellectual. So he did. Socked the first passerby on the noggin. Then he socked another passerby. Then another, and a fourth, and fifth. Our beggar considered it his rightful alms, so one after another he took money from a little girl, and a little old lady's pension, and the money a son sent home to a grandfather, and a little boy's Christmas present. The passersby got scared, and stopped walking along Red Cavalry Street. So the lazy beggar moved to Collectivization Prospect and terrorized everybody there. Then he went to Fallen Heroes Street, and Industrialization Square, and he started stealing in apartment-building courtyards. In fact, he mugged and beat up every passerby in town. The city was deserted. There wasn't anyone left for the lazy beggar to get even a little bit of alms from. Not even someone who would *give* it to him. So the beggar died of hunger, cold, and sores, because he couldn't and wouldn't earn his living, and because he was too lazy to wait for alms to be given him. And as he breathed his last in You-Have-Nothing-to-Lose-but-Your-Chains Lane, he prayed quietly and penitently, 'Forgive me, Lord, for the passersby I murdered, and send me just one traveler with a crust of bread, I beg you, Lord!' The Lord God heard his prayer and was sorely grieved, because He couldn't send anyone to the beggar, for a reason that even He didn't understand. Not knowing evil, God also didn't know that the lazy beggars of Leningrad, Stalingrad, Sverdlovsk, Kalinin, Molotov, Frunze, Kirov, and all the other cities had beat up and mugged all the passersby so thoroughly that even the survivors were too weak to walk anymore. The land was empty . . ."

Valery Chkalovich looked thoughtful for a moment, but I could tell he hadn't understood a fucking word, Kolya. So I changed the subject. "Let's get back to the credit union. On the basis of all the data available on your personality, the computer you invented has concocted a crime covered under Articles 58, sections 1(a), 10, and 14, and 167, section 2. You stand accused that, having in 1914 entered into a criminal conspiracy with a person later found to be Grigory Rasputin, you systematically corrupted the ladies-in-waiting of the court; went picnicking with leaders of the Social Revolutionary Party, at which time you also promised Plekhanov the portfolio of Minister for Australian Affairs; and in various ways sabotaged the manufacture of Katyusha rockets at the Ford factory in Kansas City. For your services to Papuan intelligence in gathering information about Lemeshev's and Zhdanov's private lives, you received an honorarium from your credit union for which you signed. Do you confess that you are guilty of the accusations hereby declared; and do you agree to a severe sentence, the maximum measure of social protection: death by firing squad?"

I wish you could have seen what came over Valery Chkalovich then, Kolya. He didn't holler or groan or faint. Just foamed at the mouth and insisted the accusation was full of inner contradictions, it was the result of incomplete algorithmization, our semiconductors broke down more often than American ones, and besides he'd never met Rasputin. But I fixed him, the scumbag.

"So it seems," I say, "you constructed a machine to dishonor the Soviet people publicly, and you're guilty of the deaths of 413,851 persons and as many still waiting to be liquidated. Now you keep yakking about 'What have I done? What have I done?' But when you decided you couldn't expect any alms from nature, that was when you should have been asking yourself, 'What am I doing? What do I want to do?' Do you know you'll be sitting next to Andrei Yanuarovich Vyshinsky himself in the dock? They've accused him of transmitting venereal disease to textile factory workers and of an attempted attack on the presumption of innocence with inappropriate methods. The party's never going to forgive you for it!"

"Cursed be the day when Mama sensed the physicist in me! Cursed be positivism! Cursed be science! Oh, what have I done? Give me a new life, and I'll beg nature for alms with outstretched hands from hill and dale! Give me a new life, and tell me please what I've got to do with the Papuan secret service!"

"You tell me what I've got to do with a kangaroo, you learned bastard!" I shot back at him. I was sick and tired of this riffraff. He was getting to be a real pain. He paced up and down, muttering crazily, and spat on all the photographs on the walls.

But not a peep from Kidalla. Quiet as the tomb. I

switch on the Telefunken and get London. Seems the All-Union Conference of Punitive Agencies is going on in the Kremlin right now. Comrade Kidalla's giving a report on the future mechanization and automation of the agency's work. We listened to the report via London. There was a discussion after it, but the British Communist Party's radio station drowned it out. As far as they were concerned, our mass repression had nothing to do with the theory and practice of the socialist revolution; in fact, it was simply criminal for socialist consciences to be shocked by it. Hands off historical necessity, they said, you scum of the international arena!

Meanwhile, Valery Chkalovich had gone off his head. I mean totally. I began to feel bad. I told him if it hadn't been for him I would have waited for my finest hour forever and never known, never guessed I was a murderer and rapist of caged animals. I didn't give a shit about his longing to penetrate the secrets of matter. It didn't make any difference to me. If he hadn't been there, some other bullshitter with eyes popping out with curiosity would have invented a computer for the KGB. And that's what ruined you, Valery old buddy. You're finished, and now you'll never see your abacuses again, or your beloved arithmometer, or your quiet cup of tea over that inflammatory *Moscow Evening News*, or those closed symposiums and open party meetings, or the leaders of the parades on May Day and November 7, or a simultaneous chess game against Botvinnik, or the lawful moral relaxation permitted on weekends, you'll never see any of them anymore. When you're fed up with counting on your fingers, you can ask your beloved electronic baby to tell you the price of a connection to Papuan intelligence using the credit union as cover. You won't have to wait long, you inquisitive mind!

When I said this, Kolya, he suddenly spat at "Pasha Angelina trying on Catherine II's crown in the Granovity Palace," then at "We say no to Vadim Kozin!" Then he stood to attention, bowed to the picture of "The agency joking and smiling," and said: "Permit me to inform you, Comrade Stalin, that I beg you to permit me to inform you that the person informing you is deputy engineer Valery Kooler. I've cursed the latest achievements of scientific thought in occupied territories epaulettes torn from Akaky Akakievich's overcoat the highest honor of the party and everyone to the shameful pillar of the workers' extra effort self-criticism. I plotted. I feigned. I conspired. I lived under cover! I led a double life under pretext of beautifying the scientific research institute rocket factory no. 8 capitalism's blemishes. I was moonlighting as a snake in the bosom of the party and the people. More than once, I insinuated myself and crossed the uncrossable barrier of public toilets, left formulas behind, simultaneously cohabited. Give me back my deposit, and destroy the working blueprints. At your orders I will shoot myself willingly!"

My poor Valery Chkalovich is stripping down to his underpants, Kolya, standing against the wall. He covers "Cooks learning to lead the state" and a watercolor of "Sweet butter to the masses!" with his body, and says, "Ready for short circuit!"

I realized his brain had gone right off the rails, just like his computer. By now I was completely spooked.

Kidalla might slap on another twenty-five years for driving a big-shot state criminal out of his gourd, and then I'd really have had it.

"Valery," I say, "don't worry! Everything'll be fine. Drink a glass of water, kid, there, I'll put you to bed. I'm sorry I pulled that dirty stunt about the credit union. But you've got to understand, I didn't like it when they made me wait almost twenty-five years for my case and then pulled a kangaroo out of the hat. I'm an internationally famous crook, you know," I say. "The way things are going, people won't think I'm a regular guy anymore."

I calmed him down, somehow, and slapped him around a little until he came to, but that was a disaster. He started cutting up the *Times* in strips, poked little holes in them, and said, "Permission to report, Comrade Beria! Ready for programming! IBM to KGB."

Then he picked up all the strips with holes in them— I think they're called punch cards—and lay down on the sofa. His yellow eyes are popping out of his head and he's saying, "I absolutely must have castor oil to economize on computer time. I'm still not economical, comrades. Look after me, Fan Fanych. Don't forget, you're my program technician. Who would have predicted that I could self-reproduce a speech mechanism, Joseph Vissarionovich! Attention! I'm recording the passage of the punch cards through the circuit. Diodes functioning perfectly! Prepare to receive results!"

I dragged Valery Chkalovich off to the john, but he just went on reporting from inside, Kolya. "It has come to pass! The press is the party's strongest and sharpest weapon. IBM reporting to KGB! Based on results tabulated, for the first time in history we can definitively say: Everything is shit! Shit! Shit! Shit! I don't believe in Man's existence! He doesn't exist! Everything is shit! It's all fucked!"

Thunderous applause reached me from the All-Union Conference of Punitive Agencies over the Telefunken via London. Get this, Kolya, you could hear Valery Chkalovich himself, along with Kidalla's commentary. "Comrades and colleagues from the people's democracies, we can definitely say that human surveillance is a thing of the past. We have the latest achievements of scientific thought instead, which make it possible for our suspects to express themselves fully without feeling hampered by the notorious shyness complex invented by that enemy of the workers Ivan Freud. The workers and engineers in the secret factories can be proud of their nimble fingers, which have brought us telecameras, tape recorders, computers, and all the amplifiers that help us hear the enemy's inner voices!"

My Valery started screaming again: "Everything is shit! It's all fucked!" but he was drowned out by the French Communist Party's vehement denials. Since the conference could hear me, I hollered fit to bust, "Intermission! Let's all stand for twenty-four hours in memory of Comrades Dzerzhinsky, Uritsky, Volodarsky, Menzhinsky, Yezhov, Yagoda, and his faithful friend and ally Ingus the dog. Head for the buffet, everybody!"

Believe me, Kolya, they pushed back their chairs and stamped their feet. The secret-service types wanted to drink and stuff their faces, too, but Beria, who must have been up on the dais, burst out laughing and said, "You can see our enemies can keep their sense of humor,

even with their backs to the wall. But our dearly beloved Stalin—the agency's oldest friend—said it first:
he laughs best who laughs last!"

Everybody laughed, and they all stood and launched
into "Masha and me at the proceedings." Suddenly
there was a rattle from the john. Something cracked
and clicked. Water gurgled. When I looked in a few
minutes later—no Valery Chkalovich Kooler.

He's an academician again now, just as good-looking,
although his hair's gone gray. He runs some center for
statistical calculations and hosts a TV show, "Yesterday
and Today in Science." But at the time I heard on the
Telefunken that the Mexican, Greenland, and Papuan
Communist Parties were hopping mad. The jerks kept
saying there couldn't have been a conference like that
in the Kremlin and it must have been put together by
refugee renegades at Radio Liberty. In other words, the
CPSU's worst enemies were trying to invent its history.

Sorry I keep running off at the mouth like this, Kolya.
I know you can't stand politics. Let's drink to tapirs,
sea lions, and warblers. I hope they get their place in
the sun when there's an amnesty after some asshole
hotshot's death—maybe you and I will, too, assuming
God forbid they don't put us away again. And then
they can grant amnesty to academicians and writers
and colonels and beer venders.

That reminds me of that clapped-out cow Niurka on
our street corner. She personally does me out of fifty
grams every time she pours me a mug of beer. What
did I ever do to her, miserable douchebag? I don't get
it. Why the hell should I have to ask her to wait for the
head to settle before she finishes pouring? I should go
down on my knees in front of her stinking tank? How

those shitheads want to humiliate you and me for the stupidest two-bit things! In their faces! Do they really think this old international crook and Kolya Paganini are going to beg for fifty grams of beer every time? Better rip off the tank and give it away to a Guards division. The doughboys can drink it and piss their lives away. A barracks is worse than a jail, Kolya—but it's still better than a zoo.

Yeah, I know I've gotten sidetracked again. But what can you do, wading through a whole bunch of preliminary inquiries and still trying to hold your head up high. You get turned into a kangaroo, you try to hang on to some humanity, finally they free you, you work like crazy at Christ knows what, and bang, you've still got to beg them to wait for the head to settle. I've never asked anyone for a favor—well, maybe just the prosecutor, once or twice, and I can't even forgive myself for that. Hey, what about some breakfast? Ah, Kolya! That stuff we called stew in the camps is just bouillon out here. Let's drink to squirrels, sables, and martens. I can't stand to see them scuttling about in their cages.

I was scuttling about like a sable in my No. 3 (Deluxe) myself. No windows, no doors. I've forgotten whether it had a ceiling again. I scuttle about, or stare at the floor, or scribble some cheerful line for the screenplay of the trial, or just try to catnap—anything so I don't have to look at all those pictures and photographs covering the walls from top to bottom. And Karpo Marx was getting hairier and hairier in front of my eyes, and his beard was getting a little gray, while Lenin was getting balder and balder. I just couldn't stand to look at those pictures. Frankly, how I stayed normal and didn't go totally bananas, I'll never understand. Those pictures were always changing. You try and imagine this, Kolya. Suddenly, for no reason at all, "Pasha Angelina trying on Catherine II's crown in the Granovity Palace" vanishes, and instead you get "The porters of Kazansky Station say 'Good riddance, Judas!' to Trotsky." Or else "Karatsupa and his faithful friend Jawarharlal Nehru" zooms from lower right-hand corner to upper left-hand, and this fucking folk dance, excuse me, just goes on and on around the clock. "On rivers of enemy blood, the *Uritsky*, the *Volodarsky*, the *Kirov*, and many other ships set forth on their maiden voyage." "We say no to the fascist terror in Spain." "A new Poland is born of great travail." "The people of Zaporozhe write a letter to Truman." "Bread to the granaries!" "Coal to the mines!" "Everyone to the elections!"

I ended up putting a blindfold around my eyes just to keep out all those dead lies, that inhuman crap of banquet toasts, just to protect them from all the awful monolithic unity of party and people, the devilish pig snouts of the leaders flattering their slaves and their slavish labor. I wore a blindfold so those profanities in my great and beloved language wouldn't gouge out my pupils or spit on my heart and soul. I didn't stir up any more trouble—no use, right?

Seemed like Kidalla had forgotten about me. Then every half hour for a week, Yuri Levitan started chanting over the radio, again and again: "The teaching of Marx is all-powerful, because it is right."

That old crook Fan Fanych crowed like a rooster when he heard this. He had a feeling his trial was going to begin soon. I can always sniff out that kind of thing. Yuri Levitan wouldn't have been chanting, "The teaching of Marx is all-powerful, because it is right" twenty times a day for nothing. No, sir! Our microphone men aren't made that way. But it's just the opposite with Marx's teaching, you know, Kolya: because it's wrong, it's all-powerful. The fact is, teachings that are right and all-powerful all the time just don't exist.

"Okay, Mr. Crook, you haven't forgotten anything about kangaroos, have you?" Kidalla asks suddenly.

"You try forgetting when you've been in a kangaroo's skin yourself," I said. "I'm ready to go out into the dock and look the world's most democratic judiciary in the eye! I'm ready to read the indictment and sign 206, the best article in the RSFSR Criminal Justice Code."

"Stalin posing for a group of Soviet sculptors" moved away from "A rat in the New York slums," and old Ugly Mug—I hadn't seen him in months—said, "Bring your things!"

I DON'T KNOW to this day
how I got to the courthouse or where it was. I sniffed
a sweetish kind of gas and next thing I knew I was
waking up in the dock, behind a bar made of Karelian
birch. The seat was okay, but it didn't have a back,
which is unbelievably maddening during a trial. I don't
know about you, but I get this horrible feeling of emptiness behind me. I looked up and peered around a little.
For a while I couldn't stand to look the people there
in the face. But it was pretty interesting. In the front
rows were the representatives from all the Soviet republics, in national dress: turbans, kerchiefs, Caucasian
sheepskin hats, felt cloaks, side-buttoned Russian
blouses, high boots, Central Asian skullcaps, caftans,
and a lot of daggers. Behind them were workers straight
off the assembly lines, wiping their hands on their
overalls. Peasants with sickles. Intellectuals with note
pads. Writers. Generals. Soldiers. Violinists. A lot of
famous movie stars. A ballerina. Film directors. Surkov.
Fadeev. Khrennikov. Behind them were representatives
of the fraternal Communist Parties and daughter
Chekas. A TV camera. Two guys are running around

the hall, full of cheerful energy, sorting out the public. Now and then they argue with each other—the bastards are taking care of the aesthetic dimension.

Suddenly Mendelssohn's "Wedding March" started playing. Some Pioneers carrying bunches of paper flowers came running into the courtroom, and Lemeshev intoned, "Court is in session! Co-ou-our-ourt is in se-e-e-ess-ion!" We all stood up, and the judge (more like a mouse than a woman) came down the giant spiral staircase, the symbol of the spiral of historical development, with her two assessors, an old bag and a big healthy kid in a Russian blouse and huge boots. They sat down on chairs with enormous Soviet emblems on the backs. They named all the members of the Politburo honorary assessors, led by Stalin, and everybody else sat down again.

The prosecutor wore a uniform. His teeth were black and yellow, and he kept tapping his fingers on the table and looking at the ceiling. The creep's expression said that he was the only person with a clear conscience in the courtroom and if he could he'd slap correction-camp sentences on everyone else without a second thought. My defense lawyer also looks like he considers everybody present an unexposed crook. The difference between him and the prosecutor is that he looks like he understands. He's sorry for them, personally. Professionally speaking, he's ready to acquit them all, or at least reduce their sentences. The Pioneers strewed flowers all over the two volumes of my case history and gave bouquets to the judges, the prosecutor, and my escort. There weren't enough for the defense counsel, so the prosecutor walked over and shared his chrysanthemums. Off we go. In the name of the Republic of

Such-and-such . . . during these open closed proceedings we're going to hear the case of the accused citizen Gulyaev, alias Martyshkin, Katzenelenbogen, Zbigniew Cherez-Sedelnik, Ter-Johann Bach. They read two whole pages of my working names. The last one was Cariton Ustinych Newton Tarkington.

The old assessor—the same old bag I met on the way to Kidalla, remember, Kolya? the one who caught me giving the Karpo Marx picture in the grocery-store window a dirty look—when she realized my name was C.U.N. Tarkington, she said very loudly, "That's disgusting!"

The mouse-judge pushed on again. Accused of a crime that our penal code hadn't foreseen even though it was the best in the world. But it could be seen as corresponding to Article 58, sections 1, 2, 3, 4, 5, 6, 7, 8, 9, 10, etc., stopping at paragraphs (a), (b), (c), (d), and (e), then express to the end of the line. The accused was charged that he did, on a night between July 14, 1789, and January 9, 1905, bestially rape and sadistically murder in the Moscow Zoo a Royal Holstein kangaroo answering to the name of Gemma, and that on the night of May 1, along with a band of hoodlums, he sawed off the horn of Polikarp the rhinoceros, born 1937, with the intention of grinding the said horn to powder in order to stimulate the sexual activity of workers in certain Moscow theaters, the Philharmonic, and the State Circus . . . The accused, Tarkington, has confessed fully to these crimes . . .

That really pissed me off. I started shrieking like a banshee: "I didn't saw off any rhinoceros horn! That's the first I've heard of it! Bastards! You want me to take the rap for something else! I see what you're up to!"

Believe it or not, Kolya, no one tried to shut me up; in fact, quite the opposite. Everybody burst out clapping, even the prosecutor and the judge, and in the background you could faintly hear an Oginsky polonaise. I froze. My morale plummeted. For the first time in my life—much more sharply, much more hopelessly than when I was in the No. 3 (Deluxe)—I felt terribly alone and defenseless. Some diabolical force was making sure the masses were going to do a happy folk dance on me in my loneliness and weakness—on my life, on my one and only life! But Fan Fanych is no Caspar Milquetoast, and I kept a grip on myself. Go on, dance away, do your tango. Stamp on him, read how the truck drove over a yogi and didn't bother him at all. Three cheers for this other yogi—they threw him in the sea in a locked trunk, but he got out and swam up from the bottom of the Indian Ocean. Keep on reading, keep on stamping, dance on my poor lifeless chest. Your yogis never even dreamed of trucks as heavy and humiliating as the ones steamrolling over Fan Fanych's soul. Let me tell you, running over broken glass or red-hot coals is nothing to walking the hallways of the Lubyanka. Drinking sulfuric acid just isn't in the same league as reading up on a crime pinned on you against your will. Your yogis never even dreamed of the five, ten, twenty trunks they stuffed Fan Fanych into to drop him down to the bottom of dead rivers and seas and oceans. But Fan Fanych got himself out every time, can you believe it, he swam up to the top, got back to God's dry land, shook himself, and said, "Praised be the Lord." And every time his poor soul rejoiced that it had been miraculously saved. So go on, have fun! Fan Fanych's ribs won't crack under your trucks. He's got tricks up his sleeve to get him out of your worst trunks. He'll fly out of hell's abyss like a swallow. You can tell your yogis if they want to train their will and strength and courage they should get over here right away. Try Soviet life with all its liberating preliminary inquiries and collective labor in the corrective camps. Fan Fanych isn't a bad guy. He'll teach those poor yogis how to reach nirvana in a night on hard bunks. I thought about all this while the judge was mumbling the charges. It made me feel a little better. It was their job to lock me up, my job to get out of it. What's the use of moaning—the show's going to be worth watching.

So I'd confessed in full to all the crimes in question, and the evidence from the preliminary inquiry indicated that the accused, Tarkington, Ca.iton Ustinych Newton . . .

I guess this indictment stuff makes you want to throw up, Kolya. Okay, let's take time out from court and deal with this rhinoceros Polikarp, who really chose a great year to get born in.

It's just before May Day. The troops are getting ready for the parade. Tanks, howitzers, amphibious cars, privates, officers, motorcycles, horses, and generals all over the place. Stalin's inspecting Budyonny's mustache and polishing his jacket buttons. Vigilance is being stepped up everywhere. Beria hasn't had a shish kebab or a drop of Tsinandali in two whole days. He's stopped doing interrogations personally. He's sitting around in his villa near the zoo and wishing it was May 2.

Don't ask me why, Kolya, but the leaders think their enemies dream about nothing but how to ruin the May Day and November 7 holidays or spoil everything just before the Supreme Soviet elections. But this year the whole country's as quiet as a tomb—quieter than it's ever been. No one's blown up Lenin's mausoleum or the bridge over the Volga, or poisoned the hero-cities' piped water. Salami and sausages aren't what they used to be before the war, but you can live with it. The frontier's locked, the key's in an ostrich egg, the egg's in the Museum of the Revolution, the revolution was in 1917, no one can turn back the course of history, and anyway who gives a shit about the ostrich. So everything's quiet as a tomb. Then suddenly, the night before May Day: "Bang-bang! Bang-bang!" The soldiers dozing in their tanks woke up and switched on the engines. Red alert! Stalin heard it too and woke Beria: "Who fired those shots?" Beria said sleepily, "Fanya Kaplan." "I mean just now, for chrissake!" "We'll find out, Joseph Vissarionovich." They found out. Beria reported, "It was Rybkin, the watchman at the zoo. He says he had an attack of DTs. Says somebody was trying to steal the rhinoceros. Not a party member. Wounded in the war three times. Drank away his war medals at the Tishinsky market. He only kept the one he got for defending Stalingrad. It's your favorite, Joseph Vissarionovich."

"There's no smoke without fire. The Whites have always been hotheads, and our intelligence agents read in that guy Hemingway's books that rhinoceros horn can turn a millionaire into a real man. I bet that's what's behind Rybkin's two shots. Have the animal examined."

They dragged out the entire Academy of Sciences for the examination. For once, Stalin was right. Some unknown hoodlums had sawed off the horn the night before the parade and the demonstration. The academicians took a blood sample, tested it, and discovered the poor animal had been given a dose that would have knocked out an elephant. The military parade and demonstration went off as usual, but the leaders on the podium looked kind of peaky. They saluted their beloved Soviet people, but you could see their hearts weren't in it, and they kept looking guiltily at Stalin. We kind of overlooked the zoo, they seemed to be saying, please excuse us, we'll fix it, we'll call a party meeting in the predators' section and find the culprits.

Of course they couldn't find a thing, but Beria quickly fixed up a conspiracy among some homos from the operetta, the circus, and the conservatory, and a bunch of middle-aged dentists. They couldn't answer the question "What do you need so much gold and silver for?" and the agency came to the logical conclusion that it was for buying powdered rhinoceros horn. The dentists broke down, naturally. I mean, they tortured them with their own drills. What did I have to do with it all, Kolya? They said I was an accomplice and got Rybkin the watchman loaded to put him off his guard. Well, I did get him loaded, but it was so I could get on with my own business in the zoo. I decided to deny sawing off the horn to my last breath. On principle. I wasn't taking the rap for some horn. The computer hadn't said anything about it and I didn't have anything about it in my screenplay either.

Well, Kolya, let's drink to that poor rhinoceros Polikarp. Okay, back to the trial. First I described where I was born and baptized.

Old woman assessor: Defendant, why are you called Tarkington?

Me: I'm half Mordvinian and half British. Now read the initial letters of my names.

Old woman assessor (writing them down and reading): That's disgusting! It's a four-letter word!

A Chukchi representative (from the audience): Why didn't you rape a walrus? *(Applause.)*

Me: I'm just not attracted to walruses. And there's a more intimate reason I'll only discuss privately.

Prosecutor: Before we turn on the projector and acquaint the court with the filmed evidence in this case, I'd like to say a few words about this radically new cinematic genre, at whose birth we all have the honor to be present. The author of the screenplay is the accused himself, C.U.N. Tarkington. Obviously the investigators, who for a short time had to act as screenwriters, and the screenwriters, who became investigators, made some corrections in the accused's criminal concept. Not everything went smoothly, and not everything conformed to the aesthetic norms of Socialist Realism, the artistic movement of the century. But the collective overcame all the problems and is submitting the fruit of its efforts to the people's judgment today. For the time being, its creators will remain anonymous. They will all receive the Stalin Prize, first class. Long live the greatest friend of the most important art of all, long live the brilliant successor to the work of Marx and Chaplin, Engels and de Sica, Lenin and all-the-Pudovkins—the great Stalin! Death to Hollywood!

Black blinds came down over the windows, the lights went out, and a newsreel came on. Someone had smelted the first ton of cast iron . . . Some peasant had voluntarily returned his paycheck and called on the entire kolkhoz to do the same . . . Mountain shepherds had discovered the meat grinder . . . London was feting Ulanova. Senator McCarthy was slandering Charlie Chaplin . . . Soviet Jews were cordially refusing to unite with Israel. Then came The Movie. I felt sick.

An enclosure in the zoo, yellowish grass trodden down by animals, a manger kind of like the wash troughs at a Pioneer camp. A dead kangaroo lying nearby. The administrators of the zoo, scientific advisers, some Young Naturalists are standing around her, weeping. Suddenly, sirens wailing, two black Volgas and a paddy wagon roll up to the enclosure. Some guards with German shepherd dogs and various specialists jump out of the paddy wagon. Kidalla, in civvies, gets out of one of the Volgas and tells them to arrest everybody there. They shove them all into the paddy wagon. Close-up. Kidalla takes a hand grenade out of Gemma's pouch and bravely rips off the detonator. The audience gasps and claps. Gemma's head and open, staring eyes . . . her paws . . . her little toes . . . the rounded nails . . . the gray-brown fur . . . the strong, streamlined hind legs . . . her tail. I shut my eyes. When I open them again, the screen's showing a half-eaten turnip, a bag of grain, and two French rolls, the tidbits I used to lure Gemma on a night between July 14 and January 9. Kidalla turned her over and pointed to the fourteen knife wounds in her heart. I shut my eyes again. Bastards, scum, assholes! Why did they have to kill poor innocent Gemma? Why ruin my goddamn screenplay? I would have admitted raping five more kangaroos, boa constrictors, crocodiles, hyenas, for chrissake, without any of this. There wasn't any murder in my screenplay! What did they have to kill her for? I open my eyes again. It's the evidence: a fly button and a bus ticket. Suddenly Kidalla pulls something else out of Gemma's pouch. A baby kangaroo! A baby, Kolya, alive! It's alive! It's moving!

The courtroom exploded in a standing ovation and I clapped too until my palms ached, wiping the tears off on my sleeve. Alive! A young woman in a major's uniform, who was taking soil samples and measuring footprints, unbuttoned her blouse, displaying a gorgeous breast, and put the little 'roo to it, with a big womanly smile all over the screen. Kidalla turned away so the people wouldn't see a Chekist cry.

The lights came on unexpectedly. The Australian Communist Party representative was sick. His face was gray and he was clutching his heart. They put a microphone to his lips, and he whispered to the court—the world, maybe—"Workers of the world, unite! The teaching of Marx is all-powerful, because it is right!" They gave him a shot and he recovered a little. Two peasant women brandishing sickles threw themselves at me in a frenzy, and a workman with a hammer was right behind them. Without my escort, I would have had it. The lights went off again. They're arresting Rybkin the watchman, so I finally get to see the guy I got plastered and whose medals I bought at the Tishinsky market.

Rybkin was in dreamland, leaning up against a hippopotamus, which was snoozing too. His carbine was lying between the hippo's jaws. You could also see a half-empty bottle of vodka and a bag of pickles. Hippopotamuses sleep with their mouths open, like winos. Kidalla wakes Rybkin up by tickling his nostril with the muzzle of his pistol. The audience roared with laughter.

Rybkin opens an eye vaguely and stretches his hand out toward the vodka bottle, but Kidalla shouts, "Hands up!" Rybkin gets up, but you can see he doesn't quite get the message. The right one goes up, but the left's still groping for the bottle. Kidalla kicks his hand and shoves Rybkin into the paddy wagon. The poor guy keeps looking around yearningly at the bottle and the pickles in the hippo's mouth as he's walking to the car. He hasn't got a clue about what's going on. I felt pretty terrible about that. Then we got to yours truly's own invention, the detective-story part. The search for Fan Fanych with only two pathetic clues: the fly button and the bus ticket missing three numbers. Cross-examination of conductors, bus drivers, passengers, a saleslady in a men's clothing store, salesmen in liquor stores.

They interrogated Rybkin. In the end he caved in, but he categorically refused to answer any questions until they gave him something for the hair of the dog. What a mensch. But I was the only person in the courtroom who clapped. The mouse-judge warned me she'd have me thrown out if I prevented people of good will from watching the movie in peace, even if I had written the screenplay.

They draw the net tighter and tighter. By now eight million Muscovites are looking for Fan Fanych with the help of the description provided by Rybkin—under Kidalla's direction, of course. Eight million Muscovites gazing passionately into one another's faces from morning till night, looking for my features and distinguishing marks. Bitter lines around the mouth, Kolya. Kind, blue-gray eyes, bold crease above the nose. Handsome dark auburn eyebrows. Slightly bald. Noble forehead.

Bullet scar and pale-blue powder burns on the left temple. An average, sometimes even charming guy of indeterminate age.

Students are combing the forests near cities from Moscow to Vladivostok. Military patrols are checking papers at railroad stations and airports. Rybkin's wartime stripes are publicly torn off, but they left him his Stalingrad medal on Stalin's personal orders. The factories that have overfulfilled their half-year quotas sound their sirens every four hours. The circle's closing inexorably, but they still haven't managed to smoke me out. Kidalla's directing the search. He jumps out of cars and into helicopters and out of helicopters and into airplanes. We watch him meeting with his co-workers, thinking and eating in his office. He sleeps there, too, or rather, he dozes with his eyes open. He analyzes my fly button for an hour without lifting his eyes from the microscope. Then we see him explaining something to Beria, who's pulling leaves off the calendar, thinking, thinking, thinking.

Then they showed Gemma's body being brought to the airport on a gun carriage. Moscow workers were waving little Australian and Soviet flags along the route. Then they carried Gemma up the gangway on a stretcher and the airplane took off for Australia while people of good will watched, sad, angry. Then Gemma's funeral in Melbourne and our ambassador's speech over her grave, followed by the opening of a memorial complex designed by Vuchetich. Finally, the whole courtroom burst out sobbing, and I was pretty near cracking too.

I was experiencing the tragedy as if I'd really been through it. Maybe I was the only guy in the courtroom who felt this way, but you know what, Kolya? As the picture went on, I noticed I was starting to root for the Chekists. That was the crazy awful powerful effect the most important art form could have on your brain. Yeah! I was on their side, I wanted them to catch that little shit Fan Fanych posthaste and make him pay, the parasite!

I couldn't help jumping up when they arrested someone in the Aragvi restaurant right in the middle of a tango, right out of his partner's arms—but it still wasn't me, unfortunately. The young lieutenant apologized to the guy and asked the orchestra to play the tango again. Then back to the Lubyanka and a long line of guys missing fly buttons. There's a lot of lonely bachelors and husbands with lazy wives in Moscow—well, they're the same thing really, right?

Then a girl comes on. She's scared to death and gives Kidalla my tie with the gold coronets on a red background, gabbling into the microphone about how I was an animal, a sex maniac, how I liked to play leapfrog in the long corridor of her communal apartment at night. You know, it's the favorite game of kangaroos and French politicians, at least up until de Gaulle. And now here's another chick! Oh, I loved her so much, I was so gentle and generous with her—you should have seen her squeal on me, serious, businesslike, angrily turning over to the agency a diamond ring, a sealskin coat, and a book of Simonov's poetry, *Friends and Foes*. Every one of those chicks squealed on me. So did two of my aunts five times removed—lock, stock, and barrel—plus a whole bunch of dealers and speculators. And I was on their side right through it all. I'd totally forgotten about myself. I couldn't tell anymore which parts of the screenplay were mine and which were the Stalin Prize guys'.

So I sit there and watch and stamp my feet and clap and bite my nails—where is that bastard, for chrissake? Now Kidalla's right there on our street, interrogating that horrible bitch Niurka who sells beer on our corner. Let me tell you, Kolya, that bag swore I waited every day till the head settled and asked her to top it up just to get at her. Lying bitch! Me, who never asked her for anything of the sort! In fact, it was the other way around; I always said politely, "Please, just foam if you can manage it." That was what drove her crazy. But, you know, this time I didn't get angry at Niurka? This time I just nodded my head, oh, you're so right, Niurka, a real Soviet citizen, that's what you are. You know what got me out of this awful state for a while, Kolya? It was you, old buddy! If God lets me die a normal death and I have the strength to look behind me at the end, I'll remember the way you looked at the photo Kidalla shoved in your face, shrugged your shoulders, and said firmly, a little scornful of cops, the way a regular guy should be who respects himself and his friends: "Never saw the asshole before in my life."

When I'm dying I'll remember your laugh when they pinned you to the wall with the snapshot (you and me in the Savoy, smiling at the waiter bringing a bottle of Stolichnaya and baked carp) and you said to Kidalla and his sidekicks, who were furious because for cinematic reasons they couldn't lay a hand on you, "If I remembered every guy I've propped up a bar with . . ."

So you got me back to normal for five minutes. But the Bolsheviks don't call the movies the most important

---

art form for nothing—it can really turn everything upside down. I'm waiting for the net to close around me yet again. They've surrounded my house and a fire engine comes. They hold a tarpaulin under my windows in case I throw myself out from the sixth floor.

Kidalla takes the loudspeaker: "Come out, Cariton Ustinych Newton Tarkington! This is it! It's no use trying to resist!"

In front of the door there are six cops with automatics, ready to pump me full of holes. The bell rings and out comes my neighbor Zoika—the one whose apartment I pushed the bedbug into—and of course she starts telling them that two days before I was going away somewhere and I pulled a bundle of cash and some rings out of the toilet cistern and threatened to rape Zoika and then kill her if she ever talked. Then I beat it. Zoika showed them a switchblade covered in blood she's found in one of her galoshes. There were some gray-brown hairs stuck to the blade. Good thing they didn't search my pad. I was jumping with curiosity, where the fuck was I, where had the scumbag gotten to? Then they showed Stalin and Molotov receiving the Australian ambassador and giving him the late Empress Alexandra Fyodorovna's emeralds as a consolation. And of course there was a demonstration. The murderer must pay! Australia, we're with you! Hands off a friendly continent's fauna!

Suddenly, out of nowhere, they're showing a meadow covered with daisies, bluebells, pink clover. Butterflies are fluttering, bees are humming, and a lark's singing in the clear sky. It's all just as quiet and bucolic as can be. A brown-and-white cow's grazing near the river. The grass is so high she looks like she's floating when she walks, you can't see her legs move. "Martha! Martha!" A healthy-looking woman—you'd need a tank to flatten her—is calling the cow and shouting something in German. She's carrying a pail. "Martha! Martha!" The cow's hurrying toward the river. The woman catches up with her, grabs her by the horns, then slaps her on the neck. The cow stands still while the woman squats down and puts the bucket underneath her. She's getting ready to milk. She takes a teat in each hand, then opens her mouth with a dumb expression. You can see she's figuring something out. Then she shrieks, *"Hans! Hans! Soldaten! Schnell! Schnell!"*

The cow's falling down. You take a guess what's coming out of her belly. It's my face—me to a T! It occurred to me that Kidalla could very likely have suggested I go through this charade while I was under some kind of dope. But I had absolutely no idea how I could have ended up inside Martha the cow. They would have had to skin her real carefully so as not to leave any marks, keeping the head and tail attached, then find a second guy for the hind legs. In fact, I'm helping him out of Martha on the screen right now. It turns out he's not a man at all; it's Zoya the movie actress. We head for the river, trampling down the long grass. The water's the boundary between East and West Germany. Faster, Fan Fanych, faster! Don't leave me behind, Zoya! They're shooting at us already, bullets are whistling over our heads, automatic fire's spraying the grass all around us. The German shepherds' barking gets closer and closer. There's the river right in front of us, if we can plunge in we'll come out in a bar in Munich at a table covered with steins of beer that the waitress fills as soon as they're empty, and adds a splash after the head's settled without your having to embarrass yourself by asking. Jump, Zoya, jump, you idiot. But she trips over a molehill. She falls down, gets up, we're through the grass, fifteen yards of bare no-man's-land to the river. But the curtain of automatic fire's slashing at our feet. I give myself up, I don't want to die. Zoya's already up to her neck in the river but she's putting her hands up too. Two German shepherds are swimming toward her. Poor Zoya's squealing with terror—this isn't *A Musical Story* or the lead in *At the Frontier*. The East German guards are frisking us when suddenly the farmer's wife comes rushing up to me and bashes me on the noodle with her bucket—bang, everything swims in front of my eyes and my head rings like the Tsar Bell in the Kremlin. I fall down and the audience practically explodes with laughter. That was the end of my screenplay, and I was sorry my movie was over—but in fact there was still more to come.

We moved on to the interrogations. We watched them for two days straight, just short breaks for lunch and a leak. I denied the charges, evaded the questions, lied, refused to admit the fly button was mine, told them I never bought bus tickets on purpose, to undermine the public transportation system, begged them to turn me over to the Ecuadorian or Swiss police. But Kidalla's patient logic and the knife in Zoika's galosh hurt my argument and finally I broke down. The old witch assessor yelled again, "It's disgusting, total decadence!"

However I try, Kolya, I can't remember a single thing about the interrogations, or the faces of the endless witnesses and broads who were allowed to throw light on the process whereby I gradually plunged toward the bloody crime, inflamed by increasingly complicated sexual fantasies. I was in a bad state to think clearly anyway. The electrode they fixed on my chest tickled my nipple like crazy. The technician who stuck it on said it was really important, but I pulled it off secretly and felt a whole lot better. Suddenly, between interrogations, they showed us the meeting between Walter Ulbricht and Gerda Brombach, who'd discovered me and Zoya inside Martha's tummy.

"How did you manage it, Gerda?"

"Oh, nothing special. When I touched the cow's udder, it was cold. They taught us Kant and practical reason in school. I know an udder has to be warm, and this one was the cold in itself. I couldn't restrain a cry when I perceived this. So I hit him over the head with my bucket. Any German woman would have done the same. Marshal Tito is kaput! Israel must pay!"

"Thank you, Gerda. You're a good German," said that fag Ulbricht.

She was pretty nice, really. You know, I was so like myself in the movie—I mean, it wasn't so much that I was like me but that I didn't have a shadow of a doubt that the not-me was me, or vice versa—sorry, I'm getting mixed up again—but at the same time I just didn't remember one tiny little bit of what I was seeing on the screen, and I started feeling crazy again. My mind just gave up trying to sort out which existence was true and which fake. It was scary. In fact, I don't know anything scarier. Remember how I savored my last seconds of freedom like a condemned man savors his last crust of bread? Those seconds were the Time of My Life! But once you're in the dock and there's no support behind your back, only emptiness, when black darkness is all around, and there's your double up on a screen in front of you, when your poor tortured soul's trying to find some bit of its life inside that double, so as not to go under forever—I hope you never go through anything like those moments, Kolya, because they're nothing less than the Time of Death. After all the terrible things I've lived through, I can tell you, suicide is a poor tormented soul's last effort to find life again. I don't know what these efforts come to, Kolya, and you probably weren't meant to know either. Meanwhile, let's wish life to guilty humans and innocent animals, life to every living thing.

I'm starting to feel I'm going crazy again, especially because they're showing some really terrible things. Kidalla's arranged a confrontation between me and a middle-aged general. His epaulettes have gone, of course, and there's just dark patches on his tunic where his medal ribbons used to be. He's got a twitch in his cheek and eyelid. But, apart from that, he had a decent face. The face of a man and a soldier, Kolya, but something childish about it, too. Defenseless. As if they'd asked him to play at fighting a war, but some war whose rules he didn't know—he was used to Finnish wars and world wars. But in this one they never let you defend yourself, they only attack.

"Citizen Tarkington," Kidalla says, "did you have an agreement with former General Denisov that he would give you a hand grenade and a general's summer uniform in exchange for a load of planks and a hundred sheets of iron roofing?"

Can you imagine my saying yes, Kolya, even if General Denisov had given me five armored troop carriers and a couple of atomic bombs right under Molotov and Kaganovich's noses, instead of a pathetic hand grenade? Of course you can't! But I'm a miserable jerk, not only did I say he'd given them to me, I even added that in return for three bags of cement (this screenplay had him building a dacha for his mistress), the general offered me a brand-new field radio station and a plan of the army's strategic retreat to the Urals in case of war with Yugoslavia.

"Citizen Denisov, can you confirm Citizen Tarkington's statement?"

The general didn't look at me and Kidalla, but he said calmly that he could. I don't know if it was special effects or what, but in two minutes he was turning gray, and soon he'd gone white right in front of our eyes. He was a true general, and I'm just a piece of shit. I felt a great hole in my breast where my soul should have been. I just wanted to leap down out of the dock and throw myself on my escort's bayonet. In fact, I didn't just want to. I jumped up, but my feet seemed to be rooted to the floor. The bastards had even thought of that. I had to stay in the land of the living. I tried not to watch the screen, but a sickening terror (the kind that makes a guy who's scared to death of heights keep looking down from the tenth floor) dragged my hands away from my face and made me watch myself lying like a rat and squealing on everyone Kidalla mentioned. Sure, I knew I must have been doped or hypnotized, but so what? It didn't make me feel any better. Whatever they were doing, they were doing it to *me*, not some other asshole. Waiting for Kidalla to ask about you was the worst. He had to know about some of the scams we'd been in together and he definitely knew we were drinking pals. He wasn't going to pass up this chance. But the bastard didn't open his mouth.

The investigation was coming to an end. They'd done lots of experiments. I showed how I'd raped Gemma on a stuffed model of her body. I pointed out the bench where I'd sat for hours in front of her enclosure, hatching my crime. But Kidalla never said a word about you, Kolya! That vomit of the saviors of mankind didn't say a word. Why? I think I can guess. Probably there's something about guys like you and me, Kolya, that Kidalla just can't get to the bottom of, for all his power and cunning. He knows that great "something" is there, all right, but it's too deep for him. There's another possibility, too. Kidalla thinks guys like us are just rotten to the core——human deserts, not living souls, and dead, deserted bodies can't have a God, or any friends. Those are the only two reasons we were spared, Kolya.

So who the hell's up there on the screen? Me or not-me? Kidalla's the only one who can tell me. You see, I could toss off the rough draft of the screenplay, but I couldn't have squealed on General Denisov. He wasn't even in my screenplay, and neither were a lot of other characters. But you're right, Kolya. When you're Fan Fanych, international crook, you don't collaborate on screenplays. Let them write it themselves. Anyway, slander and fakery—that's their job, right? It would have saved me a lot of heartbreak over Rybkin the watchman, not to mention myself. Who is he really, anyway—some famous actor they created the role for, or a real live watchman? You just sit in the dock and rack your brains about it. When they took Rybkin away, he only put one of his hands up. The other was still groping for the bottle of vodka in the hippo's jaws. An actor could never have thought of that one. In fact, the more brilliant an actor is, the more you can see he's playacting. Maybe it was the director having a little joke? You never know. So I sit playing guessing games, while they interview more and more people, from simple folk to the more complex. What would they do to me for my bloody crimes? What would they sentence me to?

You have no idea how cruel and dense a lot of people of good will can be, Kolya. They didn't waste a second worrying whether I was guilty or not. About ninety percent simply said my legs ought to be torn off my body. The remaining ten percent thought up original tortures, but only so I'd have to scream with pain for a good long time. Not one of them bright enough to suggest *eternal* pain and torture. I guess men always envy anyone any kind of eternal existence, even an agonizing one. The complex people—writers, artists, export managers, journalists, the rest of the dreck— every one of them proposed pouring vodka down me from morning till night without ever letting me get over my hangover, until my heart just stopped. A horrible death, sure, but it needs complex people to think it up. The simple ones—and that's why I love 'em, the assholes—they'd never let you die like that. They'd help you through your hangover. Thank goodness for them.

The interviews just went on and on. Finally, for the nth time, Troshin, an actor from the Moscow Art Theater, announced, "We declare, we declare, we declare . . . an intermission!" After the intermission, in which they exhibited me at the Museum of Justice, they showed the latest newsreel. Then they showed the following short episode, to scare off people who might want to try concealing dangerous criminals.

I'm walking down a platform in the Belorussky Station, dressed in a general's uniform. I can tell you, I looked pretty spiffy. Very classy. It's too bad you haven't seen how being a general suits me. I'm limping elegantly, as if I've got a war wound. I walk up to the sleeping car of the Moscow–Berlin express and I feel really great. So far, this is definitely like me, Kolya. I get the feeling I actually must have been through this. I say to the conductress, "Hi, cutie, *guten Morgen*," and climb in. In the corridor I run into Zoya. Apparently, we've known each other a long time. She whispers something in my ear. I'm nodding and winking. I go into my compartment. You better believe it, there's a very pretty woman, about forty-three, in there. She doesn't pay any attention to me, just goes on reading a magazine with a picture of that slob Walter Ulbricht on the cover. I bow and get a cold nod back. I love it—this is where things get interesting. I sit down opposite her and take off my cap. I give a little sniff, just to check my feet don't smell. I hate smells in a train compartment. Mine are bad enough and other people's are worse. But everything's fine. Even my tiniest gesture's perfect. I'm not getting anywhere, so I stroll out into the corridor, looking cold and distant. I look out of the window for two straight hours, until the lady's beginning to worry I'm never coming back.

I come back, finally. Quietly open my suitcase. Take out a bottle of Armenian brandy, caviar, and a lemon. With her permission I spread all of this on the table and ask her, in German, if she'll do me the honor and kindness of joining me in a glass and a snack of the good God's gifts. "It's strange to hear a military man talk of God," the lady says. I'm a little disappointed when she grabs a glass like an old hooker. We drink up and get acquainted. I chat a little and suddenly sneeze. But you see, Kolya, I've never sneezed in my life. I'm just made that way, don't look so surprised. I've never sneezed— that's all. No, I don't know why. Stop pestering me, I've got a hang-up about it as it is. I envy people who can sneeze so much, I even fell in love with a woman once because she could sneeze seventeen times in a row. I can't. I guess it's my distinguishing feature. And Kidalla didn't know it obviously. I mean, who could give a shit about whether I can sneeze or not? You just assume people can, right? And that's where Kidalla blew it. Finally, I knew it wasn't me up there on the screen. Too bad it had to happen just when things were getting really interesting. It was unbearable to watch this fake Fan Fanych sit himself down next to the lady, undo the buttons on his uniform one by one, and then grab hold of her knee when the train braked. It must have been the first time in the history of jurisprudence the dock got polluted with semen—by me. Yeah, I came, just like I did when I was a kid in high school with a crush on the botany teacher when she gave me private lessons about pistils and stamens. She used to sit next to me, and I'd feel the warm touch of her elbow. Overcome with lust, I gave up trying to remember which were the pistils and which were the stamens.

Did I have to find out it wasn't me getting laid up there? They've certainly learned how to mock the human ego, the bastards. Suddenly Kozlovsky bleated, "Intermission!" They yanked me off to a cell to change my underpants. The creeps with the instruments had told them what I'd done.

I lost interest after that. Who cared about watching how General Fan Fanych lived in the apartment of the wife of an old communist underground agent, or watching her take him and Zoya to her hometown near the frontier, or seeing her dead—poisoned with potassium cyanide—in the forest. As she lay dying she managed to gasp, in three languages, "Good people! Be vigilant!" That part was not only uninteresting, it was a load of untalented crap. Then the representatives of the union republics started cross-examining me.

A Georgian: Say, buddy, did your mama give birth to you?

Me: Sure. Lydia Andreevna, my mom.

A Ukrainian: Women weren't enough for you, huh?

Me: Sexual perversions will survive until the death of imperialism, dear comrades!

An Estonian: Have you had any other domestic animals?

Me: A turkey, a crane, a cat named Alice, and a gelding named Flicka.

Prosecutor: Please enter in the record that a crane isn't a domestic animal and Flicka is a mare's name.

A Russian: You really didn't feel sorry for Gemma when you put the grenade in her shopping bag—I mean pouch?

Me: I had to destroy all the evidence. Sex and morality don't mix.

An Armenian: Who did you dedicate your crime to?

Me: Churchill, Chiang Kai-shek, Truman, and Marshal Tito.

An Uzbek: Did you treat the kangaroo to a pilaf?

Me: No, I don't know how to make it.

Defense Counsel: I would like this extenuating circumstance entered in the record.

Prosecutor: What's the name of the human being or animal who first aroused your sexual feelings?

Me: Joseph Vissarionovich Stalin.

*O*H, THE HELL with all the questions, Kolya. Let's go on to both sides' summation. The next day we got a short lecture on the international situation. Then the prosecutor took the floor.

"Dear Comrade Judges! Dear comrades! Dear defendant! We've all had a difficult time coming to grips with everything that's happened here in the last few days. We're witnessing a trial of the future. We're trying Citizen C.U.N. Tarkington for a first—a crime designed by a computer, using all the available data on the parameters of the accused's a priori criminal personality. We're trying Citizen Tarkington for a crime predicted by a machine, committed by a man, and discovered by our splendid Chekists. [*Thunderous applause. All stand.*]

"In this creative development of Marx's teaching on law, you might say we've freed our punitive hands from the shackles and snags of legal procedure. We've made the preliminary inquiry mighty and crude. Above all, as Mayakovsky says, we've made it visible. Visible and therefore comprehensible to everyone. Comrades, for how many years have we forgotten to use the art of cinema—in Lenin's view the most important art form—in our efforts to purge society of every potential enemy? Too many! Today you're all witnesses to the greatest moment in legal history, when life and Socialist Realist art converge. We can now inform our beloved party, our beloved government, and especially our beloved Stalin, that the problem of crime and punishment is settled before sentence is passed. We're happy to say that all progressive people of good will groaning under the yoke of capitalism are cheering our achievements. They're waiting hopefully for the moment when the proletariat in their countries takes power into its own hands and lays the foundations for a new life. A life with no place for crime, a life that'll celebrate Punishment with a capital P! [*Thunderous applause. All sit down.*] Nothing's more encouraging than seeing the splendid faces of the representatives of Communist Parties and popular liberation movements from all over the globe, aglow with hope. Because we've created this marvelous new legal model for them, too, grudging neither effort nor time [*General shout: "Peace! Friendship!"*] We're also informing the party and the people that we've conducted various psychophysiological experiments during this judicial session. We've obtained valuable data on the way the accused perceives the indictment and on his reactions to the questions from the representatives of the union republics—from the entire Soviet people, in other words. Soviet jurists have cooperated amicably with engineers, scientific scholars, the accused, and his guard, and discovered a new group of biocurrents in the brain and especially the upper extremities of the criminal when he experiences strong aversion to the inquiry, the trial, and the indictment. We've investigated the phenomena of sexual instability, spiritual demoralization, and unreasonable cheerfulness. Despite a short breakdown, we've successfully tested the RRR—the recorder of reactive repentance. Now we can say for certain that the recorder has registered all the impulses of repentance and resolution in recidivist structures, as exemplified by the defendant's psyche, under the influence of everything we've seen and heard here—the whole legal-aesthetic-political complex. We've recommended that C.U.N. Tarkington be awarded the medal of an Exemplary Worker for Soviet Justice for his conscientious participation in the experiment!"

Needless to say, the black-and-yellow-fanged prosecutor then went on about my remorse. They'd found out I'd torn off the RRR electrode and stuck it back on again, but the remorse it was registering had nothing to do with the kangaroo. No, I just couldn't believe that because I had nothing better to do I'd been dumb enough to write the screenplay for the trial while I was sitting around in my No. 3 (Deluxe). I couldn't forgive myself for that! Anyway, the prosecutor was a shit. But my defense counsel was such a bozo I ended up laughing and applauding hysterically.

"Comrades! In a country that's already well on the road to communism, lawyers should have become a weapon in the struggle with criminality long ago. For Marx–Lenin–Stalin, defending means attacking! Well, now we've done it. The defense has nothing more to say. I can't even think about the fiendish dogmas that have fettered my work for the last forty years without a shudder. But that's all in the past. Now prosecutors and defenders can shake hands in friendship and take the high road to Justice! Give them the green light! I'm through!"

This joker collapsed trembling and sobbing into a chair. I was laughing so hard the guards' commander made me drink a whole vial of valerian. But even then I was as happy as a clam. I knew which me was me and that this whole farce was just a trial of the future. We don't know what the future will actually be like— it's none of our business, and a good thing too.

"Defendant Tarkington! Do you have anything to say?"

I stood up. I leaned my elbows on the Karelian birch barrier and looked at the friendly brown knots in the polished wood. They reminded me of one of my best girls' elegantly shaped eyes—shit, she sold me down the river, too—and suddenly I needed a beer so bad, my jaws were twitching. I kept thinking about the beer, and somehow I started wondering about what it meant, my right to a final statement. Why final? Who should I say my last words to? You? The high boots? The Russian blouses? The Caucasian fur caps? The Circassian coats? The quilted jackets? The caftans and daggers? Black-and-yellow choppers? My bozo defense counsel? The mouse-judge, constantly riffling through my case history? The representatives of the peoples' democracies and fraternal Communist Parties? Maybe my escort and Kidalla? Or the Politburo, headed by Stalin? So who *should* I say my last words to? Oh, go suck a dick— it'll keep your heads from wagging! Well, of course I didn't say that, Kolya, or those would have been my last words. At that moment, my natural sense of dignity wouldn't let me say a single word, not even one little letter or comma.

If you're very lucky, you say your last words to your mom, your pop, your children, wife, girlfriend, drinking buddy, holy father, or whatever. In fact, you can even say your last beautiful, majestic words to your hangman, and whatever they are, at that moment they will be your whole life. But say my last words to all these assholes? No, Kolya! *Jamais!*

I said to myself, You're guilty of writing a draft of the screenplay for the trial out of deadly boredom. You got what you asked for, jerk! I shook my head to show there's no point yakking, everything's clear enough. Anyway, my mouth's watering—I just kept thinking, Let's get to the buffet! I shook my head again and sat down. I was given a standing ovation. Then they got up and trampled each other in the rush for the buffet. The ones doing the rushing were the unenlightened spectators. But the judges, those stinking lawyers, the journalists, the writers, the academicians, the generals, they all shook hands and kissed each other on both cheeks. And some reporter, who seemed to think he was at a hockey game, hollered into the microphone, "Victory! This is Nikolai Ozerov reporting from the trial of the future. Till we meet again over the airwaves, comrades!"

They turned off the electromagnets under the soles of my feet, and me and my guard went through a private door to a private buffet. Guess who was serving in there, Kolya. You got it! That douchebag Niurka. The guard led me up to the counter, and the trial bookkeeper, Nina Petrovna, checked her list and gave me a ruble coin with the daddy of the state stamped on the obverse. I say to Niurka, "A bottle of Riga beer and a salami sandwich."

Niurka acts as if she doesn't recognize me and says politely, "To eat here or to go?"

"To eat here."

She picked up a mug, the cow, so I couldn't rip off the bottle for the deposit, and poured the beer from the bottle into the mug. But she couldn't get it all in because of the head. So she said, "Wait for it to settle."

I said I could start drinking and she could pour the rest in afterward. But Niurka said, "A full glass should be a full glass, or you might drink this and then say why didn't you get a full mug. And then I have to do the explaining to the controller. So wait."

She won't give me the mug, Kolya. She just loves watching me squirm. I wait. The third warning bell rings. But the head on bottled beer's thick, not like draft. It's not settling. My throat's dry as a bone, my mouth's watering like crazy, and the escort's pushing me out. I say, "Listen, let me drink it straight out of the bottle, you stupid bitch!"

"No, it's not allowed. This is a trial of the future, not some wino hangout. Bug off. You can come back after the sentence."

"What if the beer's flat," I said, politely, "and gets as warm as camel's piss in the desert?"

"Then I'll open a new bottle for you."

"You mean I'll have to wait for the 'future' again?"

"Of course you will. I can't help it that they send us foamy beer. Maybe in the future they'll invent beer without it."

"All right. Here's the cash. Give me a bottle to take out."

"You can't take it with you," says the guard.

"Then give me a salami sandwich at least," I whispered, almost bursting into tears.

"No sandwiches without beer. We're trying to fight

alcoholism, you know," says that slimy Niurka. This is how you drive a guy crazy.

The administrator, a brisk little guy called Arkady Semyonovich, is flouncing up to me, exclaiming feebly: "Fan Fanych, old fellow, what are you up to? The court's waiting, you know. People are getting impatient!"

"Start the newsreel without me," I say.

"We can't do that. After all, it's your trial, not ours! Get back to the dock, there's a good fellow."

You know me, Kolya. In my own way I'm kind of an aristocrat. I couldn't get steamed in front of this bunch of scumbags, turn ugly, stand up for my rights—but don't forget, I'd renounced my right to a final statement simply to get a drink sooner, before they took me away. I mean, it could be the last time in my life I'd ever drink a nice cold beer with a Poltava salami sandwich. And this filthy bitch was torturing me, dumping on me right before they pronounced sentence! So in the end I left to hear what they had to say, hungry and thirsty. Niurka hissed after me, "You should have been screwing chicks, not kangaroos! You freak!"

Cheers, Kolya. Let's hope all the animals in the zoo get fed and watered whenever they want or need it.

When I get back to the courtroom, it's half dark. Everyone's already sitting down. Click. They've switched on the magnets under my feet. During the intermission the judge's table and the chairs with the Soviet emblems have been pushed aside to reveal a transparent wall. It's another first, Kolya. We get to watch the judges passing sentence in their deliberating room. The mouse-judge is braiding her hair into a thick pigtail in front of the mirror, holding hairpins in her teeth. She's listening to the old ratbag assessor droning on. I listened too. It was pretty interesting. Seems a bunch of guys like me lynched her husband during collectivization, just because he had a good party member's nose for sniffing out kulak grain caches, and one day he confiscated all the grain in some village and the kulaks' kids starved to death. So she thought the party ought to commute my jail sentence to execution. Especially because when I was young I scoffed (see my case history, p. 10) at 1920s enthusiasm, I debauched cranes by taking cynical advantage of their constitutional peculiarities—I hadn't even balked at a cat and a gelding.

Without even taking the hairpins out of her mouth, the mouse-judge asked what she meant by cranes' constitutions, because everybody knew there was only one true constitution in the world, Stalin's.

This threw the old bag for a moment, but she knew you didn't get into arguments about the constitution. Then the big clumsy assessor in the wading boots opened his trap for the first time since the trial started. "We shouldn't shoot him just because of a crane. If they stayed in their swamps and didn't hang around the villages . . . It's their own fault they get butt-fucked."

The old woman moved away from him snootily, wrinkling her nose as if he was polluting the air. "I'm for the firing squad," she said. "You've got to realize that everyone who supports us, every fighter for peace is expecting it. If we're softhearted, Tarkington's example could be catching. Look at young people nowadays. They're only looking for degeneracy, they go crazy about every decadent miasma the West sends our way. Today kangaroos, tomorrow Przhevalski's horses. Then—we can't shut our eyes to the problem—it may be gibbons, gorillas—primates! What next? Us? Humans?"

"I think we should shoot the watchman at the zoo, not Tarkington. It's guys like him who did in Chapaev. How could he fall asleep when he was on guard?" said the other assessor. "Maybe the gelding liked having relations with a man. We can't shoot him for that. That leaves the alley cat . . ."

The mouse-judge suddenly shut up Big Boots. Too bad, I was getting to like him. She stuck all the pins in her hair, and finally decided to bring her colleagues back to earth. "Comrades, you're forgetting something. This country doesn't have a death penalty. We have a labor shortage. We need everyone we've got to get the economy back on its feet."

I was the first one to clap, Kolya. It was great fun and so interesting. I hadn't been seriously bothered by all this stuff about the death penalty. I knew Stalin had dragged all the Politburo members into a meeting when the war was over. When they'd had a drink and a bite to eat, he said, "Guess what I'm going to do next, Vyacheslav."

"You're thinking of a local confrontation with imperialism—global, even," Molotov said. His face is so flat, Kolya, it looks as if his daddy used to pick him up by the feet when he was a kid and bang his head against the wall. He probably had a premonition about the kind of asshole his kid would grow up to be.

"What about you, Lazar?"

"You're always thinking about one thing, Joseph—our general line. Moscow *is* communism. Ha, ha!"

"What have you got to say, Georgie Malenkov?"

"Excuse me, Joseph Vissarionovich, I'm just an ordinary mortal party member, but whatever your idea is, we'll do our best to carry it out."

"That's a good answer. Can you guess, Anastas?"

"I don't want to put one over on you, Joseph, I don't know what you're thinking of. But I have an idea it's something to do with the food industry. I'll tell the party the people are going to be well fed soon."

"You've been telling me that for twenty-five years. But nobody's guessed my idea."

"Maybe you want to invade Africa, Joseph Vissariono-vich?"

"You've never been too bright, Nikita, but the way you're going you'll be a complete cretin soon. [*Roars of laughter.*] Forget about Africa. You should be worrying about the anti-Soviet jokes they're telling about you in Moscow. Klim, what about you?"

"We'll have the H-bomb in time for your seventieth birthday, Joseph."

"I'll believe that when I see it. What's the matter with you, Shvernik, what are you so down in the mouth about? Haven't you decorated anybody recently? Bored? We'll find you another job. You can go to the Ministry of Land Improvement! I mean, your waiting room is just chaos. All those women and kids crying—tsk, tsk. But they bother you about as much as a dripping tap. So you can get into land improvement instead. The president of excrement! [*Roars of laughter.*] You tell them what my idea is, Lavrenty. I can see you've guessed by your pince-nez. Go on, don't be scared."

"I think you want to abolish capital punishment," said Beria.

"Exactly. On the nose! Dance, Nikita. We'll clap hands. Make a circle!"

Nikita danced, thinking, "He's just an animal. Not a man, just an animal with an ugly mug. But just wait!"

Stalin explained he'd never forgotten the people personally. It was time to stop shooting them. "Of course, it's never too late to shoot somebody. But we'll stop for the time being. The Soviet people are the first in the world to build communism, but they're not used to working. They get to work late. They fool around. They rip off everything. What's the point of shooting the work force? We've got plenty of prisoners of war and traitors from occupied territories. Why send a Stakhanov to the uranium mines when we can send an enemy? Enough bloodshed's enough. We'll swap death for labor. Communism's everybody's vital concern! And uranium ore, new hydroelectric stations, factories, mines, and bombers are the fabric of communism. Let our enemies make the fabric. We've had enough shooting. Let's get down to work. But no need to mix up executions and a little . . . bang-bang now and then. You get me, Lavrenty?"

In other words, Kolya, I didn't have to worry about some old bag who'd been a party member since 1905 asking the mouse-judge to send me to the firing squad. Stalin had abolished the death penalty and that was that. But this douchebag has the nerve to try some kind of threat: "I think you've forgotten this is a trial of the future. The recent abolition of capital punishment is obviously only a temporary measure for the party. In the future, when we've fulfilled the projections for the economy, we're definitely going to reinstate it. Think about it, Vladlena Felixovna! What's the matter, dear, cat got your tongue? Let's shoot him! We've got to create the future today!"

"If you look at it that way, you're right. We can shoot him," Big Boots agreed. Dead silence in court, Kolya. I can tell you, I was numb—more dead than alive. I couldn't stop humming in my head a little rhyme I heard from a kulak in Kazakhstan once. Couldn't have remembered it at a worse time.

> Don't cry, my dear,
> I'll see you later.
> I'm off to be shot
> By a little dictator.

So this is what Comrade Kidalla set me up for. Very neat, buddy. What can I say? Hats off, fellas. I haven't got a hope. No nice doctor in a white coat is going to come into this courtroom and say, "Well, children, back to bed now. Cariton Ustinovich Newton Tarkington, alias Fan Fanych, please come to me for your discharge. That's enough playing at mass psychosis!"

So this is it. My life's going to end like this, in front of this horrible bunch. Who would have thought it, Kolya, who would have thought it . . . The mouse-judge is scurrying around the deliberating room, saying something first to one assessor, then the other. I can't hear what they're saying because the audience is clapping and chanting endlessly, "Shoot-him-dead! Shoot-him-dead!"

An electric cart rolls in, piled high with letters and telegrams, all of them, private and collective, demanding that the court wipe me off the face of the earth. They pushed it into the deliberating room and the old bag read the requests. She was crying, she was so happy and she felt so close to the people and the party and the Komsomol and all the men of arts and letters. Big Boots was reading them too and they kept waving the letters at the mouse-judge. I just sit there wondering how they'll finish me off, guns or poison. Poison would be less hassle. But of course they won't do it that way. For humanitarian reasons, you know. Just a quiet bowl of barley soup and I'm dead—no way. Afterward they'd have to pulverize me, body and soul. Better shoot me full of holes like in the good old days. I sit and wonder which you notice first, the bang-bang or the bullet in the back of the neck. This way I try to deaden my nerves so I won't remember anything or snivel or regret anything or love anything anymore. The quicker my soul gets out of this dirty, smelly dormitory, the better. On the third day it'll stop off somewhere. My soul can have a nice cup of tea at a quiet railroad buffet, a soft roll maybe, suck some hard candy. Not a soul about except mine. And on the third day, my lovely, you'll eat a lonely dinner in some freezing bar, but the borscht'll be hot and the lamb with kasha like it was in tsarist times. So eat up, get yourself warm, have some junket and a cigarette for the road. You've got more than a month's flying ahead of you, forty days without stopping. And when you get to your unknown destination on the fortieth day, then . . .

"Court in session!" Maxim Dormidontych Mikhailov chanted, and we all leaped to our feet. The sentence, Kolya! But the mouse-judge Vladlena Felixovna didn't announce it. She and her two assessors just stood behind their table. It was Yuri Levitan himself who announced, "All Soviet radio stations are standing by!" The gabble

went in one ear and out the other. "Charged that he did
. . . being guided by . . . not guilty . . . sawing off a
rhinoceros horn . . . liberate from the guard . . . case to
be examined further in the hero-cities . . . the crime . . .
at night . . . viciously raped and murdered . . . a hand
grenade . . . material evidence and the testimony of witnesses . . . completely damning. Twenty-five years' deprivation of freedom . . . taking into consideration countless requests of workers, guided by revolutionary Soviet
criminal law . . . Tarkington, Cariton Ustinovich Newton, born . . . capital punishment: to be shot!"

They're going to shoot me, Kolya. Don't goggle like
that. Don't act surprised or tell me there's no retroactive
law. Don't bother. Bourgeois laws aren't retroactive. Our
law's different. It's not a dogma, it's simply a guide to
action.

"Defendant Tarkington! Do you understand the sentence?"

"Terrific sentence. I couldn't have hoped for anything
like it. But I'd like the court to petition Stalin in favor of
execution by hanging in all the capitals and hero-cities
of the Soviet Union. Thank you, unaccused comrades!
Till we meet again over the airwaves!"

I gabbled this and they clapped quietly, but then the
two stage managers went running sternly through the
crowd turning the smiles and jokes into afflicted expressions. Some kids gave me an elegant edition of *Lenin
and Stalin on Law*. Then two more electric carts rolled
in, weighed down with red-and-black souvenir folders
with zippers down one side. They gave them out to the
audience and played cheerful music, some medley of
Dunaevsky's stuff. "How can we stand still? In our
daring we are always right," etc. Every bit of this crap

is more appalling, no, better, it's more disgusting than death.

The guard took me away to a lab cell. I wouldn't drink a glass of pure alcohol. I didn't eat lunch. I signed the experiment log and a statement agreeing not to divulge anything.

"Who can I divulge anything to *there*?" I say.

"Well, anything could happen. That's the regulations."

I also signed a bunch of lists and documents concerning the removal from service of various pieces of equipment. And at the lab technicians' request I wrote a declaration to the Minister of Machine Construction saying I'd wanted to screw the country one more time, so I'd smashed a bottle of alcohol with a steel bar. The lab guys wrote it off in the inventory and then drank the lot.

Sᴜᴅᴅᴇɴʟʏ I'm floating again, floating, so fast I don't have time to wonder whether I'm croaking or not. I came to in the condemned cell, bare-ass naked but not shaking with cold, don't ask me why. I don't even want to open my eyes. What's the point of waking up? I should just kick the bucket and that's that. No more worries for any of us, and society'll piss in its pants, it'll be so happy to get rid of this ugly monster who's good for nothing but getting in the way of its onward march to the shining heights. I just lie there without moving, Kolya, trying not to laugh, if you can believe it. I'm a funny guy. For a second I could imagine society getting really close to the heights, which are shining like crazy; in fact, a lot of the people are blinded by the unbearable dazzle already. But there's a few who are a bit smarter—they're wearing sunglasses. Society keeps going and starts disturbing the shaky slopes. Here come landslides, snowdrifts, avalanches, the Lenin glacier rolls down on society with all its ice-cold might, with smaller glaciers behind it: the Karpo Marx, the Budyonny, the Dzerzhinsky, the Stanislavsky, and the

Valery Kooler. A moment later the blind, deaf flood of humanity smashes into this raging element—thank God, it doesn't know all the ridiculous names men have saddled it with. The leaders and their slaves look around, totally at a loss. It was their helpless perplexity that made me laugh, I swear, Kolya, it wasn't because this picture of pitiless retribution could make me less scared of what was coming. My soundless laughter wasn't revenge—I'm not so stupid I believe everything's going to happen like I imagine it. But just for a moment, the helplessness and perplexity turned the cattle I knew back into people, or rather children, fated to be possessed by arrogance forever, to curse themselves for it at the Last Judgment and smile feebly and pray to God for salvation. Oh, Lord, I thought, how much older I feel, standing like this at the summit of this moment, than those who've already rotted and those whose time to rot will come too. It's so great not to be dying in the crowd, it's so great to be all alone and by myself right now, Lord! I don't want a pardon, I don't want to fool around with an appeal, I don't want anything anymore, I just want to go on lying here until they take me away with my things and I take my last steps on earth—this earth of reinforced concrete, red tiles, emptiness . . . emptiness, Kolya. It's so great to be all alone and by myself!

What a hope. Somewhere a march starts playing. "We're conquering space and time."

"On your feet, Tarkington! Get up, you rat, look around a little. You think we're all playing games here?" says Kidalla. "You think we don't know you're awake? On your feet, pig! I got a party reprimand because of you! Why didn't you make a final statement at the trial, jerk?"

"We hadn't talked about it," I said, getting up. I took a look around the walls. Behind glass was exhibited every implement you could want for committing suicide: soaped ropes, poisons, razors, knives, pistols, sleeping pills. So they want to see how I react to this kind of decor, specially designed with the condemned man in mind—after all, he's probably just dying to cut his waiting time by hours if not days. Okay, fine. Whatever you say, fellas! At your service! I'm looking for something sharp, but my cell doesn't even have any corners, let alone a spoon like the Count of Monte Cristo found. Just all these instruments stuck under glass. I know they're gawking at me, studying my psyche for the judiciary of the future, so I try lifting up the glass front of the case with my nails. I prowl around like a wolf, drooling so they think I'm just desperate for something, even if it's only a nail. I'd shove it into my heart and that'd be that.

Then they started scrambling the time. I heard the march again. I lie down on the bunk. Far as I'm concerned, they can think I've fallen for their little game and I think it's evening already. That's what they get paid for, they even write dissertations about this sort of crap. I know it's still daytime. I only woke up a couple of hours ago. I know it for sure: my left foot always starts to itch toward evening, I get this urge for a cup of tea with rusks and blackcurrant jelly. So I'm snoring real pretty, to make it look good, and I hear Beria's voice:

"Your experiments are enormously important to us,

comrades. It won't be long, Stalin said yesterday—we were eating shish kebabs, just the two of us—till our country's flying to the stars. But getting to even the nearest star—he pointed out—takes longer than twenty-five years in a camp with deprivation of civic rights. So we've got to find out how to change the human organism's biological clock so it can survive extended flights. Joseph Vissarionovich stressed that the human organism's biological clock is also relative: it's totally dependent on the will of the party and the will of the people . . . Anyway, buzz this scoundrel off to hell somewhere! He's been taking up space on earth for too long!" ordered Beria.

They played the same march again. I get up, stretch, yawn luxuriously, take a piss in the can, and say, "Are you thinking of feeding me, jerks? Or do we have to kick the bucket on an empty stomach in your glorious future?"

Nothing. The suicide instruments are still hanging inaccessibly behind the glass. My bunk disappeared into the wall and a hologram appeared instead. It's Ilyich, staring at Mr. H. G. Wells, propping his chin on his hand. He blinks a lot and says, "Oh, Wells, Wells!"

Suddenly a clock starts ticking loudly somewhere. Tick-tock, tick-tock. A screen lit up in front of my nose. The seconds flashed by. 60 . . . 59 . . . 40 . . . 36 . . . 30 . . . 20 . . . 10 . . . 3 . . . 1 . . . lift-off!

I hear a distant roar, I try to keep ahold of myself, obviously nothing can be worse than dying, you can't get out of it, I've been through a little, it'll take more than that to shock me, don't be scared, Fan Fanych, you'll come through . . . But my knees are knocking at the unknown, I can't help it, what have the pigs thought up this time, how long are you going to torture me? Suddenly there's a window like an airplane porthole in the wall. I look out—and I can see Red Square floating miles and miles away from me, and Lenin's tomb getting smaller and smaller—it's simply fascinating. Now Moscow's completely hidden beneath the clouds, and I'm above them, above the cloud snowdrifts, above the ice cream of my childhood, and there's a big round yellow cookie, a little pitted, with the word VANYA on it. I can see the moon, Kolya. I figured they'd decided to send me off to the devil as an experiment, instead of shooting me. I try and remember if there's a diabolical constellation in the universe. Which is better, death or a flight like this? I give up, and I get down on my knees and say, "Lord, don't leave me! Give me the strength to exist!"

I still have no idea how you and I would have gotten through the Soviet regime if we hadn't believed in God, Kolya. Our lives would just have been a miserable, humiliating, everyday hell without Him.

Well, I'm flying. I've said goodbye to earth. I'll tell you what I thought and felt then some other time. I do all the things they tell me to do over the radio, I listen to the latest news from Yuri Levitan: the thousandth FD locomotive has come off the rails, etc. I listen to music by Soviet composers, I eat—well, I fill my tummy with various pastes squeezed out of tubes—in fact, I live the way the Popoviches and Tereshkovas do now. I doze off and wake up once every hundred years by the electronic calendar. I take a peek out the porthole. It's pitch-dark outside except when a star or a constellation flashes by from time to time.

Oh, you're so right, Kolya, I was a stupid schmuck

---

who believed he was flying through space to hell. But in those days I didn't know what being weightless was—and if I didn't know that, how could I tell whether I was flying or not? Or whether I was out in space or in a laboratory in the Lubyanka? Especially because something kept rumbling behind the picture of Lenin and Wells, the little lights on the instruments kept flashing on and off, a bunch of arrows and indicators went crazy, and so forth. So I must be flying, right?

Anyway, time didn't exist for me, and, thank God, I didn't think about life or death anymore. I did have an idea for a while that maybe they had done me in after the sentence, and this flight was actually life in hell. But even that couldn't go on endlessly, forever. There has to be some kind of end of ends, even if it's only some tiny country railroad station where poor peasant women wearing eternal black plush jackets sell home fries and onions. There has to be. Hang on, Fan Fanych!

I think the electronic calendar's on the blink. The time's gone incredibly fast since I took off from earth. The speedometer says we're doing 60,000 miles per second. Well, what the hell does it matter what my speed is now? I catnap, wake up, fly past some kind of gray stone planets, with holes like Swiss cheese, doze again, and wake up again. Sometimes I laugh hysterically— I'm a weird, strange kind of guy. I'm beginning to understand a whole lot about what's happened in my life, Kolya. But what I don't get is this deep, warm, quiet laugh at what you'd think would be the worst moments of your life. What does it mean? My soul's alive and well, undamaged by the devil's worst weapon, despair? It's alive and chortling over the forces of evil's frantic activity, safe, knowing it's invulnerable? Is that it or not?

Sorry, I got sidetracked again. For a moment I really did despair. I didn't have anything better to do, so I decided to work out how fast time was passing by the growth of my beard and nails. But they just aren't growing. My face stays clean-shaven and the nails on my hands and feet are just as short every time I wake up. But by my calculation and that useless electronic calendar, I've already been flying for a thousand light-years. The earth must have already got to the stage of communism, the glorious future—and probably kicked the thermonuclear bucket as well. Oh, stop lecturing me, Kolya. I didn't know then you can slow down time when you're orbiting at almost the speed of light, and all that jazz. I was just getting jumpy. So would any normal guy in my situation. What was wrong? Was it that my beard and nails just weren't growing at all? Or had the Cheka snarled up time for me so badly that a day was like eternity? Maybe they doped me every day to shave my beard, and cut my nails once a week? So what? They could do it as much as they liked. But what if they really had blown my brains out, or just shot me in some ultramodern way so nothing would ever grow on me again? All I've got is an extraterrestrial life, which is obviously no better than a living death. And if that's it—then my number's really up. Fan Fanych liked a laugh when he was alive, but he doesn't give a damn anymore if he's dead. Yep, Kolya, that's sheer despair. Doesn't happen often, thank God. Mostly I can grin quietly to myself, so the Creator knows Fan Fanych is doing okay and He needn't worry about his health and spirits, despite a life spattered with sins and a pretty awful end.

Thousands more years passed, Kolya. Then one day I open my eyes and feel some kind of scratch or pimple itching on my leg. I rub it. A scratch! Where did it come from? I hardly dare find out. I lift up my left foot like a monkey, but the nails haven't grown. Disappointed, I lift up the right one. It's one of the greatest moments in my life when I see the little toe's grown a big healthy nail. I've never seen such a lovely nail—or maybe I did and just never noticed. So! You creeps are shaving me and cutting my nails to study my sense of time. But one of your colleagues had a bit of a hangover, right? He just forgot one little nail, skimped on the job, and now you can all go to hell! I'm alive and all right, and I don't have anything to be ashamed of.

When we were kids, me and my little brother had contests to see who could manage to bite his little toe. He always beat me, Lord rest his soul. But this time I was so damn happy, somehow I managed to bend right over to my little toe and give it a big kiss, gorgeous little thing. Thanks! I jumped up off the bunk, happy as a clam, and took a peek out the porthole. It was all dark except for two stars, one a bit bigger than the other. I yelled, "Kidalla! You putrid skunk! Your stars are a fake! Your cosmos is a rip-off! You've been pulling my leg for a couple of months, not thousands of years! Can you hear me, you crazy jerk? Let me tell you, I feel great! My pulse and blood pressure are normal, I'm ready for any of your experiments! How about that? Time's passing just the same as it always has, the earth hasn't floated off to hell, and I'm still on it, alive and well on death row! You won't get rid of me that easily, you bastard!"

I yelled at him some more—yelled my lungs out—and launched into a gypsy dance. *Chavella! Oom-papa-*

oom-papa! Chavella! Go on, try and glitter just a little, fake stars, twinkle your little shoulders. Hey, brother, kiss your guitar, spread the sound, *chavella*, that gold and silver sound! Fan Fanych is dancing a gypsy dance in the depths of the Cheka's fake universe! *Chavella! Oom-pa, oom-pa, oom-pa, oom-pa-pa-pa-pa!*

Suddenly a buzzer went off, three long, two short, a purple light flashed, and "Prepare to land" came on the screen. One of the stars in the depths of the porthole started to float toward me. Even though I knew it was phony I still got a cold feeling in my groin when the bogus descent began. Everything floated nearer and nearer. The moon came into view, half hidden by clouds. First the clouds were black, then purple, yellow, white—finally, the long leaves of some strange trees were brushing the glass. A hideous kind of lizard came out from behind a tree and headed in my direction. It bumped against the glass with its dragonish foot and dreadful long tail. It was a real monster, not a fake. It had heavy, wrinkled eyelids, just like Kidalla's. I suddenly noticed the glass cover had fallen off the suicide weapons. Take whatever you want, Fan Fanych! Take a soaped rope, tie it in a fashionable knot, and kick the bucket. Swallow the potassium cyanide, slash your wrists, put a bullet through your head, get yourself out of here. But I just hollered again, "Kidalla! You dirty skunk! You think my name's Ordzhonikidze, you think I'm going to do myself in? It isn't my life, it's a gift from God! Play with your toys yourself if that's what you want—I'll dance along with you! *Chavella! Oom-pa-pa-pa-pa! Chavella!* You won't make me give up this easily!"

Suddenly everything in the porthole vanished—the

collected works, from scratch, in twenty-four years and six months, no more, no less. Sorry, folks, but I lost half a year in preliminary imprisonment. And if you can, run over to Irkutsk Central and bring me the first Sofia Andreevna you come across to be my helpmate."

You can tell, Kolya, I'd missed the sight of ugly old human faces in my No. 3 (Deluxe) so much you couldn't stop me yakking. And it gave me the chance to warm up inside the watchtower. The boss guard writes down some of my demands just in case. And I get to the barracks happy just to be alive, my arms and legs are crowing, the sky's still there over my head, the earth's still bearing me, even if it does belong to the state. Above all, the worst's behind me, and *que sera, sera.* Thank you, my guardian angel, my good friend. I'm sorry you got saddled with the job of keeping a guy as hopeless as I am away from the devilish jaws of death and despair.

So I walk into the barracks with Dziuba, the boss guard. His eyes are really dark, but the whites are yellowish-red. On his way out he says if I make trouble he'll fix me himself. He's personally shot or driven to suicide, through painstaking investigations, 1,937 men —in honor of that glorious year—and he's not going to shrink from the thirty-eighth, even though he's already been retired for a year.

While we were walking across camp to the barracks, I'd had time to ask Dziuba if any of the enemies he'd shot were famous. Turned out there were some— Kamenev, Tukhachevsky, Blücher, Count Sheremetev, Countess Orlova, the Durnovo boys; mostly high nobility and the clergy, in fact. They gave him the job when he got rid of his greatest-ever target without fumbling:

---

little Tsarevich Alyosha, whose quiet innocent gaze scared all the Chekists.

"They gave me another prize for shooting the author of an arithmetic textbook, Shaposhnikov, and the writer Simonov," he said.

I said, "Listen, Citizen Dziuba, you can't play me for a sucker. They're still alive and well." But he said even if I was an internationally famous crook, I was a sucker if I didn't know that both the textbook and "Wait for me, I'll come back" had been slapped together in a secret workshop after the executions.

"What did you do them in for?" I asked.

Well, I found out why they'd retired him, when Dziuba said Shaposhnikov lied in his arithmetic book and that was why Dziuba's son still couldn't learn his multiplication tables after three years, and Dziuba's wife had screwed his own brother while the phonograph played the song Simonov wrote, "Wait for me, I'll come back." The bastard had totally lost his marbles.

We go into the barracks. Everyone stands up like kids in first grade, but very slowly. Dziuba says, "Here's your monitor, fascists! Get out your international arenas, or it's a strip search and twenty-four hours in the slaughterhouse! Jump to it!"

Some of the zeks are hauling out some kind of little boards and rags with little arrows and circles all over them. They couldn't live without some kind of politics, so they spent their time arranging all the international powers on these little boards and scraps and rags.

"How many times do I have to tell you scumbags, no gambling? Where are the chips? Come on, let's have all those monopolies, concerns, cartels, colonies, bourgeois parties, et cetera . . . You've lost capitalism's economic patsy out of me. Anyone who tries that won't live another day. Pull down your pants, bend over, get that world crisis chip out of your ass! What did I tell you—will you look at that? You even sneaked the national liberation movements up there! And you managed to stuff Socialist Realism in, too! Hey, listen, monitor! Every time you catch these jerks arranging their forces on the arenas instead of sleeping, you come straight out and tell me! Bedtime, assholes! Lights out!"

Dziuba beats it, and Chernyshevsky comes up to me and holds out his hand. "Were you arrested a long time ago, comrade?"

I say it's been six months since they put me inside, and they throw themselves on me like ants on a dead beetle. Just try fending them off. "What's the news? What's the news? What's the Leningrad party organization saying? Are the cadres still deciding everything? Is Mayakovsky getting published? Are there still long lines outside Lenin's tomb? How's Stalin doing? Is Mikoyan still running food and export? Is Kaganovich still running the Ukraine and the subway? What about young people? Comrade, please, just a few words on the enthusiasm of the masses and the international situation, please! And above all, does the so-called free world realize where it's headed?"

I have to admit it, Kolya, the conditions these poor suckers lived under were really super-tough. They never got near a radio, and they'd forgotten what a newspaper looked like. Well, I gave them a crock of shit.

"Churchill's being tried in Moscow City Court for his Iron Curtain speech. Ukrainian secret-agent partisans—guys with a clear conscience—have seized power in Switzerland, and we're in possession of almost all world

138

capital. What else? The Leningrad party organization thinks its leader was taken away just in time, and for good reasons. We've sent air balloons over Africa to drop tracts inciting the overthrow of the white colonizers. Latin America's in turmoil. Everything's going to collapse, basically because of the foundation of the People's Republic of China."

They went totally nuts when they heard this. "He was right! Ilyich was right! Even if he is a boor, Dzhugashvili's still a genius when it comes to getting things done! Hurrah! Let's get a sheet and make a new international arena, so we can see how things are going now! But first, let's sing the 'Internationale' to ourselves!"

It was Chernyshevsky who said this. They all stood up, completely overcome, tears running down their cheeks, their Adam's apples so jumpy that one of them had a seizure and they had to lay him down on a bunk. But they sang their hymn to the end. When they finished, Chernyshevsky—the wiry, yellow-faced one— announced a party meeting. They chose an honorary presidium consisting of Karpo Marx, Engels, Lenin, Stalin, Bukharin, Budyonny, Jacques Duclos, Thorez, Togliatti, Mao Tse-tung, Nikolai Ostrovsky, and Yezhov. They passed a resolution approving the Politburo's action. Some were for it, some against. The speakers sipped water from the kettle from time to time. Everything done by the rules and according to rank. They obviously didn't live by bread at all, just meetings. Then Chernyshevsky asked me to tell the group about myself.

"I'll be brief," I said. "Your era's intellect and honor and conscience can all go to hell as far as I'm concerned. I've never wanted to change the world. I've never taken alms from nature by force, I've just expropriated what the big guys don't need. I've ripped off a lot of governments, but I've never touched ordinary people. And I could have—I know six and a half languages. I refuse to help build such a dubious future on principle. I left behind me outside a whole museum of all the wallets, briefcases, and monocles I've swiped from big political activists from Poland, Rumania, England, Japan, Morocco, Germany, Costa Rica, et cetera. I've had the clap twice. I raped and viciously murdered a kangaroo called Gemma in the Moscow Zoo on a night between January 9, 1789, and July 14, 1905. That's why the People's Court in Krasnaya Presnya put me away for twenty-five years. And now," I wind up, "benefactors of mankind, friends of the people, night-night, it's sleepy-time."

They muttered to each other, went into a huddle, and finally passed a resolution which said that jailing a recidivist criminal alongside the most senior members of the party, the men who stormed the Winter Palace and fought at Lenin's side, was horrible cynicism and violated the Geneva Convention's ruling on treatment of political prisoners. They resolved not to shake hands with me and not to call me comrade, but rejected Chernyshevsky's amendment proposing a Red Terror against me. They said it went against Leninist norms of polemical discussion with an ideological enemy. I told them a whole lot more about the country's internal situation, starvation, imprisonment, the greatest commander of all times and all peoples, who should have been hauled up before the law for killing and dismembering millions of soldiers, about making you do time for being late for work that an animal shouldn't have to do, about how the peasants were starving to death while the big guys told them fairy tales about serfdom and the glorious kolkhoz life. I told them how an ordinary guy who has to go from one end of Moscow to the other to get to work squeezes himself into streetcars and not enough trolley-buses, scuffles with other poor bastards just like him, worried to death by government loans and meetings, puts in the extra hours when they have elections to the people's courts, all the time getting madder than a hungry wolf. And it's only because he's afraid they'll shove him inside that he tucks his tail between his legs and just bares his teeth after a little glass of vodka.

"Maybe, but we've got the cheapest housing in the world!" said Chernyshevsky to me, his dull eyes suddenly shining.

Well, then I told those saviors of ours a little about the population density in communal apartments, and about how mommy and daddy couldn't sleep together with dignity in their room because the kids would wake up and cry or giggle, not understanding the heartfelt, simple, great event—greater than Stakhanov's record—going on in their narrow bed. Newlyweds don't have anywhere to go when they want to pop their cherries—where's the fun in doing it in the same room with all your relatives? Before Kidalla called me, Kolya, I gave a lot of my neighbors advice on interrupted sexual intercourse and permanent frustration.

"The cheapest housing!" I said. "You should see the most advanced people in the world nagging each other in their tiny kitchens in front of the one and only faucet, or standing in line to piss and shit! You should see them spitting in their neighbors' borscht, scalding them with boiling water, hounding each other, wearing each other out, persecuting each other, stopping each other singing songs, counting the empty bottles. Before I was arrested I left my neighbor Zoika a bedbug, out of respect for living creatures. You fucking specialists in popular liberation movements, you should see how your New Man loathes his fellow men to the point of craziness, or rains insults on their poor miserable faces, their poor embittered broken hearts! You should see! As for individual apartments," I go on, "well, there are individual apartments for individual comrades—you can count them on your fingers—and various people's artists, alias *Battleship Potemkin*, *Mister Twister*, *The Rout*, *The Iron Flood*, *The Worker and the Peasant Woman*, *Communists at the Interrogation*, *Happy Kids*, the atomic bomb, *The Sabre Dance*, in other words—the glorious dawn of our motherland."

But Chernyshevsky just won't stop. "The entire world envies our free medical services, free prescriptions, free hospital beds! You don't believe that, either?"

"No, I don't," I said. "I've had five girlfriends who were doctors, and what they told me about our free medical services made my hair stand on end. You see, they don't have time to look after sick people. They push them through quicker than parts on a Ford assembly line, and you end up paying the highest price for your free services there is—your health. And if a doctor gives a worker too much sick leave, they haul her up in front of the party committee. My last girlfriend they just put inside for sabotage—yanked her out from under me at 4 a.m. She hadn't sent some fitters' foreman back to work quick enough. They started boozing on the job without him and didn't get the pictures of Beria and Molotov hung on the big shots' apartment house in time for May Day. So shut your trap, Chernyshevsky, alias *What Is to Be Done?*"

Oh, you should have heard him holler, Kolya, he went wild: "But the enthusiasm of the twenties! The enthusiasm of the thirties!"

I told him if you subtract the enthusiasm of the twenties from the enthusiasm of the thirties, all that's left is ten years for counterrevolutionary agitation and propaganda. "And listen, you bunch of suckers," I told them, "you don't know how lucky you are to be here playing your silly little games on your prison bunks, your cops and capitalist robbers and your I Spy the Crisis and never knowing a goddamn thing about the real world. Your very own blessed party saved you—its most sensitive members—saved you the terror of looking at the new world built by the Nobodies who became Somebodies. Have you got that, you dummies? Do you know I came here specially to say a little thank you to you, because who do I have to thank for everything that happens to Fan Fanych, a regular guy, if not you? Historical necessity, maybe? You can't shake hands with it, can you? Chernyshevsky, you say your concept was good but you're not responsible for the lousy execution? I don't like cursing, buddy, but that's horseshit. Let's say I decide to mug the German diplomatic courier on the *Titanic*, for instance, and so I try to notice everything going on. I know he's more worried about all his crappy notes and memos and peace treaties than the dollars in his wallet. I notice he's more nervous before lunch than after dinner. I listen to my intuition, I think about the disasters that can happen at sea, and in the end I say to hell with the dollars, they're a dead loss. My heart's telling me there's something nasty in the air and I should get myself out of here, as far as possible from the historical necessity of ripping off the diplomatic courier. Well, you all know what happened to the *Titanic*. That's the point of thinking about an idea and not putting it into practice! You have to know how to find the flaw in your concept!"

Four guys suddenly gave their party cards back to Chernyshevsky and lay down on their bunks.

"The trip's tired me out," I say. "I want to sleep, too. Tomorrow will come soon, and then back to work!"

Kolya, my dear old buddy, let's drink to antelopes, monkeys, and red foxes. When you think how we feel in the camps, imagine what they go through. God, it doesn't bear thinking about. It's especially bad for the antelopes. How are they supposed to get away from lionesses? And what about foxes? They pace about jumpily in their cells like lifelong crooks, thinking about all the hens and roosters they've swiped. The only thing a monkey's interested in is when he's likely to turn into a man. But they're still a whole lot better off free, especially because they take a lot longer to turn into men than when they're in the zoo. Oh, cursed mankind, guilty before microbes, snakes, butterflies, whales, grasses, birds, elephants, water, mountains, and God!

But that first night in camp, Chernyshevsky simply wouldn't let me sleep. He started them discussing whether I ought to be killed or not. Believe it or not, my arrival was threatening their underground cell's unity. I'd poisoned the members' consciousness with the virus of liquidationism and right-wing opportunism. In fact I, Fan Fanych, symbolized all the meanest, nastiest aspects of petty-bourgeois man: the kind of guy whose main aim in life is a ride to work on an empty trolleybus, hour after hour spent with all his favorite scabs, arteries, and cancers in the doctor's office, strolling around stores bursting with produce and goods of primary and secondary necessity, which petty-bourgeois man cynically opposes, in what he calls his soul, to historical necessity, beloved by party and government.

"*Mister* Tarkington and the *gentlemen* like him," says Chernyshevsky, "couldn't give a damn about all our problems or all the reactionary intrigues around us. They couldn't give a damn that the best sons of the people of the U.S.A. are languishing in torture chambers or about the tragedies in Spain, Portugal, and Lichtenstein. They couldn't give a damn about the war wounds our Komsomol volunteers are healing, or about the most brilliant discovery of Marxist economic thought, the workday. They couldn't give a damn about the state commission's plan for the electrification of Russia, or about Leninist simplicity and modesty, or about our secret-service men, who work in difficult conditions, sometimes even groping in the dark. They couldn't give a damn about the Exhibition of Economic Achievements, the All-Union Central Trade Union Council, the Department for the Struggle against the Embezzlement of Socialist Property, the Russian Soviet Federal Socialist Republic, the Institute of Marxism–Leninism, the Central Aero- and Hydrodynamics Institute, the All-Union Library of Social Sciences, or the United Nations. They couldn't give a damn about Stakhanov, Kozhedub, Eisenstein, Khachaturian, the Kukryniks, and least of all about the voice of Yuri Levitan, the world economic crisis, or the Gorky Park of Culture and Rest. No, just take everything from the party and don't give anything back except black ingratitude for free medical services and the lowest mortality rate and cheapest housing in the world. In a word," says Chernyshevsky, "that's the new opposition's aim. You can see why, for want of anything better to do, it degenerates to the point of fornication with representatives of exotic species, sent to zoos by the party and the government to save them from being completely wiped out in the wild by multi-millionaires' sons and by that terrible writer, that murderer Hemingway. Perhaps when Mr. Tarkington wakes up," says Chernyshevsky, "he can tell us how many pieces of silver he got out of the Marshall Plan people for his loathsome, malicious caricature of our communal apartments—those prototypes of the communes of the future? Now we have to put two resolutions to the vote. The first is to co-opt head guard Dziuba to the Central Committee, since, in our present delicate internal situation, he serves as liaison between us, the subjective victims of a tragic objective error, and Stalin's Politburo. The second resolution is that we, the Old Bolsheviks, who risked our lives to storm the Winter Palace and fought at Lenin's side, have decided to liquidate Tarkington, C.U.N., the liquidator who's infiltrated our ranks, the opportunist and hardened kangaroophiliac. Who's in favor? I propose we vote on both resolutions right away."

Chernyshevsky counts the votes, wipes his pince-nez, tugs at his little beard. Everyone seems to have abstained except him. He voted to co-opt Dziuba to the Central Committee and to liquidate me. He asked the meeting gloomily, "What is to be done?" and answered the question himself. "Nothing. The party's decision must be carried out. We'll have to make a concession of principle to Nechaevism."

I have to admit, Kolya, it was kind of interesting to be at a party meeting for the first and last time in my life. I couldn't make it till the end. I dropped off. I slept a whole lot better on my bunk than on the sofa Yagoda swiped from Riabushinsky. But I had a really terrible dream. I seem to be grazing on the hot asphalt of Melbourne, looking for green grass in the cracks. My chamois-soft lips are burning, my nose is dry, I'm longing for grass, but they're pushing and shoving me, and it's hot in my fur coat, and I'm choking from the gasoline fumes. I don't know what to do. But I need to bring back grass to my babies, preferably fresh green grass. They're waiting for me. I left them for a little while in Shvernik's waiting room on Mokhovaya Street. Then I realize with horror I've got one foot here in Melbourne and the other over there in Moscow. But that's not the worst part. In the end I find some grass. It was growing by the escalator in the subway, between the teeth of the steel comb that constantly swallows up the steps. I have to keep hopping backwards against their flow to tear up the grass. How did it get there? Feet, feet, feet, trampling on it all day long . . . I've torn up the grass and stuffed my pouch full, when suddenly I feel someone else sliding a hand in there. I grab the bastard and it's you, Kolya, and you ask why I didn't tell you about my pouch, I could use it to take beer and sunflower seeds into the soccer game. I'm so mad you've gone rummaging in my pouch and my babies are dying of hunger in Shvernik and Kalinin's waiting room that I howl loud enough to echo right through the subway station. The escalator stops and I go bounding down the steps. Down and down, but it seems like I'm never going to get to the end. I howl again. *Woo-ah-ah-ah!*

Suddenly sparks were spitting out of my left eye. It hurt badly and I woke up, thinking Chernyshevsky's attacking me, and ready to tear him apart. Don't take me for some liberal type, some Witte. My name's Fan Fanych and I'm just an ordinary guy. Well, I wake up all right, but the barracks are like some scene from the last days of Pompeii. You can't see a thing, there's an incredible racket, teeth gnashing, growling.

I light a match. About twenty guys are sprawled all over each other in the spaces between the bunks, having a collective epileptic fit. Total madness, just imagine, Kolya . . . What's up? Are you pissed because I dreamed about you? But you didn't swipe my grass—you didn't even know if you were sneaking into a human pocket or a kangaroo's. Let's face it, pal, I didn't dream about you on purpose. Hey, you shouldn't get depressed about anything so stupid—it's not good. I'm going to stop yakking about my life story for a while. I just remembered a terrible story Kidalla once told me when he was high on chifir.

He'd hired a one-time high-society fortune-teller as a stoolie. She used to interpret the dreams of the tsaritsa and her ladies-in-waiting. I don't know if she was a Freemason or not, but she still got the wives of a bunch of high-up workers as clients—even intellectuals sometimes. It was unbelievable what people dreamed about in those days. Charlotta Gavrilovna repeated all the dreams they told her to Kidalla. On the basis of Pavlov's teachings that dreams represent the effort our brains make every night to chew over our daytime thoughts,

Kidalla got together a bunch of great case histories. They nicknamed him "the poet of the agency." A diplomat's wife told this Charlotta Gavrilovna she'd dreamed about her hubby and two secretaries from the embassy in Italy. They were grabbing first Molotov, then Kaganovich, Kalinin, Mayakovsky, Mikoyan, Voroshilov, Vodopyanov, Mamlakat Mamaeva, and other members of the Politburo by the arms and legs and throwing them out to jackals, hyenas, and vultures in the forum of the Colosseum on Constitution Day. They were dedicating all this tossing to Stalin. It was his birthday in sixteen days. But for some reason the jackals and hyenas and vultures wouldn't eat the members of the Politburo and turned up their noses and turned away their fanged muzzles. Stalin was sitting there in a box, wearing a dirty sheet and sandals. He said to Mussolini, "Excuse me, Comrade Duce, some low-grade gladiators seem to have infiltrated our ranks."

Charlotta interpreted this dream very favorably. She said it meant a meeting, money, a wedding in a party summer-vacation house, and the defeat of General Franco. Then she reported the whole thing to Kidalla. All he had to do was summon the lovely lady's husband and his secretaries back from Italy and accuse them of conspiring with the Italian fascists to abduct all our party big shots and a lot of the lower-ranking activists. The guards took turns screwing the lady who'd told her dream right in front of her husband, until he cracked and squealed on his accomplices. At the end Kidalla told him he should be grateful to the investigators for not accusing him and the secretaries of attempting to throw a bunch of comrades to the lions and tigers at the circus, during a performance in honor of the delegates to the

Victory Congress. Because that was the big one—finito—not just ten measly years with disfranchisement and confiscation of property.

Well, like I told you, Kolya, there's total chaos in the barracks. The moon's shining through the window. On the watchtowers the guards are shooting at that white moon, just in case. The epileptics had heard the shots and fallen off their bunks in convulsions, groaning, screaming, biting their tongues, grinding their teeth. Someone should have put pillows under their heads, freed their bitten tongues with a spoon, held their arms and legs, petted them, wiped the sweat off their foreheads. But Chernyshevsky just sits on his bunk, smoking a straw from his mattress and saying to me, as if nothing was going on, "We got this epilepsy epidemic from Dostoevsky. I can't think why Belinsky and I didn't liquidate him then. None of this would have happened."

In come the guards with kerosene lamps. They stand around heaving with laughter, holding their sides. Some of them even bring their wives and children along for a look at this spectacle. With the four guys who turned in their party cards before, I start trying to calm the sick men. We were busy till morning. It was awful just to look at them. Blue faces, bloody mouths, barely breathing, and all of them with miserable, inhuman eyes, almost dead already. You could see Lenin's little lamp shining in those eyes. They lit up again toward morning.

You can see I didn't get much of a chance to sleep anymore that night, Kolya. The bell rang for reveille. On your feet. They dished out the bread ration and a bowl of brown slop. I went over to Chernyshevsky and told him if I ever once caught him trying to attack me I'd have him eaten by ravenous mad dogs right down to the bare bones, and when I got out again I'd take his skeleton to the Museum of the Revolution and swap it for the remains of Makhno and Rodzianko, or some other political corpse. He swallowed the whole thing and said they'd talked about me at the meeting, but there was no question of attacking me, they just wanted to get me interested in studying party history, which was the equivalent of liquidating me, and maybe even more effective.

"Now you tell me, Comrade Tarkington, what's new outside? What's happened to the United Nations? Does it still do whatever the U.S. says? Doesn't the party realize that murderer Vyshinsky, that Okhrana agent-provocateur they have at the UN, is a compromiser? We're compromising ourselves constantly!" Then Chernyshevsky grabbed me by the shoulder, grinned like a village idiot, and said, "Well, okay, okay. We've found you out. You're an English comrade. I sense Gallagher's hand in this. A master. I wouldn't be surprised if we heard one day that the English royal family's joined the party. Where are your credentials, Tarkington?"

Well, I acted real nonchalant and threw myself into it. I congratulated them for not giving in to provocation and still being great activists in the Comintern and the International Workers' Assistance Organization. "You're here for your own protection, on Stalin's personal orders, with the agreement of Thorez, Togliatti, and Thälmann. It's total war outside the camp, all over the world. They want to wipe out all the Old Bolsheviks, all the guys who stormed the Winter Palace and fought at Lenin and Sverdlov's side. Even inside our country there are certain forces—difficult to expose—that'll stop at nothing. So, as always, the party had to find a brilliant and simple plan. In the name of the Politburo and the Communist Parties of thirty countries, I have the honor to inform you, the heroes of our time, that you aren't here to be punished. You're just being carefully hidden, comrades, and neither the Gestapo nor the FBI nor the Sûreté Générale, nor even our own intelligence service, nor any secret police, however great it is, can get its bloody claws on you!"

At first I was just spouting off because I was so mad and depressed, but after a while they're sobbing at what I'm saying, those poor little Bolsheviks; they're holding hands, and even the ones just coming out of their fit brightened up a little, breathed a little deeper, poor bastards, came alive a little more. Their blue lips got some color back in them.

They stood up again and mumbled their hymn, and their voices were breaking with emotion. The earth shall rise on new foundations . . . Sing, little birds, sing, build yourselves a new world on your homemade international arenas, turn the old world inside out like an old coat under the direction of Karpo Marx, your chief pattern-cutter and bookkeeper of the world revolution.

Let's drink to every captured, crucified butterfly, and to beetles, and to the live birds that somebody stuffed, and hope you and I'll never have to have our old suits and overcoats turned.

J UST BETWEEN you and me, I have to admit I once did have a suit and overcoat turned, in Berlin, 1929. Inflation was going crazy, and I couldn't keep up with it. I'd rip off a million marks, say, and by the next morning they weren't worth zip. My clothes are falling apart, so one day I drop by Rosa Luxemburg and Karpo Liebknecht's and ask them, "What shall I do?"

They said I ought to have all my clothes turned. We moseyed over to Solomon the tailor. He did a fantastic job on my overcoat and suit, Kolya. They came out looking like new. I take a walking stick and stroll down Unter den Linden, but my spirits are strangely low. I'm not feeling a man's usual happy, proud independence from his temporal clothing on this earth. Definitely not.

For some reason my whole body's twitching inside the suit, as if there's a flea biting me, or a sharp little splinter scratching me. I keep looking in store windows and surreptitiously examining my reflection. I stand in front of mirrors pretending to adjust my necktie but really trying to crush my coat and suit into submission with my piercing stare. What in hell's come over you, you ass-holes? Why don't you like being worn by me? You look so great! You're pressed, you've got a chrysanthemum hiding the scar your breast pocket left. What's it to you if something that was left is right now, and vice versa? I'm the one who fumbles when I unbutton my fly because I'm not used to it this way. What's got into you both, for chrissake? But they won't say a word, the jerks, just go on hanging on me like they're on tenter-hooks. This hostility's starting to make me nervous when I'm supposed to be working. I jump. I keep looking around me when I should be looking all the valets, butlers, secretaries, and so forth straight in the eye. Whether I'm at a sit-down dinner or a buffet, I don't know what to do with myself.

I check out Hindenburg's nanny at the symphony—you should have seen the diamonds in her ears. I listen to Shostakovich yet again, and I'm sweating. My back's dripping. I can tell my rotten jacket's doing it on purpose, just to make me look like an idiot, and my pants are giving it moral support. They're riding up my knees in creases, and keep rustling. And my pockets are moaning like seashells, "Oo-oo-oo." I keep fidgeting on my chair, which, to make things worse, is collapsible. Some fascist whispers politely to me, "You came to listen to the music. If you don't like it, go find yourself a whorehouse!"

I don't say anything. I try to control myself. But I can't stand the irritation and twist a button off my jacket and scratch away at my fly. Then the conductor, Toscanini, turns around and shakes his baton at me: Ssssh! I wonder how the hell he can have noticed *mein Kampf* with my wardrobe when he has his back to the audience. I didn't make any noise twisting off the button, my pants didn't scream with pain, my goddamn jacket didn't fall off me in a faint. There aren't any mirrors in front of Toscanini. Maybe somebody in the orchestra squealed on me, I think. No, when they're not staring at their music, they're rolling their eyes at the ceiling because they love the music so much. Toscanini really amazed me.

Meanwhile, my suit's cooled down a little. It's curled up in a little ball, crying. Go on, cry, rat, cry! Just you wait! If you don't shut up I'm going to burn holes in you with matches and douse you with caustic soda!

Intermission. I didn't go to the buffet, just strolled around the foyer with my monocle on. But I can tell everyone's staring at me, whispering to each other, razzing me. My suit senses it and starts heating up my back again. I'll spare you the armpits—it was like carrying around a sauna. God, my knees! You don't usually expect your knees to sweat, Kolya, right? They were streaming, just to make me miserable, and stuck to my pants. I kept having to sneak my hands in my pockets to yank my pants legs straight. In other words, the intermission was even worse than the concert.

I leaned against a pillar. I hated my suit with deadly loathing. But my fucking jacket's fighting back, stabbing one of its pig's bristles through my shirt. I pull one lapel away and the other one goes for me! I try to arrange myself in an empty space inside my jacket so I won't touch it at all. I'm wriggling and writhing all over. But the third bell's ringing and I haven't fixed a damn thing.

I get back to my seat. The stabbing's still going on. The bristles get sharper and sharper and suddenly tickle me all over at the same time. I waved my arms like a steam locomotive, scratching and giggling like crazy. The fascists shushed. Toscanini looked over his shoulder again and stared me up and down snootily as if I was a piece of macaroni. The orchestra trumpeted something and everyone forgot about me, thank God. Only the same greasy fascist behind me whispered, "If I were you, I would've gone to the whorehouse hours ago. I'm telling you, you'll have a good time!"

I scribbled a note that sounded as if it came from some German in the audience and passed it to the fascist's lady friend. Then I broke for the exit, feeling like the whole audience and Toscanini and his orchestra were all staring at my back. You know what my miserable jacket had done? Only ridden right up on my shoulders. My pants had just been waiting for this and worked their way into my asshole so deep and tight you'd think I'd done it myself by sheer willpower. While I'm walking out, I bend over and jiggle all the muscles and flesh in my poor ass, but I know it's hopeless. I ducked behind a velvet curtain, yanked at my pants ass so hard I really pinched myself, and wiped my sweaty face with the curtain. I peeked out from behind it. The fascist's lady friend read my note, stood up, and whacked the fascist in the face. A buzz. Toscanini shuddered with fury and threw his baton at the orchestra. The woman ran sobbing toward my curtain and out the door, grazing me with hip and bosom on the way. Someone in the audience hollered, "It's time to put a stop to this filthy Social Democratic agitation once and for all. We Germans have always been famous for our appreciation of music! We're a nation of philosophers, not Jews." I looked at him: he had a forelock, and a little black mustache right under his nose.

The greasy pig who'd gotten slapped in the face yelled out, "Heil, Hitler!"

I ran like hell to my pad on Boulevard Hegel.

As soon as I got home, I ripped off my pants and whipped my little Gretchen in the face with them without a word—thwack! thwack! thwack! Then I started swatting flies with the jacket. Yeah, I know I'm a shit, it was bad, it wasn't fair to the poor woman and the flies. But that's the way it is, we always take out our anger on people who've got nothing to do with our fury or screwups or persecutions or desperate grief . . . I stamp on the suit. I'm foaming at the mouth. Then I throw myself crying on the couch. Gretchen's crying, too. We're both crying. You know, you can look at it another way. If we took out our anger on the guys who're really to blame for all the shit in our lives, who could we apologize to afterward, who could we ask to forgive us, who could we suffer for? We made up. In the morning she pressed the suit. It looked terrible. Maybe it's going to be different? What a hope. When the coat and suit are in a reasonable mood they act kind of cold and hostile toward me, but at least I get a little respect. But when they get mean and sassy, boy, are they vicious. The jacket's favorite game is losing the chrysanthemum or carnation I use to hide the scar where the pocket's been turned. It's as if it's saying, "Look! *I've* got nothing to hide! Look over here! *I'm* not ashamed of myself! I may be only a poor jacket, but I'm honest!"

Kolya, I know you've been through a lot. You've been in Vanino transit camp, the bastards have gone after you with their pikes, you've been tortured by bedbugs and hunger while you lay in solitary, you've rattled around half dead in prison trains with less water than the

Sahara—at least the desert has mirages—but you've never felt how consumer goods and products can blackmail an ordinary guy during inflationary times, the motherfuckers, and I hope you never do.

Not long after the concert, I ran into a real aristocratic little lady in a museum. Aristocratic, yeah, but poor. She was trying to look more elegant by being just a little too clever with her outfit. As you know, a woman's getup is much more complicated than ours—it's made up of a lot more different things. Under inflation us guys could always darn our underpants, say, or just forget about them altogether. But what's a pretty girl with no money to do about stockings? Or shoes? She ages five years the first time they're reheeled and twenty the second. It's just no fun to walk around anymore. Don't even mention stocking runs. Those runs make a woman's heart bleed like real wounds in men's hearts.

The lady and I were both feasting our eyes on a yummy still life. I pretended I didn't notice how the poor lady in the severe suit with the moleskin muff—well, her mouth was watering like crazy. She'd pulled off the lobster tail already and was wondering what to wash it down with. There was a hell of a lot to choose from. Oh, Kolya, you should have felt my heart jump and seen me blush when I realized her spiffy little suit had been turned—and brilliantly, too. And I was the only one in this crowd of Germans who'd noticed. I'm no sucker. When the inside of a piece of cloth suddenly turns into the outside, without knowing how or why, the goddamn thing starts acting outrageously chic—it gives you a blatant come-on. And the better and more expensive the material was before—gabardine, maybe, or some kind of tweed—the more this awful wrong side, with its unhoped-for new career (thanks to inflation and human misery), crudely throws its weight around and acts like it owns the world. From being Nobody, you see, it's suddenly become Somebody. But also the wrong side never forgets, even when it's drunk with this kind of happiness, that it's got no glorious future ahead of it. Zip. It'll never be looked after by a tailor again, and its owner certainly won't re-turn the suit or overcoat himself. Besides, the faithless material's own nature won't let it be done. But they're long-lived bastards, these wrong sides. I don't know if it's because they're afraid of their inevitable ends, or if it's just incredible economizing, but somehow they manage to hang on to life a lot longer than the right side ever does, a *lot* longer.

So the soft cream-colored wool of the little lady's severe suit is shining with joy in its new life, the lady's little paws are warming each other inside their tiny moleskin nest. She put a little glycerine on the fur before she went out so it wouldn't look so old and balding. We're alone in front of the still life, and we've gobbled up everything that was in it. All that's left are the pheasant wings, the pineapple tops and lemon peel, and the lobsters' and crayfishes' bright red armor. We gobbled the lot and eyed each other, feeling good and full. I followed her into the other rooms.

"Look at that, jerk," I say to my suit. "There's someone who knows how to behave in society! What's stopping you being as nice as that? The lady's suit's been turned just like you have, but you can see how it carries itself! A marquess, a baron, practically a general!" My suit keeps its trap shut and doesn't sass me. The jacket settles on me a little more comfortably. The lapels bring their little points closer and the buttons stop moaning about being separated from their old buttonholes and forcibly wedded to new usurpers. My pants' creases suddenly appear, and the legs float freely like boats on a lake, overtaking each other by turns. I can walk with a lot more dignity.

Just then, which was pretty unfortunate, the lady and I come to an exhibit of nineteenth-century costumes. Every kind of suit, camisole, cloak, and frock coat, and dresses trimmed with fur and jewels, a hundred years old or more, they all look young and gay and self-respecting—they could care less about us. The lady and I feel every kind of cloth—silks, velvets, et cetera —just like we're in the trade. We're looking to pounce on the littlest thing that's been turned. But there's nothing. Suddenly, out of nowhere, the little lady clasps the bemedaled breast of a black-and-gold Talleyrand uniform to her cheek and bursts into bitter tears.

"Excuse me, Frau, did you lose something?" She shakes her head sadly. "You're not feeling so good?"

"I'm just so sorry these aren't ever . . . never . . . nothing's ever going to . . . anymore . . . it's all so terrible . . . terrible . . . terrible!" says the lady, and drops her handkerchief.

Believe me, Kolya, some voice inside me was already saying, "Don't bend over, whatever you do!" But the situation was too touching, and I bent over with the feeling something irreparable was going to happen, and was I right. My blasted pants split right down the seam on my ass, with a malicious ripping sound. My suit's won. The jacket shouted, "Bravo! Bravo!" I straighten up. I give the little lady her handkerchief even though I'm so ashamed my face is burning up. I try to hide my worse than bare behind. What I went through, Kolya! God!

"Thank you. That's very kind of you."

"I'd be so happy to call on you at a more convenient time, Frau," I say.

"Here's my card. *Auf Wiedersehen*. I don't feel well —it's the naphthalene. Please don't come with me. Here's a safety pin," says the little lady. She's figured out the tragedy.

She heads for the exit. What could I do? I try to put together the two halves of my pants. I'm hiding behind a Hofmarschall of the Austrian court in parade uniform. I get the halves lined up finally. With the other hand I bring the safety pin through my fly to join the two trouser halves from inside—I'm pouring with sweat from the tension—and suddenly yell loud enough to bring the roof down. "Aa-aagghh!" I've finally managed to stick the pin in my ass.

Here comes the attendant. *"Was ist das?"*

"What a fantastic exhibit! The fashions! The accessories! And not one of them's been turned!"

"You're right, alas," said the attendant. "But please could you keep your enthusiasm a little quieter? *Gut?*"

"Gut," I say. I'm in despair. I may as well leave the museum with a ripped rear end, but I just don't have the moxie. My suit's practically pissing its own pants, seeing me in this agony and humiliation. It's wriggling all over the place, totally crazy, and trying to turn itself inside out—I mean, back to its old outside, the asshole. "Don't worry, I'll teach you to scream 'Bravo!' I'll teach you and you'll be sorry."

I try to pin the halves together again, this time from

the outside. Carefully. "You don't mean to tell me you can't pin up your pants—you, the guy who took an entire set of platinum dentures with diamond fillings out of old Baron Broschke's mouth without his noticing anything, when he'd been gawking at the Mona Lisa in the Louvre with his mouth open for two hours straight?" I tell myself.

"Ow-ow-ow-ouch!" Of course I've stabbed myself yet again. I'm so mad I shove the pin right up the ass of the Austrian Hofmarschall. In a flash I discard this petty plebeian state for a really inspired aristocratic one. It's the only condition that helps us accomplish miracles in life, dangerous jobs, the circus. Don't forget I was a tightrope walker once . . . M. de Rothschild himself was standing on the Hofmarschall's left, wearing a black suit of very fine cloth. He had a little derby on his manne-quin noodle and a cane in his dead hand. The placard said:

A Suit of Baron Rothschild's. From the private collec-tion of Prince Yusupov.

Rothschild's build and mine were pretty similar. With the sort of daring that comes from terrified excitement, I pick the right moment to take off my pants, lift up the weightless mannequin, yank the pants off Rothschild, and put them on, pronto. They pinch—they're a little tight. The cut's pretty weird, but I can't tell you, Kolya, how great the touch of that delicate, imperishable mate-rial felt on my ass and legs. I just can't tell you. My teeth are grinding with hatred as I stuff my pants inside my jacket, say sorry to Mr. Rothschild, and head calmly for the door. I look back. The mighty financier looks pretty pathetic. You can tell he's never been tortured by his own wardrobe—as for inflation, he wouldn't know what it was if it hit him. But I don't take any pleasure in his posthumous humiliation. An awful grimace is distorting his black frock coat, which is trying to tear itself off the mannequin and come running after me. I can see bitter tears running down from its mother-of-pearl buttons. There's a lump in my throat, and I beat it out of the museum.

Let's drink to birds of paradise and peacocks, who have to spread their tails in jail . . .

So I beat it and went home. I dropped by my neighbors' apartment, sat down at their sewing machine, and sewed up the ripped pants four times, keeping the needle in for a long time. "Well," I say, "what do you think of that, creeps?" My Gretchen pressed them again so hard they actually smoked. Second-degree burns. I stashed the Rothschild pants in the pantry. In the evening, with my mind on the little lady, I moseyed over to the Soviet embassy to celebrate the anniversary of our great revolution. I stuffed myself sick. I drank myself silly. The former-working-class-turned-diplomatic-corps knew how to party all right. My suit felt like its old self again. I grab a little sturgeon, some olives, a piece of cheese, and put in a call to the little lady, but they told me, "She passed away two hours ago."

Later I found out she'd gassed herself. Yes, it's very sad, Kolya . . . The next morning I read an announcement in the paper: "Anyone returning Baron Rothschild's trousers will receive a reward. Call . . ." I got a few billion marks—insurance, of course—from the museum director. Gretchen, Karpo, Rosa, and I dined out on them.

My clothes won't stop razzing me. Where do you think my fly came unbuttoned and the end of my necktie stuck out for everyone to see? In the British embassy, where I'd dropped by for a snack on King George's birthday. Did I say snack? I stuffed my face. The chief of protocol comes up to me and mumbles something, looking snootily down his nose. I don't get the message right away, so I keep looking around the room, wondering what he's mumbling about. I've waited a long time for George's birthday—I want that juicy roast beef, I haven't had any in days, and just when I'm bringing the fork to my lips, my nostrils flaring, I finally get the idea. I look down and see the end of my tie poking out of my fly. Mortified, I put down the two-pronged gold fork with the piece of meat. I haughtily give the guy to understand I've taken the hint. Thank you from the bottom of my heart. I'm leaving right now. Please make my apologies to everyone. Greetings to the royal family. I take a quick look around before slipping out discreetly, head held high, to swig a few drops in the john for my devastated heart. No one's drinking or eating at the buffet, not a soul. They're all gawking at me, right down to the portrait of King George. Jesus, what I went through then! I beat it, forever shamed in the eyes of the Berlin diplomats.

Later on, Rosa Luxemburg and Karl Liebknecht explained that I should have just gone on eating and drinking as if nothing had happened. You see, when real high-society types spot something weird about a stranger's getup, they pretend they haven't seen a thing. Then they took me to see a doctor, Dr. Freud. A nice guy, but unbelievably nosy. He even asked if I sniffed my fingers after I wiped my behind when I was a kid, if I bit my toenails, if I ever surprised Mama and Papa in the act together or in any combinations with their friends. Then he told me to tell my entire life story without hiding anything. It took five days to tell him the whole thing, and all the while my suit and overcoat fooled around on the floor in the vestibule.

His diagnosis was real simple: inferiority complex due to inflation. Walks in the fresh air before bedtime. Charcot showers. Galvanic therapy. Absolutely no looking in the mirror for any reason.

The next day I have yet another chat with the doctor. But it's weird, Kolya. I keep trying to get back to my suit and overcoat, hoping to get Dr. Freud interested in them, but he just goes on and on about my childhood. Did I remember coming out of Mommy's tummy, Mommy nursing me, did I stay on the potty a long time, did I let the cat play with my weewee, or did I just want to boil it up in soup with dumplings or swap it for a doll with long hair and tiny panties? Well, he went too far when he asked if I called my fur coat a tushie, a beehive a peepee, Mama Papa, and did I piss on my reflection in puddles.

"Okay, Dr. Freud. Hold it," I say. "Maybe you know all about potties and abnormal people, but you obviously don't know shit about what's really important to a guy, sometimes a lot more important than broads. We'll settle up when this inflation's over. I hope you get lots of clients."

Then I left. I walk down Friedrichstrasse. My overcoat's soaking wet—the shoulder pads have swollen and stick up cheekily, sneering at me. I hiss at them, "No umbrellas, no way!" I roam through the puddles, drenching my pants. I'll show 'em. I feel bad about my shoes,

while the crooks' chat went on. Mustache talks the most, and some of it's kind of interesting.

"Damn, I'd give ten Himmlers for a hit man as good as Stalin. Don't forget that, fellas, he's going to go far. But don't worry, your Führer'll double-cross him, too. He rubs out his generals personally, but he does in his *Parteigenossen* in the camps and the Gestapo. He calls his Gestapo the Lubyanka. One of our guys sent us a plan of the Soviet camps. I have to admit, the Bolsheviks have a genius for some things, but we're taking on the problem of liquidating every degenerate the German way. We leaders only live once, gentlemen, and living a poor but honest life is just too much agony." That was the last I heard for the moment. I slipped away, my suit and coat on their best behavior. I went through the wallet—three grand in dollars and pounds—in the women's john. I read some lines by Walter Mayakovsky on the wall: "The party is a million-fingered hand, clenched in one enormous fist. Yesterday I pissed here, comrades, please forgive me if I missed." So I took the dough out of the wallet and went back in.

Suddenly the fat pig, Goering, throws himself on me like a long-lost relative. "Thanks, pal! You were just great at the Philharmonic! Your little note got rid of that stupid bitch once and for all. Her cunt was diseased and her clitoris was as hard as the trigger on a Luger. A real bitch, man. Thanks again. We're a nation of lovers, not Hegels and Kantoroviches!"

What I said in the note I sent the pig so his lady friend would read it was: "Hey! Can't I ever rely on you? You said you'd never show up with that ugly bitch again. I'll see you at the whorehouse. It's really *great!*"

"Thanks, buddy! Join our party!" the pig proposes. I

suddenly noticed all of them, Mustache and the rest, looked like their faces had been turned. In fact, you can see the wrong sides in all their rotten speeches and gestures.

"The important thing is to have a party at all," I say evasively to Goering. "It's never too late to join."

"Long live the party!" Mustache shrieks. He shakes my hand too and says I left the concert hall like a hero, and showed the German soul's organic hostility to the Modernist–Marxist epidemic in music. If he, Hitler, were to take power, he'd appoint me director of the Philharmonic and head of the Repertory Committee right away. "I don't know what exactly, but something about you appeals to me," he said. "You've got an Aryan face. Are you interested in astrology?"

"No," I said. "I'm just an international crook on tour from country to country—a gangster, if you like. And I don't want to get involved, on principle."

"What do you mean, 'involved'?" The Führer didn't get it.

"I mean, I don't want to work," I said. He asked me to explain, so I told him I couldn't give a flying fuck about building capitalism or communism, it was all just one of mankind's mistakes, along with our suicidal technological progress, gradually murdering every living thing— air, rivers, seas, and jungles. I wouldn't touch any of it. "I just help myself to what the guy who's stuffed himself doesn't want. So I don't offend anyone. I'd like to be a farmer in the Antarctic, where they still don't have any political parties."

"That's our kind of style—Wagner could have said it! But you're a little limited, Fan Fanych, if you haven't tried National Socialism. We fascists are going to turn your individual protest into every German's philosophy, the philosophy of the New Germany. We're taking what the Jewish plutocracy doesn't want, we're going to smash Bolshevik Russia and ransack the coffers of all the great decayed European families. We Aryans'll stuff our faces and let all this scum do the dirty work. Have you ever been to Russia?" asked the Führer. He put another beer in front of me.

"Yep," I said. "More than once."

"Did you ever see their Führer, Stalin?"

"Yeah, I've met him a couple of times," I said. "Once in Baku and once in Tiflis. He was holding up banks. He and his gang used to go after the mail trains. He wasn't a bad crook, but he got out of the business. Became General Secretary. He acts like a pig, sucks the peasants' blood, rubs out noblemen, rips off the government. Has to have his blood ration. But that's just the beginning. The real stuff comes later."

The Führer looked pretty thoughtful for a moment. Then he said, "It's going to be rough, real rough. But I'm used to Wagnerian and Nietzschean action—no Bach for me. I'll fix your Stalin."

"Let me read your palm," I say to the Führer. I can smell something real nasty about him. He gives me his hand, palm up. "This line," I tell him, "shows you liked to eat shit when you were a kid. But it's also your line of luck and success. You're going to make a big splash in history."

"That's right!" the Führer said happily. "But look, shut up about the shit. I never ate any. I'm an artist, Fan Fanych. A great artist."

"You just don't remember it. It's the kind of thing that happens in early childhood. It shows you're a powerful personality, a man apart. Besides, that line says brown's your favorite color. Say, it wasn't you who drew a swastika in the Reichstag toilet with your finger, was it?"

"You're a magician!" said the Führer. He went white. "I'm going to draw more, and they'll be in blood this time, not shit! In the Louvre, Buckingham Palace, the Kremlin, the White House! Everything stinks! Everything stinks of humanism! Feh! I'm going to burn this pigsty of a world to the ground!"

"Maybe you should learn to draw first," I suggested. "With inflation the way it is now, you can get lessons from Van Gogh himself for a song."

"My vocation is giving lessons, not taking them!" Hitler snapped. I wondered bitterly how many of these crazy mixed-up professors we'd had dumped on our poor heads this century.

We sit there drinking our beer. My suit and overcoat are just wonderful. They're dry, they're not stabbing me anymore, and my pants aren't pressing into my groin. Maybe it'll work out, maybe they'll get used to it and I'll be able to wear them till things get better. What a hope! Goering, who was getting shitfaced, nudged Hitler, who poured his bacon omelette and beer all over me with a jerk of his elbow.

"Don't worry," he said. "You'll be wearing our uniform soon. You'll look good in it. Not like that garbage you're wearing now."

"No, thanks," I said. "A real crook won't go near uniforms. I'm no fascist."

Just then I notice there's a procession going by outside, with a catafalque up front, pulled by eight horses. Everyone's walking in silence, heads low—they look like they're thinking and thinking about something.

There's a coffin on the catafalque, and about ten mourners, including my pals Rosa Luxemburg and Karpo Liebknecht. They're both crying. I yell out the window, "Luxemburg! Liebknecht! Rosa! Karl!"

Hitler says, "Where are they? Where? To arms, citizens! Present—mugs!"

If I hadn't told the fascists that Rosa and Karl were just my pals' nicknames, not the communists, I hate to think what could have happened. Kurt and Magda got their names because they broke into a lot of villas and apartments that belonged to factory owners. It was the only honest way they could find of expropriating surplus value.

Hitler finally noticed his wallet was gone. He climbed up on the table and really let loose. "A nation capable of stealing its Führer's wallet will go far! I promise I'll make the poorest part of Germany spit blood! We've had it up to here! It's time to burn down the Reichstag, boys! The cradle of the Judeo–Bulgarian mongrels must burn with a blue flame. To the barricades!"

I said, "Not me, folks!" and beat it. I caught up with the catafalque as if I was flying on wings—I don't know where I found the strength. Over every inch of my body, I felt my suit and overcoat shivering the gentle shiver of the last throes. "Who are you burying, Rosa?" I asked. You'll never guess, Kolya. It was Solomon the tailor. He got so depressed by all the masses of orders he was getting for turned clothes, he hanged himself. I took off my overcoat as I walked along, then my jacket and pants, leaving just my underpants. I laid all the garments in the coffin, next to the body of the guy who'd turned them. My heart was sad but peaceful. I'd done my duty by my insulted and injured clothes.

We should never turn anything, Kolya. Let them live and die at their appointed hour, or at least from natural misfortunes—forests, jackets, states, shoes, literature, overcoats, mountains, cats, mice, neckties, and people. You know what? No one on earth knows that if I hadn't ripped off Hitler's wallet from his raincoat that time, maybe he never would have burned down the Reichstag. I tell you, Kolya, you should never turn anything. I certainly don't want to get to the Last Judgment to find me and Karpo Marx accused of trying to change the world. No thanks! The world doesn't forgive men who try to turn it inside out. It'll grip you in the crotch like a pair of pants and press on your chest so hard you can't breathe . . . I'm not proud about the Führer, Kolya. It's my one really terrible mistake. You should have seen the look on his face when he realized his wallet was gone and told his gang, "That's it! That's the last straw!" You'd understand that the blood and blasted lives of millions of people are on my conscience, Kolya. Let alone our ravaged planet. I've heard some people say it's Hitler, and Stalin even more, who's to blame. That's total crap. It's Fan Fanych who's to blame for everything, Fan Fanych alone and nobody else. And he alone has got to atone for it, too. Not for the case Kidalla made up with the computer, but for his own, the real one, the biggest case of all. Lord, forgive me! I don't have anything to say in my defense . . .

So you want to know why they didn't draft Fan Fanych for the front line, Kolya. You could figure it out for yourself, I guess, but I'll explain anyway, because the whole business is connected with an important moment in my life. And, if we dare dig a little deeper, with life in today's world. We won't dig any deeper than that.

It's exactly ten days since 4 p.m., June 22. I'm waiting for them to get moving—what else?—wondering which article they'll get me on, and what twists they'll give my case. If I were Kidalla, I would have busted myself on Day 2 of the war, for attempting to poison the lunches and dinners of the Central Committee's top-level private dining room (the big shots eat breakfast at home). One massive dose of potassium cyanide in the party bosses' stomachs—and at a critical point in their history our people are deprived of Intellect, Honor, and Conscience all at once. Gee, too bad. It's too late! Hitler's road to India is wide open. Kidalla goes off and reports all of this to Beria. And Beria tells the boss, who snickers in his mustache and says: "Well, we've settled things on the home front. Time to deal with this fiasco at the front lines. Dump Budyonny. This is a patriotic war, not a civil one, and we're going to call it that from now on."

So, I want to shed my blood for the motherland and the unhappy Soviet people. One day I got up—didn't even wash or eat breakfast—and strolled down to the recruiting office. There's a line like the one at Lenin's tomb—mostly men, a few women. There's even a line *here*, for chrissake? You can't croak, you can't shed your blood in peace. You still have to ask, "Where's the end of the line?"

"Good morning, ladies and gentlemen," I say, kind of tired but tough. The idea is to act like I'm some big shot in civvies. "Are you volunteers?"

"Yessir!" A veteran, about seventy-five, white mustache, answers for the whole bunch. "We can't have any red tape here. They need soldiers at the front. Let me tell you, I've been through the Russo-Japanese War, World War I . . ."

His arms and legs are shaking. This is no fighter. He's just a little old guy.

"You go home, granddad," I say. "You're wanted on the home front. They're thinking about making you chief of Solyanki Fortified District. Go on home now. You just forget about going to the front. It's a different kind of front they have now. It's the biggest front that ever existed in the history of fronts. Got it?"

"Yessir! Permission to leave."

The old guy shuffled off and I went right up to the military commander's office. The guy was a real butcher; on the take and puffy from booze. Let me introduce myself, alias, alias, alias, alias Legashkin-Promokashkin. Why didn't you send me a draft notice, creeps? Wanted

---

175

to get to the front yourselves? Listen, you snakes, I can straighten this business out in a hurry. I want to shed my blood, so put a gun in my hands right now!

Three Stripes took a look at some piece of paper and dialed a number. "Good morning, Comrade Major. Paskov here. I have one of yours in my office . . . Legashkin-Promokashkin . . . Wants to go to the front. Okay. I'll put him on. Right! Yes! Yes!" The ugly creep hands me the receiver.

"Hi, Comrade Kidalla," I said. "Hey, congratulations on your promotion to major, old pal."

"Hello, scumbag. Like hell you're going to the front. You're working for the agency. Just wait, and keep out of trouble. Stop worrying about your blood. We won't be spilling it so much as spoiling it. Just wait, will you? Understand? Wait!"

"What if I make a complaint to Stalin?"

"Go ahead, complain. I'll tell you the answer myself right now: Wait, faggot. If it weren't for the agency you'd have been rotting in Kolyma long ago."

I wasn't giving up yet. "What if I'm still waiting and the Führer rides into Moscow in a black Mercedes? He gets out at Red Square, climbs on Voroshilov's white stallion, gallops up to Lenin's tomb, and says, 'I'll show you how to rip off your leaders, you bastards!' Then what?" I went on. "I'm still waiting, and where are you? Switzerland? Argentina? It's a joke—our victory's inside a turtle egg, the egg's inside a turtle, the turtle was in the Moscow Zoo until they made it into soup for Kaganovich. And what can you do if that stinking Kaganovich likes turtle soup?"

When Three Stripes hears this his jaw drops, but

Kidalla only paused for a moment and said, "Our cause is just. Your time will come, not the Führer."

I'm not finished yet. "Yeah, but just suppose in a month the Führer's throwing a big bash in the Bolshoi Georgievsky Hall with Dzhambul in person playing the harp for him and Oistrakh on accordion?"

The room's packed with officers, Kolya. One of them pulls out a revolver. He's giving the commissar a look that says, Tell me to shoot his lights out right here, but the commissar kind of hisses at him. Kidalla says, "The time will come when you'll curse this moment of doubt about our defeat of fascism. Go home. Stock up on chow. Soon there won't be anything to eat at all."

So finally I say to Kidalla, "Listen, if they beat us, I won't keep you waiting. I'll rip your legs right off your ass and stick Koch's bacillus up there, you yellowbelly in fancy uniform. I hope you get a massive fucking coronary! I hope a three-ton bomb falls on your precious Lubyanka!"

"Till we meet again, Comrade Etcetera."

No use going for Kidalla anymore, right? So I hung up and yelled at the officers, "At-ten-*shun!*" They all whip their hands down by their sides. Dead silence. I leave. The line outside stares at me like I was Molotov or someone. They all gather round. I give the command: "Women, children—all volunteers—about— face!" The line turned around in confusion. "Go home until they tell you to come with all your things. Quick —march!" I did the right thing, Kolya. Armies of soldiers going to the front just to get captured, scads of them, and they were throwing these volunteers like lambs to the wolves to save their own skins. Workers, professors, old tsarist vets, legally blind people, sclerotics, cripples whose fingers couldn't pull a trigger, poor little girls. So I saved a few people from a useless death—thank the Lord.

Okay, that's enough. Wartime. Misery. The State Mint sent me a shitload of papers: passports, travel warrants, testimonials, wound certificates, general's orders. So I'm traveling through the length and breadth of our boundless motherland. I see some people suffering, burying their families, swelling up from starvation, searching for food in the fields and factories and camps twenty hours a day. And other people just stuff themselves, they swallow up sausages and bank notes and foreign currency and gold and diamonds. Now I can see the monolithic unity of the Soviet people: it's misery, Kolya, sheer misery. The whole thing's fucked. Forget wartime for a moment, let me tell you this: there's no Soviet nation in nature. Just individual people like individual sausages. And you can't get sausages in the provinces now for love or money. If they ever turn up in Tambov, Torzhok, or Tula, the line forms when the national anthem comes on the radio at dawn and everyone stands there reading books about our flourishing Soviet society. Sorry. I got carried away. My heart's like an old kettle these days—everything all mixed up and bubbling around in it together.

Well, finally, 1945. Stalin has victory in his grasp, I guess, the world's at his feet and he knows it. With Hitler it's just the other way around: the world certainly isn't at his feet, and he doesn't know it. But in Moscow the atmosphere's gloomy as hell. Vodka's rationed, people don't give a shit anymore—they just sit around playing shell games in the peasant markets. And my old neighbor Zoika has a really tough job at the post office, what with all the packages coming in from Germany. She gave most of the stuff away to privates and junior officers, but you can bet she kept something for herself. The guy who was screwing her, Minai Igorevich—he's a tailor's cutter who invented a new kind of military greatcoat—he was bringing home ten packages a day. There wasn't a spare inch of space in Zoika's apartment with all that china and porcelain, and this bitch mopped her floors with Gobelin tapestries—she hung them in the goddam *toilet*. The whole apartment stank of German misery, Kolya, all those gorgeous things in the hands of those louts.

I try Kidalla one more time. I call and tell him I can start right away as a top-class agent. Damn, I can get straight to the Führer himself. We're personally acquainted, we can discuss his strategic plans. We can save hundreds of thousands of soldiers, I tell him. They send back all these packages of clothes and stuff and then they just get wiped out in offensives again and again. Isn't it a shame? The death notices come along right behind the packages!

"So you do believe we're going to win now?" says Kidalla. "And you wanted this jerk, this acquaintance of yours, to smash our Joseph Vissarionovich. You wanted him to ride into Lenin's tomb on a white mare."

I was straight with him. "I just want to see both Führers in one crystal coffin, and that coffin chucked in the stinking Yauza River, and I hope it floats on waves of shit and filth and piss. Then ships of every nation will come to visit us."

"Loudmouth. I was right about you. Just wait, buddy, will you? You call me one more time and I'll rub your face in horseradish. Okay, smartass?"

Believe me, Kolya, if it had been up to me I could have crossed the front line, no problem, pinched some big shot's uniform, called the Führer's headquarters, refreshed his memory about me, and—excuse me— fucked the brains of the entire Wehrmacht into pea soup. But I never got to the front. For some reason I ended up in the Crimea. I made the trip in civvies, but I had the entire uniform of a lieutenant general of the MGB forces, from cap to kid boots, in my elegant valise. My ID was the real McCoy—representative from HQ. Authorized to carry out observations on the establish- ment of new frontiers in liberated Europe, with plenary powers as high as the sky. Station commandants and Cheka officials broke out in a cold sweat just reading my papers.

I stopped off on the way at Bryanshchina. Aunt Lisa's old estate . . . I was fourteen—went swimming and caught a cold. Tea and raspberry jam . . . and my aunt —she was thirty-two—in a nightdress . . . she's rubbing my chest with goose fat, sitting next to me with her thigh warming my ribs and skin and my chill melts and flies out of my chest, but . . . Oh, God, you can't go back! I remember as if it were yesterday the fear, the tingling in my spine, the sweet taste of sin. I was a jerk and got embarrassed—but believe me, Kolya, I never caught a cold in my life since then, not once. It's a medical phenomenon, right? Anyhow, you know what happened to my aunt's estate. It's not there.

There's a white marble column lying in the dirty

snow daubed with a red-painted slogan: THE WHOLE HARVEST TO THE FRONT! I head for the little village. Jesus. Women and children blue, almost black, swollen right up from total thirst and hunger. The huts were crooked and cross-eyed, their windows were blocked with rags like cataracts. Tears on their lashes. Not one man around, not even old men. But in front of every hut—there were only nine—there were standing these bronze busts of two-time Heroes of the Soviet Union on brand-new pedestals, and the bronze was shining in the sunshine, rays of light flashing off the busts of pilots. Some had already fallen in battle, some were still flying. As soon as the Germans had been scared off, a special detachment came to the village on Kalinin's orders. They put up these bronze Ivans and Fedyas and Seryozhas, molded by our rotten Phidiases and Michelangelos. They made their own countrywomen give them receipts, so if the busts got damaged, the women could be taken to this great country's courts. Then the detachment took off again for the capital, fucking anyone they ran across. It was horrible, Kolya. There were these black huts and the bronze burning in the sun and a girl hanging on to one statue howling and howling and some little kids screaming too and tugging at her skirt but can't pull her off. You get the picture? I gave the women 300,000 rubles and took the spunkiest one with me to Bryansk. Boy, I stuck an enema up the district committee second secretary. A fat retard with an ugly hangover. So I'm yelling at him:

"Let's see your party card, pig. The countryside and the peasants are the pledge of our postwar renaissance! Why aren't you out there feeding the peasants? You better report to Mikoyan right away on the beginning —no, continuing—famine. Did you forget chapter 4, scum? You forgot the law of the negation of the negation? You forgot that if the seed doesn't fall into the ground and die, nothing's going to grow at all! At-ten-shun! I should be out there, establishing new frontiers, and instead I'm screwing around here doing someone else's job! Transport seed to the kolkhozes! Supply the population with proteins! When I come back I'm taking the whole district committee to court. Let's smell your breath. Lush! I'll smash every one of you and deliver the bones to the Politburo. The people have to be fed! Understood?"

"Yes, yes, understood, sir. We'll feed them within the week. Please, sir, won't you come to dinner at my house before you leave?"

No way I was going to eat in his house. I pushed on to the Crimea. The sun was shining, naturally. It was quiet—the cypresses stand there like they always have. The water was still cold, though. Stones with holes were scattered all over the beach. There's none left now. They took them all away, and the sea hasn't had time to make holes in the ones they left. They were taking the Tatars away in convoys, men and women and little kids—they were screaming all over Yalta. You can understand it. I mean, not even a guy from Papua would like to be taken away who knows where —and that goes double for a Tatar, let alone the rest of all the peoples and nations they have in the Soviet Union.

You know, a lady from the Central Statistics Board told me once in an intimate moment that there wasn't supposed to be one member of our empire of states that didn't have at least one representative who'd done a stretch on Article 58 and all its wonderful sections. But the lady also said the Soviet authorities had screwed up. They'd never jailed a single Eskimo on 58. They busted them for stealing seal blubber, concealing reindeer skins, false registration of walruses, nonfulfillment of the plan for numbers of white foxes killed, getting to the tundra late—fine. But stuff like agitation and propaganda, sabotage, diversions, terror, attempts on leaders' lives, collaborating with Greenland agents—forget it. The Eskimos just didn't do it. And they never got busted for betrayal of the motherland—their motherland was the North Pole. To my knowledge, even Andrei Yanuarevich Vyshinsky, who should copy down the RSFSR criminal code in his own blood in hell's kitchen till the end of the world, couldn't imagine how you could, say, betray the North Pole to the South Pole. Maybe the Eskimos weren't capable of understanding what Soviet power really is. Or else for them it was kind of like a gale on dry land, or a fake Northern Lights, or an endless blizzard or eclipse of the sun. Something you just couldn't fight. I don't know, Kolya.

So. It's warm. It's spring. The almond buds are out and little lilac pimples are breaking out on the gnarled, knotty fig trees. The cypresses are basking in the sunshine. They give off a hot heady smell, like a naked woman after a pine-scented bath.

Just at a moment when maybe thousands of soldiers from Prussia were croaking in dirty snow and blood and gulping their last gasps of air—and they wouldn't let me shed my blood—Fan Fanych dropped into the empty Livadia Palace. I walk through the drawing rooms, the hallways, the bedrooms, I sing my favorite little ditty.

> The streetcar floats across the sea,
> The phonographs sound sad.
> Inside his little railroad car,
> The tsar resigned. Too bad.

I went down a secret little stairway somewhere and came to a secret little chamber. Could be the place where Rasputin shtupped all the ladies-in-waiting. Suddenly this loud, crude, military-style voice comes in from outside the window.

"Cymbaliev, get into that cedar! Zykov, you're in the rhododendron. The rest of you scatter through the park. Stay camouflaged. If you meet You-know-who—freeze! Okay, scatter! Don't let a fly get out of here alive."

Yeah, I've really landed in it. I take a quick look around the room. Lilac silk upholstery decorated with white chrysanthemums. Sofa, little tables, little chairs, little ottomans, a lot of Karelian birch and a tiny toilet in the wall behind a bamboo screen. Two little windows just below the ceiling, behind wrought-iron bars. Trellised grapevines beyond the bars. So I'm in a cellar. Audibility—excellent. The same loudmouth soldier's still walking around above me giving orders.

"Bedbugs, cockroaches, and moths—to be executed. Check all residences for ongoing tarantula and scorpion situations. Poluverko! Password!"

"Halt! Who goes there! Is matter primary?"

"Response?"

"Always, Comrades Kutuzov, Suvorov, and Nakhimov! Death to Hegel!"

"Okay, scatter! Blow Zelinsky-Nesmeyanov gas through the ventilation system!"

I stretch out on the sofa. What the hell does all this mean? Nothing to do but wait. There couldn't be all this hoopla in Livadia just for some shindig for Kaganovich and Beria. Hey. Maybe You-know-who is old Suliko with the mustache. Maybe he wants to warm up his little old hands, cramped from hanging on to the wheel of state and party. Every hour I'm more certain that's it. Cars zip in and out. I smell salmon in the air. People bring live pheasants, geese, ducks, pigs right into the palace. A giant sturgeon yanked itself out of the hands of the six guys carrying it and landed up against my wall beating its tail. Boom, boom, boom. In short, it looks like they're getting ready for an incredible blowout.

I wait one day. Two. I'm hungry. Suddenly I hear people in the yard talking English. It's our guys, with some Yanks and Englishmen. They're yakking like diplomats do—the weather, the laurel trees, the heat. They say there's a place in the sun for all the Allied countries. That is, if capitalism will ever understand that it's historically fated to pass the torch to its gravediggers, the proletariat. They're laughing. Laugh, you classic diplomats, laugh. They'll truss you and stick parsley in your ears and eat you on May Day at the first World Proletarian Banquet in the Bolshoi Georgievsky Palace.

Finally a dead silence fell on the tsar's palace and the park, Kolya. The only sounds were Cymbaliev panting in the cedar and Zykov in the rhododendron.

———

Silence. Then the heavy soft sound of car tires on the crushed red-brick drive. You can hear the crunch of the tiniest chips. A ray of sunlight darts off the chrome hubcap and hits me right in the eyes. I blink but just keep looking straight ahead through the trellised vines.

The door of the Lincoln opens and four boots get out on each side. First one foot in a laced boot, breeches striped down the seam, comes poking out the door and then another. The left. Its black-leather expression looks more like a right to me. Both feet are standing in front of my little window. You can tell the right one's intimidated by the left. It's trying to keep to the side and stay out of the limelight. Somehow the left one's moved three or four steps further forward than the right—and just then I heard that voice we all know and love, Kolya.

"It's so quiet here. And warm! Peaceful, eh?"

My Very Best Friend. He's standing too close for me to see his face and mustache. He lights up. A small, dry, pockmarked hand. Gentle? Forgiving? No. The pipe just smokes away in his all-powerful, strong-willed hand.

"Come over here, Vyacheslav," says Stalin.

Two more feet move toward us. Ugly feet in low yellow shoes. Custom-made—the bony phalanges of Molotov's big toes spread sideways and bring up bumps like blisters on the leather. When Molotov walks over, he rubs the blisters against each other and you can tell they itch badly. You don't notice him rubbing much, I guess—maybe he doesn't notice he's doing it. Sores have a life of their own sometimes. And Molotov has two, so they won't get lonesome. Imagine life for a duodenal ulcer, all by itself in the nice, healthy company of the heart, lungs, stomach, liver and spleen, appendix, rectum . . . All alone—and an ulcer as well! That's rough. I'm wandering again, Kolya. Sorry.

"Listen! Who's banging?" Stalin asks jumpily. "Don't you hear it? Go see who it is."

It was the sound of a shoemaker hammering, I could tell. Eight military and civilian feet stomped by my grating and disappeared somewhere. I watched the black Stalin lace-ups crunching on the red-brick chips as he walked around silently. Molotov brought him a wicker rocking chair and he sat down. His right leg bent and braced itself, while the left one rested across it like it was the boss. It hung right over and took a look around with the toe of its shoe. Molotov just stands there. Fan Fanych, have you ever dropped straight into the frying pan! Fate's flipped the king of diamonds into someone else's deck. No joking, they'll lynch you as soon as look at you, and no Kidalla's going to save you from the pockmarked paws of the Ace of Spades and his goons. Don't be a fool. You'll crunch like one of those brick chips and no one'll even hear the noise you made—there's cannons out there, bombs blowing up, bullets whining. Put you on trial? Don't make me laugh. Even the Soviet criminal code doesn't have a clause about eavesdropping on the conversations of Politburo members. You'll get the maximum measure under "social protection of leaders from the people"—curtains.

I take a look outside. Now the eight military and civilian feet, a little dustier, a few scratches on the kid leather, are marching in with one pair of bare feet dragging in the middle. Skinny, blackened by the sun. The legs are bare to the knees, which are covered by a leather apron. I like the way those feet walk. Dignified.

No rush. He isn't shitting his pants. Nice feet, around seventy years old each. They stopped near the Stalin lace-ups and Molotov's shoes with the bulges by the big toes. Yuck, Kolya.

"Good afternoon," the old guy says—in Russian, but my guess is he's a Tatar.

"Do you know who's sitting here before you?" says Molotov.

"Military, I guess. And high-ranking," says the Tatar —yeah, he's got an accent all right.

You won't believe this—*I* could hardly believe it— but Stalin suddenly grinned, this big, leering grin, and laughed fit to bust, like a murderer who's got away. Molotov seized the chance to lift first one foot and then the other and scratch his leather bumps.

Stalin giggled, his sooty bronchials whistling, and he asked again, "So my face is both absolutely and relatively unfamiliar to you?"

"Your honor, we've never seen each other before. So it's unfamiliar."

"Do you read the newspapers, old fellow?"

"I can't read at all, your honor."

"That's it, then. You—can't—read. Happy man. You'll have a long life . . . You've never read anything?"

"No, your honor."

"You listen to the radio?"

"I don't have a radio. I listen to the words of Allah. What He says I listen to."

"Where do you work, old fellow? What do you do?"

"Your honor, I'm a shoemaker. I repair the old stuff and stitch up the new. And I charge reasonable rates."

Stalin rapidly shifted his left foot off the right one. Silence—dead silence, Kolya. Stalin doesn't utter a word for ten minutes. Molotov's knees are trembling, the jerks. Silence. Oh, yeah, sure, the bastard was re- membering his daddy. Maybe he's remembering the way his old man used to stick a dozen nails in his mouth, under his mustache. Our modern Lenin, remem- bering his pa's hammer and his pa's fingers, eaten into indelibly by the black wax. The Bolshevik dragon's hideous head, remembering how the curved knife sliced cleanly through the beautiful piece of leather and how the smooth sole gazed at the sky for the first and last time while Pop pushed in the wooden pins and scraped off the little roughnesses with a file and fixed the heels— you remember that, you old wolf? An old wolf is what you are, the worst of the lot. A regular wolf just kills one sheep, eats till its belly's full, and runs off into the Bryansk forest until it's hungry again. But this one, the worst of the lot, it snaps its jaws and kills every single goddamn sheep though it can't eat all of them and they weren't meant to die that day. Killing indiscrimi- nately, nibbling a mouthful, watching the blood gush out . . . Silence. He knocked the pipe against his right heel. His little green box of Herzegovina Flor tobacco fell on the ground. Molotov bent over and picked it up, and for a second I saw his face upside down. Yuck.

"Do you have a family?" says Stalin.

"Yes, your honor. A wife and a son."

"A son, eh?"

"Yes. A son."

Silence again—and more silence. Who the hell knows what Stalin was remembering then. Probably the time when he was a boy.

"What does your son do?" he asked in a muffled, nasty kind of voice.

"My son's a mullah. A mullah. Works in a mosque."

"He worked for the Germans," Molotov butted in quickly. "He's an active collaborator. A quisling, sir."

"My son served Allah and us—the Tatars. The Germans have a different god, Hitler. My son wouldn't serve him."

Right then, Stalin started tapping his left foot. I could tell the shit was boiling up inside Our Leader just in the place where an ordinary guy has a soul. Bubbling up and boiling right over the edge. But he spoke as leisurely as he had at the Eighteenth Party Congress.

"Allow me to inquire of our counterspies: Why is that former stronghold of the White bastard, the Crimea, still not purged of traitors of every stripe and their so-called mullahs?"

A dusty pair of kid boots marched up ceremoniously and clicked heels. "Comrade Commander in Chief, at this moment in time all activists up to age fifty-five have been arrested. We're waiting for a special train for the deportation of their families."

"Have Kaganovich give the green light to the special trains," ordered Stalin. "It's time we reinforced the Russian people's historic victory over the Tatar–Mongolian hordes—that pathetic Romanov dynasty couldn't do it. Hands off the Crimea! Put up a bronze bust of a Tatar pilot who's a two-time Hero of the Soviet Union in Alupka, so we won't look biased . . . That double-dealing mullah son of yours is going to be shot, old fellow, and you'll die like a dog in Kolyma yourself. You'll never bang your hammer before the start of the Yalta Conference again! Take away his last, hammer, nails, thread, awl, file, knife, and all the other shoemaker's tools . . . What's the news on the uranium extraction project? Why isn't Kurchatov talking? What are those brilliant young men of his doing?"

The old guy's feet had instantly gone gray with the first awful shock. The kid-leather gang surrounded them and dragged him off somewhere. Stalin's left foot twitches slightly, the way I do with a bad hangover.

"All physicists are bastards," he muttered. He shuffled toward the palace like a very old man. He stopped just two steps away from my grating again, tapping his unloved right foot, turning it till the anklebones cracked, knocking the toe on the marble curb. Then he put the foot down—seemed as if he was listening for something. Suddenly, Kolya—you don't have to believe this if you don't want to—Stalin's right foot spoke. Quiet, but with a mean laugh, and a lot of spunk.

"Hey, Stalin. You're a shit."

"What? What?" said Stalin.

"A shit, an asshole, and a dope," the right foot said again, quickly. The left one stomped on it, but it wouldn't shut up. "A dope, an asshole, and a shit!"

Stalin's tongue flapped and he groaned loudly, "Uh-uh-h-h."

Molotov said, "Maybe you need a rest after the trip?"

"Fuck off," Stalin said, as quiet and logical as if he was standing on the dais at a congress. Then he started screaming insults at Molotov. "Where'd you get that ugly flat face? You look like a flounder with a pince-nez. Prime Motherfucker! Minister of Foreign Affairs! Churchill's got Eden—there's a *real* minister. He's good-looking, at least. What are you standing with your legs spread for? I'll get the Politburo to deal with you, and we'll amputate both of them. Don't ever scratch your bony bumps at a conference again! Tsarist spy—faggot!"

"Everything's going to be fine," Molotov mumbled diplomatically. But Stalin's right foot started cackling again as soon as its owner shut up: "You're a dope! Asshole of all time! Shit of all peoples!"

Stalin started pacing up and down at a gallop, to try and trip it up, I guess, but the right foot just kept on mouthing off, not missing a beat. "Stalin's an *ass*hole and a *dope*, and a *mis*erable piece of shit! *Stu*pid dope, *stu*pid dope, soon you'll breathe your last and *die!*"

Stalin stopped dead in his tracks. I hear his hoarse breathing. He's lying to his goons. "Sounds like an engine knocking someplace, comrades." Four boots ran up on tiptoes, yanked the Leader off his feet, and carried him off sitting on their hands. "Drop high-explosive bombs from our strategic reserve on Berlin!" he snapped.

"That won't make you feel any better," his foot chipped in sadly.

God had it in for the bastard. I was beginning to realize just how monstrous and unbearable Joseph Vissarionovich Stalin's grief and evil were. Our Prince of Darkness wielded power over nearly half the planet. Every blessed day of his life he could eat mutton soup with diamonds floating in it instead of barley. He could give an order to pour gasoline over the barracks in a hundred camps and burn up the enemies of the people with a blue flame. At a wink and a flick of his little finger the motherland's oldest virgin, Yablochkina the actress, would come running, her saggy cheeks wobbling, and declaim: "Comrade Chairman of the State Committee for Defense, I am yours!"

Try to imagine it. Here's the almighty representative

of the most humane nation that ever existed on earth, Mountain Eagle No. 2, and suddenly some stinking little right foot—not *anybody's* right foot, oh no, his own, the bastard traitor—says, "You're a shit, Stalin! Soon you'll breathe your last and die."

The really terrible part of it was, you couldn't close its mouth with a blow. You couldn't *make* it shut up. You can make your conscience shut up—that's how most people deal with it. But a foot isn't a conscience. So what to do? Tell the president of the Supreme Soviet to amputate Comrade Stalin's right foot, uh, temporarily? Well, okay, that's settled, let's cut it off, we'll attach a prosthesis. What then? Can you rely on the left foot? Nope—enemies and traitors are everywhere. You can't be too careful. So you have to liquidate the left foot, too, and ride around in a wheelchair like Roosevelt. The Politburo members, ministers, generals, Stakhanovites, Ivan Kozlovsky, Yuri Levitan, film directors, Ilya Ehrenburg, the actor Aleinikov—they'll take turns pushing you. Anyway, to be a successful statesman you need your head more than your feet. But what if my head starts going back on the basic postulates of historical materialism? Say, what if my head says it isn't matter that's primary, that the most important thing is—freedom of the spirit? An interesting situation. A real dilemma. Well, I can deal with my head. It stays quiet just the way my privates do.

But what if I'm giving my usual report at a party congress, and my right hand slides into my breast pocket and whips out my party card and throws it from the dais onto the floor of the Bolshoi Georgievsky Hall? Liquidator and deviationist! And then both hands clap thunderously. What do I do then, answer me, dear

Vladimir Ilyich, tell me please what do I do if my internal organs start talking? What if even my asshole gets fresh and tells my intestines, with true Bolshevik candor, that Stalin ruined its life and it's better being a blind gut than having to sit dumbly by, watching Stalin's unique personal self being destroyed. What to do, Stalin thought gloomily. Put a bullet through my grim, deeply harmful-to-myself forehead or my self-hating heart?

But he took himself in hand. He made his decision. Mr. Brain, Messrs. Ass, Heart, Liver-and-Spleen, your attempts are doomed to total failure. The great might of our national medicine—maybe even supplemented with foreign assistance—will be unleashed on you!

This is all buzzing in my head when, outside the window, Molotov shouts from above, "Get Professors Vovsi, Egorov, Vyshinsky, Burdenko, Marshak, and Aleinikov the actor. Right away!"

"Yes, sir!" someone said. The place was as quiet as a morgue, except when Cymbaliev, still sitting on his cedar bough, asked the commander of the guard, "What do I do when I really have to go, Comrade Major? Scout's honor, I can't last any longer."

The major thought for a while. "Do it in your pants. We'll worry about it later," he said.

So that's what happened to the old bastard, Kolya. He got what was coming to him (I mean Stalin, not Cymbaliev stuck up in his tree). But your old buddy Fan Fanych was in a pretty tough spot. No way out, nothing to eat—I'd never even dreamed of such torture. So I went to sleep, to save energy and stop worrying about finding a way out of a hopeless situation.

When I wake up and look out of the grating, it's

daylight. A Crimean breeze is wafting a wonderful scent toward me from the flower beds—thanks, breeze, I won't forget what you did for me. But Molotov's standing right smack in front of my grating. His feet are bare and he's wearing army underwear tied at the ankles with yellow drawstrings. Fucking creep. He's spreading his toes and wriggling them. I never saw such hideous toes, not in any bathhouse or on any beach: they're a kind of murky yellowy-green, and the big toes are all bent and twisted like right-turn and left-turn road signs. The muscles are locked rigid and the veins swollen up. They change color every two or three breaths, as though the veins carried violet ink and runny shit by turns instead of blood.

A Dodge rolled up. I recognized it by the balloon tires. Some pretty strange characters got out of it. One in bedroom slippers, another in women's felt shoes, a third wearing odd shoes that weren't tied, etc. How'd you like to be dragged out in the middle of the night?

"Good morning, Comrade White-gowned Murderers," says barefooted Molotov. It was true. Some of the people disgorged from the Dodge were minus their pants, but they all had white gowns on.

"We've always appreciated your subtle sense of humor," said the one in shoes. "Why are you barefoot?"

"How do you feel?" various items of footwear asked. "What happened?"

"You're here to examine Joseph Vissarionovich's general state of health. And for consultations. Also—"

The man in bedroom slippers interrupted. "May I express my indignation? I told them, if they take me— excuse me, summon me—to Stalin, I have to be able to measure his blood pressure with something, for

God's sake. Instead, that officer over there, who's clearly suffering from Down's syndrome, insists that there can be no pressure on Stalin. *He's* the one who puts pressure on *other* people—flattens 'em like lice. So now I don't have my instruments. I might as well have no hands. This is ridiculous."

"The Marshal's blood pressure is normal. Why do you think Colonel Goregliad has Down's syndrome?" said Molotov, very interested. Two pairs of general's boots and blue-striped breeches moved toward the bedroom slippers before you could say "knife."

"I've never been wrong. Look for yourself. That can only be Down's."

The boots and Molotov's bare extremities moved to the left. I'm staring too, and thinking: Those size 9 kid boots were doomed three minutes ago. Three minutes ago the creases in those uppers were glittering in the sun, glowing with power and the sheer joy of being one of the gang. Those creases were so artistically carved the colonel looked as if he was shod every morning by great sculptors like Tomsky or Vuchetich or Manizer. And the welts! It wasn't some bootmaker with a saw-tooth wheel who cut out those welts, it was a ballerina running her sharp little teeth around the edge of the new sole. Right before my eyes those boots were drooping, and dimming, and those beautiful kid creases were melting into pathetic wrinkles of fear and hopelessness and impotence.

We never really knew how these Chekists concocted their little spy games. The lace-ups lumbered off inexorably toward the boots, and you could see that in a half hour—an hour at most—the boots would have to confess everything. Everything. Right down to the years of work with "Down" in British intelligence, and the assassination attempts on Stalin and Molotov in order to add the chairmanship of the Soviet Union's Council of Ministers to Churchill's other offices. For such plot twists Romain Rolland himself would have taken Alexei Tolstoy out for a good meal!

Meanwhile, back in the Crimea. The sun's shining. It's the decisive moment of the war. The peoples of Europe are starved for freedom. The entire Soviet high command's been caught red-handed meeting with their allies at Livadia Palace. With the help of ace secret service agent Down, they're putting a turban on Stalin's head and a garbage bag on Molotov's. They're tying all the rest of the gang to the conference table and *voilà*. Goodbye Marshal Stalin. They shove him and the Politburo members into a Douglas and the plane melts into the blue yonder—the Pacific Ocean. Maybe there's a fire on board—and all those sharks down there, Kolya. And so enemy intelligence tried to write the last chapter of our party's history. But it didn't really happen that way.

The kid boots had gotten involved in a nasty business. They knew the score, so they let the goons march them off to the Dodge without protesting.

"You blew it, Down," the lace-ups said in a parting shot. "Your attempt to prevent us from taking Stalin's blood pressure has been thwarted!"

"You wait, it'll be your turn soon," the boots whined gloomily.

"Shut up, you sonuvabitch of Albion," a second pair of lace-ups yelled.

The Dodge roared into life and pulled away. Something was happening to my empty stomach: it felt as if a squirrel was running around in it to take its mind off the boredom, like they do on those little wheels. This is it, Fan Fanych. You're going to get so weak you'll be languishing like Snow White in a tsarist dungeon. You're going to die, just peg out. The worms are going to stuff themselves on you and your corpse'll stink up the whole of Livadia Palace. As a matter of fact, Kolya, thinking about this took my mind off being hungry— I'd found a pretty interesting problem: where do the worms that eat corpses come from? No, seriously, where do they come from? I never saw anything about it in *Knowledge Is Power* or *Le Figaro* or *Pravda* or *The New York Times*, not even in the Moscow crematorium's wall newspaper, *Prometheus*, where I got into reading the columns like "Our Efficiency Proposals" and "Readers' Letters." I did find out from there that "lowering the electricity grid tension by only 20 volts can enable you to burn an additional 43.4 bodies per quarter with the energy thus saved. If the force of the current is *raised* 5 amps the body capacity increases by 11 percent."

I read myself sick on insane answers to insane questions. For instance: Engineer M.'s on his way to fight at the front. He asks, "Can you leave your wife a warrant to get back her aunt's jewelry from the ashes after the cremation? She swallowed them and swore she'd take them with her to the grave." Their answer was short: "The administration is not responsible for any cremated valuables found in remains." So there. R. had been a party member since 1896. He wanted to know if there was anything in Engels that said it was okay to scatter one's ashes over the Kremlin. They told him to address his request to the Moscow Soviet. Lots of people wanted to know what you could burn along with yourself. This was the administration's policy— objects accompanying you on your last journey *couldn't* be: metal, plastic, glass, leather, any other rigid alloy, enemies, close relatives, or messages with military or state secrets. Crematees might under no circumstances conceal in their pockets bills, official notices, letters of advice, matches, or makhorka tobacco. They couldn't wrap their heads in electrical tape or soak their clothes in kerosene. It was categorically forbidden to cremate yourself wearing overcoats, fur coats, sheepskin coats, heavy jackets, felt boots, or quilted vests. From what I could see, Kolya, you could take a flower with you, or maybe a handkerchief. But the administration thought all of its crematees were a bunch of crooked cutthroats and con artists—that much I'd already figured out—so they cited this terrible example:

Colonel Yelagin, Tsarist Army. b. 5/18/1855. d. 9/11/1943. Will declared null and void. Presented for cremation twice. Administration twice discovered hand grenades dating from 1912 in his riding breeches. Yelagin denied cremation for systematic infraction of the regulations. Buried in Novodevichy Cemetery. Order No. 1405.

Just picture that Colonel Yelagin dying, going over the possible variations in his mind, busting himself laughing. The sad moment as his body enters the oven. His relatives and loved ones have complied with his will and made their getaway. The comrades are switching on the crematorium plus electrification. It's hot . . . shit, it's burning! And bang! A crack, the chimney collapses, the blind fiddle players run for cover, and Gogol's blessed headstone shudders in the Donskoy Monastery's quiet graveyard. You get the picture? And his excellency the colonel guessed the second variation right, you see? The final frisking; the grenades discovered; Soviet bureaucracy's radiant smile; cremation denied; and they lay your dear old carcass to rest in the grave in God's own ground. And your soul, at peace about your body, flies around on its own far-off business in other parts of the universe undisturbed.

Let's drink to Colonel Yelagin of the tsarist army, Kolya. Let's drink to that great tactical maneuver, goddamn it, let's drink to his victory over the worst enemy of the lot—winning in the last fight with Death itself. May our nearest and dearest carry out our last wills and testaments just the way the colonel's did. Here's to us, old buddy. Now back to the worms.

So where do the bastards come from? I'll give you my three basic hypotheses (I'm starving, don't forget). One: the worms are inside us all the time pretending to be something else, either way deep down in our organisms looking like they're cells, or else floating around like white or red blood platelets. Anyway, they're faking. And when we give up the ghost they all come crawling out of the woodwork. Revealing themselves in their true colors, right? So our job is to expose this kind of Freemason-type cell—foreign bodies, fermentations—for what they are. Expose and destroy. So there's at least one point where I totally agree with our party program: we have to—we're obligated, even—to follow Lenin's example in everything. If he's indestructible, we are too. And if he isn't, why the hell—excuse my French—do we have to deal with all these global screwups and problems? What's the point in *not* being immortal like Lenin, just burning and rotting away?

Two: the worms exist outside us till the moment of truth. They're *really* invisible—I mean yours and mine, Kolya, our own personal little worms—there's no contact with them, except maybe in abstract thinking. We've got our Creator to thank that when we're alive our minds aren't granted the power of imagining some of the things that happen to our poor deserted bodies when we're dead. So I think if my hypothesis is correct —and I'm almost croaking from starvation—it's essential we set up an experiment to study the mechanics of the worms' appearance after the body's sent out its sad signals that disaster's on the way. In fact, we can locate the moment of the signal itself! I mean, physicists can catch photons from Cygnus and signals from dead galaxies. Do we have to fuck around forever—excuse me, Kolya, but it makes me mad—with those little creatures just waiting for the chance to gobble us right down to the bones? I don't care if they're inside or outside. But seems as if we have to. Till the end of the world. Till the final resurrection.

Three: we all know the number of microbes in our bodies is beyond infinity. What if some tiny little microbe—some little hidden beast or virus—which seems harmless when we're alive, little fifth-column bastard—what if it turns itself into a worm the moment you're joining the angels? How about that? Or how about human smells—good and bad? Maybe one of them gets stimulated by the last low-frequency magnetic vibrations from the corpse and is transformed into a swarm of little beings that eat up our bodies when they've done their stretch? Our smell isn't any old scent or stink. It's probably made of tiny particles, the way light is. And everyone knows deceased people start to stink right away.

I lie down, I try to think, but I have this terrible desire to eat, and no inspiration. Spies are all over the place—kid and leather boots keep running up and disappearing into bushes and flower beds. Then I heard his footsteps. No mistaking them for anyone else's. He's headed for the wicker chair, a few yards from me. Snake. He's trying to cozy up to that sassy freedom-loving right foot. The wisest-and-greatest-of-men is scared stiff it'll make a big scene on this lovely morning. Everything around is green, though it's only February. The sea's murmuring below us, the weather's warm. He sits down in the chair. He's worried—doesn't cross his legs. Doesn't want to pinch either one of them. But his pet, the left one, has sensed a change in their relationship. It acts up and jiggles the hooks on its boot. Stalin slaps his knee. It shuts up instantly and stretches out. Here comes Molotov in light-rat-colored Min. of For. Aff. pants.

"Everything's ready, Joseph. We can start the consultation."

"I don't see the actor Aleinikov. Where is that brilliant mind?"

"Aleinikov categorically refused to fly until he and Boris Andreev had had a few drinks for their hangovers. The plane was ready, they'd called the professors, and Aleinikov stayed in Moscow. He says you can all go to—"

"That's a desperate and daring man," says Stalin. "With men like him, I would have taken Berlin long ago, maybe even Paris . . . Get them started on the sequel to the movie of *A Great Life*, and start preparing a tough critique of it. Okay, over here, you miserable Hippocrateses!"

The medical luminaries gathered around Stalin. They ask him questions about his heart, throat, ass, liver, and both hemispheres of the brain. Stalin listened and said shortly, "It's my foot." Then he sighed, quite humanly. He raised his right foot slightly. Suddenly it muttered spitefully, but cheerfully: *"If tomorrow it's war, if tomorrow we march. If dark forces threaten us . . ."*

"Do you feel anything in your foot?"

"Is the pain localized?"

"Is it cold?"

"Does it tremble? Twitch? Is it numb?"

"Do the joints crack when you walk?" asked the bedroom slippers, the felt boots, and various shoes, boots, and other footgear. Stalin just said monotonously, "It bothers me. Bothers me. Bothers me." And the goddamn foot just went on chanting like crazy: *"We don't want a foot of anyone else's land, but we won't give up an inch of ours . . ."*

The bedroom slippers couldn't take it any longer and said roughly, "Comrade Stalin, in the final analysis, you're just a patient to me. I have to know exactly what it is you're complaining of. What is wrong with your foot?"

"It's an asshole, an asshole, an asshole!" yelled the left foot. It couldn't stand the humiliation any longer.

"It *bothers* me. Do something," said Stalin.

"Hypodermic!" said the bedroom slippers, and the foot abruptly stopped droning songs by Soviet composers.

"Forget the hypodermic. It's not bothering me anymore," said Stalin with relief. In a flash of humor, he asked, "If you amputated it, it wouldn't bother me at all, right?"

"It's a little early to be discussing surgical intervention," the bedroom slippers butted in sharply.

"But if it starts bothering me during the conference," and Stalin stroked his right knee, "I'll ask Burdenko to chop off all of your heads. He's a pretty good brain surgeon."

The left foot tried to go for the right one, but got brutally kicked away.

"Please, Comrade Stalin, give us some urine and stool samples for analysis," said the felt boots. They feared the Leader more than anyone.

"Major Aganalov deals with that kind of thing," said Stalin. Someone reported something to Molotov, who passed it on to Stalin right away. All the footwear around him disappeared like magic and Stalin got up to greet somebody else. Two more men stationed themselves behind his chair. Which is how I lost sight of him. Somewhere people were jabbering in English. A cameraman with a tripod and a huge behind totally blocked my view. I took a big risk and hissed, "Move to the left, cretin of the most important of the arts!"

He moved instantly—didn't even look round. Forests of generals', diplomats', and foreigners' pants and feet crowded around the chairs. Finally in came Stalin's lace-ups and (I guessed) Churchill's brown half-boots.

Between them was a white metal chair rolling on bicycle wheels. Roosevelt was sitting in the wheelchair. His legs were covered with a Scottish plaid. An interpreter was pushing the wheelchair.

"I would have been happy to push you along the pathway myself, Mr. Roosevelt," said Stalin, "but I'm afraid your so-called free press would turn our harmless stroll into a symbol—Russia pushing America God knows where. Ho, ho, ho!"

Roosevelt and Churchill chortled too. Roosevelt was lifted into an armchair. Stalin and Churchill sat down on his left and right. Stalin was in a peaceful kind of mood—praising the Crimea, talking about Tsar Nicholas and the orgies he used to have there, just shooting the breeze and telling his big-shot guests to breathe the piney sea air more deeply. Churchill, like an old seadog, growled that he thought the wind from the southwest was bringing the odor of dung. He hadn't smelled such a stench since 1918. He asked the President and the Marshal to try it and tell him if he was wrong. Roosevelt, nicely and politely, said he was allergic to the pollen in the air and had a cold. Stalin, a little surprisingly, agreed with Churchill—he was right, it smelled like dung, just the way it did at Zinoviev and Kamenev's interrogations. But it was coming from somewhere above them, not the southwest. He called the commander of the guard. The commander comes running. Heel clicks against heel.

"Comrade Marshal, commander of the guard Major-General Kolobkov, present and correct!"

"Which one of you's stinking in that tree over there?" asked Stalin.

"Lance Corporal Cymbaliev, Comrade Marshal."

"Take him off his post and get him downwind of us."

"Yes, sir!"

The major ran over to the cedar. "Lance Corporal Cymbaliev, leave your post! Move very cautiously downwind!"

"Yes, sir, moving downwind!"

I can see Cymbaliev. He's hanging out of his tree, he wants to jump but his breeches are bulging where he dumped in them—too much top-brass food. Yeah, time for a crap, Comrade Stalin, and you and me haven't even had a bite to eat yet. You have a better time of it, Cymbaliev, whatever you say.

"You understand military management remarkably well," says Roosevelt to Stalin.

"If I may say so, I hope your guards would not leave their posts under any circumstances, either," says Stalin. "Have you fought in battle, Cymbaliev?"

"Sure thing. Wounded in the belly three times."

"Well done. General Antonov, demote Kolobkov and station him on the cedar branch. He can try a private's life—he's never been at the front. Give Cymbaliev a medal for courage and make him an officer. When the war's over, he can be secretary of the Writers Union. They need guys like him. Now *scatter*—the wind's changing."

Churchill was tickled. Everybody relaxed.

"I feel in a very good mood suddenly," says Stalin. "What about you, Mr. President?"

"I feel just fine. I think our meeting's going to be a success. The only difficulties I foresee—let me say this without diplomatic euphemism—are likely to be over Poland. The questions of the UN reparations, the liberation of Europe, your homesick prisoners of war, et cetera—I don't think they're any real problem. And if they were, my advisers and I would rather not think about it."

"Agreed," says Stalin, and his right foot, in great sympathy, taps Roosevelt and Churchill in turn. The left one's curled up under the chair like an offended cat.

"Ah, the Polish question, the Polish question!" says Churchill. "Won't you have a cigar, Marshal? They're Havanas."

"Thank you. On some questions you could call me conservative."

"Ho, ho, ho!" rumbled Churchill. "I can just imagine postwar Europe if the Marshal, appalled by the horrors of Hitler's extremism, because that conservative in political matters too . . . if Russia emerged from the crucible of war a democratic Great Power. You know, gentlemen, right now the golden age of international relations hardly seems a utopia to me. Isn't it time we ceased hostilities for good and all?"

"I can understand the Prime Minister's notion," says Roosevelt. "America's ready to be Russia's peacetime ally. An ally in the business of restoring and reconstructing Europe. Naturally, the Great Powers' common aim must be peace and prosperity for every nation on our long-suffering planet. What do you say, Mr. Stalin?"

Stalin was thinking hard. His right foot must have been desperate to be in polite company for years. It sidled up tenderly for a moment to Roosevelt's left foot, like Little Orphan Annie. Then Stalin's left foot stepped on Churchill's right shoe—it looked like an accident. Churchill stepped right back on it and said, "That's so we won't quarrel, Mr. Stalin."

"Stalin, old pal, listen," shrieked the Leader's right foot. It jumped up and down on the left one. From what I could see, all these visions and high hopes had been too much for it—it was high as a kite. "He's talking business, don't you see? Quit messing with your scummy Marxism–Leninism. You're almost seventy, you prince of pricks—how long can you go on living in a hole with a bunch of shit-eating douchebags like that fishface Molotov and that moron Kaganovich and that sneaky creep Malenkov? Get rid of them! Tell Beria to expose the theory of bases and superstructures for the big lie it is, give the land back to the peasants, loosen the knot around the economy's throat, *live* a little for the rest of your days—be a man, have some fun! You can get it up again like you haven't been able to since the civil war, every church in the world will forgi.e your bloody sins, your glory will shine forth—the real thing, not a fake anymore! Soso, please, I beg you, make a U-turn! Do it! You'll see your real friends come out, strong men weep with gratitude. Make the turn. You know you can!"

The Leader speaks. "But what if it's really impossible now to even imagine Stalin reforming Marxist–Leninist teachings, or going back to NEP—let alone admitting the immortality of the soul or what they call the Demiurge?"

"But why's it impossible, Soso?" the foot demanded passionately. "Just use your imagination!"

"My imagination's pretty poor, but I can see it myself," said Churchill. "That kind of idea goes to your head like Armenian brandy."

"An amazing notion!" Roosevelt agreed.

Stalin was beginning to get the picture too. "The

---

leaders of the Great Powers would take turns carrying out the duties of General Shepherd of World Nations," he said dreamily, after a long pause. "GSWN . . . GSWN . . . for short."

"It's fun being a subjective idealist, Soso. Even if you only do it for a week on Lake Geneva," his right foot went on. "Get a little tan, eat shish kebab with Charlie Chaplin, suck Ingrid Bergman's chocolate tit, Marlene Dietrich's lemon tit. Sing 'Suliko' with Caruso . . ."

Stalin was listening hard to his liberal limb, with a pretty wistful kind of look on his face. Molotov walked up to him, took him aside, and whispered something in his ear. Stalin butted in on the Chief Tale-Teller with a few questions: "He admitted it himself? He named his connections? Was there any kind of physical destruction in the plans?"

Finally he turned to his allies. "Gentlemen, peace will be preserved and strengthened when the peoples of the world can take the business of peace into their own hands and defend it to the finish. You imperialists wanted to soothe us communists with all your talk about the golden age of international relations—at the same time as you're flooding the Soviet Union with your agents. Mr. Churchill, just today our organs dealt with your spy Down. He had insinuated himself into my immediate vicinity. Tsk, tsk! We'll be expressing our regrets to your British Intelligence Service."

"Believe me, Marshal—" Churchill was about to protest when the right foot was off again.

"Stalin's an asshole and a dope! Soon you'll breathe your last and die! Shoot Vyacheslav Mikhailych! Where are you, my Suliko-o-o?"

Stalin groaned and rubbed furiously at his right foot.

"Let's forget about clarifying relations for now, gentlemen. Time we had some lunch and started the conference."

"You're not feeling well?" said Roosevelt.

"My damn foot's bothering me again. Mr. President, I envy you. You're living proof that great statesmen can manage fine without their feet. Well, gentlemen, I'm expecting you for our snack." Stalin got up and limped out of view. They pushed Roosevelt away and Churchill stomped off for his lunch too. I was so hungry, Kolya, I didn't even have any spit left. I drooled out a couple of drops. I couldn't even chew on my shoes. What could I do? I dug a piece of carpenter's glue out of the sofa and chewed that—but it just filled in a couple of cavities. Well, that was a good thing, but I was damn sure I couldn't last too long this way. I went to sleep again. Stalin woke me up. He was yelling at the professors.

"I'm asking you: when will it stop bothering me? Are you doctors or enemies of the people?"

"We're going to prescribe some complex measures that'll do the job, Joseph Vissarionovich. We'll dilate the blood vessels, have a massage, take pine and milk baths," said the big boots.

"But without panic," snapped the fearless bedroom slippers. "No suspicion. We won't threaten that steel-hard spirit of yours. Just rub the foot with a little brandy —I always do it that way myself. A little massage and your foot'll just feel like the greatest part of your body."

So they rubbed Stalin's foot with brandy, Kolya.

"Well?" said the bedroom slippers. "How are you feeling, Patient Stalin?"

Boy, you've had it, dear professor, talking to him that way. But after a moment Stalin said, "Well, Stalin really is a very sick man, even though the whole party, the whole country, thinks he's as strong as an ox. Patient Stalin," he repeated with a little grin. "My foot isn't bothering me. It's warm. What kind of brandy was it?"

"Armenian. Dvin," reported Molotov. The boots and bedroom slippers and galoshes and all the other kinds of shoes started to slip away quietly. But the brandy-logged foot started coming to and singing in a voice soft but full of iron logic:

On the broad plains of our motherland
Our pride and beauty waft unfettered,
And no one in the world, Andryusha,
Can live in sadness better!
Lenin is our falcon!

"All right," Stalin said evilly. "Now we'll see who gets whom. We'll see!"

"We'll twist them around our little fingers, Joseph," Molotov interrupted. "We can look like classic diplomats too. We can soothe the Allies' consciences—and that way win over public opinion in their countries. Look. We agree to a coalition government in Poland, free elections, et cetera. We demand our prisoners of war, and then . . ." Molotov rubbed his leather-covered toe bumps together. The kind of noise little boys make when they rub old rubbers in their little wet hands.

"You're a moron, Vyacheslav, but sometimes you say something intelligent. In the end we'll turn all the agreements they ram down our throats into condoms full of holes. That's true. But just for now we'll be nice, we'll go along with it, we'll act realistic. Transcend our class. What's the news of Kurchatov? Is it so hard to split a goddamn uranium-235 atom in this day and age?"

"Soon, Joseph, we'll have our little toy! The work's going ahead full speed," Molotov assured him.

"Tell them we're finished without it—there's no Russian miracle that'll save us. Without it, we're just dumping in our pants, like that guard. And Churchill will win his little game. Then we'll be tried at a second Nuremberg."

"Stalin's an asshole and a fool, and a miserable piece of shit. Soon you'll breathe your last and die," the foot butted in. "And then you'll rot. Even a thousand atom bombs won't help you any. You think you're going to spend your whole death lying next to Lenin, don't you? Well, I'm telling you, your faithful comrades-in-arms won't let you. Soon you'll breathe your last and die. For a little while you'll be laid out next to your teacher. And then they'll throw you out of the mausoleum like a rat, cover you in garbage, and dump you in a sewer. *Nightingales, nightingales, don't disturb the soldiers . . .* You know who's going to drag you out of the limelight and shove you down the toilet? You don't know? Guess. You can't guess? Ha! I told you not to write *Marxism and the Nationality Question,* asshole, I told you not to go running to that bald devil Lenin with it. You could have grabbed yourself a million and been sitting in a restaurant in London with Ordzhonikidze by now. You could have been Churchill's adviser on the Russian question. You could have been feeling up Crimean Tatar girls. But no, you wanted to play with fire worse than Goethe's Faust. But now you're a sucker—not the commander of all time and all peoples. Give me some more brandy, I've got a few more things to say to you. You'll turn blue when I'm finished with you, pockface."

"You tell me, Vyacheslav, before God," says Stalin. "What are you bastards going to do with me when I pass on?" You should have heard the forlornness of it, Kolya, the tremble in the steel voice.

"Excuse me for saying this, Joseph, but you've been unreasonably depressed lately," said Molotov. "You're going in the mausoleum and you know it. I'm telling you this for your own good. You have to pull yourself out of this depression. Come on, things are going better than ever on the home front and on the battlefield."

"The home front. I left Beria to deal with the home front, but when he propositions an underage girl he doesn't even remember which district of Moscow the Lubyanka's in, let alone the home front. 'I'm going in the mausoleum.' My minister of foreign affairs makes the picture look pretty rosy. What a diplomat."

"I'm telling you, they'll gut you like a sheep," said the right foot. "They'll take out your brains and compare them with Lenin's. Don't worry, there won't be a single worm in your body. But you have a Judas all right. One of those comrades of yours is going to drag you in shame out of your glass coffin and dump you in the dark earth—you can be sure of that. Bloodsucker, murderer, miserable piece of shit!" the foot sang. "You poor lonely turd!"

Right at that moment someone in the cedar tree above them farted deafeningly, like a blast from a cannon. It took Stalin's mind off his tortures in eternity. He said, "Hey! Who's stationed up there?"

"Private Kolobkov, Comrade Marshal!" barked the demoted major up above.

"Well, how do you like the private's life? Did you crap in your pants? Tell the truth!"

"Yes, sir. I couldn't hold it in, Comrade Marshal! I'm guilty. It won't happen again!"

"Why not? You can let it happen again—just don't do it in your pants. Take Kolobkov off his post and promote him back to major's rank again," Stalin ordered. Just when he seemed to be getting in a better mood, his foot must have decided to push him past the point of no return.

"You stinking autocrat, try ordering yourself to feel happy. But nothing can do that—you'll *never* be happy! Never!"

"Don't you worry, me and Joseph Vissarionovich will leave something behind us, even if it's just the deluge," yelled the left foot.

"Don't fret, Vyacheslav, don't fret. We'll see who gets the last laugh," said Stalin, with terrible glee. He snapped an order at Molotov: "Prepare a strategic plan of assistance for Mao Tse-tung. We'll conquer Japan, set up those teeming Chinese millions, and then we'll see who gets the last laugh!" Stalin roared and then burst out laughing. Jesus, Kolya, I finally saw how, just for the hell of it, this wicked bastard was planning to make a laughingstock, total suckers, out of the immortal Soviet people after he died. Just like he had out of the immortal Soviet government and our beloved Communist Party. At that instant Stalin really was the craftiest, most farsighted crook of all time and all peoples. If you've got a moment, just take a look at China, our comrade and brother, our yellow-faced Cain—

with its degenerates and Cultural Revolution and hydrogen bombs and rockets—and say a prayer that it doesn't set its horde of communards on our unhappy superpower.

"*On June 22, four o'clock precisely, they bombed Kiev and declared war,*" the foot crooned. Stalin added: "Send military and scientific advisers to China, Vyacheslav. They can start a center for nuclear research. Russia needs a powerful China. I want to leave it the legacy of a great friend and brother. Ha, ha, ha!"

"It won't make any difference. They'll still denounce you. They'll let all your enemies out of jail, and one night they'll carry you out of the mausoleum and wipe their asses with your *Short Course*, chapter 4. Sucker," the foot said drunkenly. Just then Roosevelt came along and interrupted Stalin and Molotov's chat.

"Good afternoon, Marshal. How's your foot?"

"It's still bothering me, but I'm trying to forget it exists."

"You're absolutely right. I have to tell you, Marshal, I'm shocked by something here that some of the members of my delegation who know Russian told me about. For instance, a gardener was cutting the laurels this morning and saying, 'Up your ass, America!' And later our chauffeur finally managed to get the car started and made a similar exclamation. My advisers heard it twenty-three times. Your chef asked his assistant if the pheasants and chickens had come—he said they had, which didn't stop the chef saying, 'Up your ass, America!' We're allies, Marshal. I demand an explanation. You have to admit we can't sit back in the face of what may be your people's unconscious aggression toward America. How can we guarantee peace worldwide if one of the permanent members of the Security Council can't stop wishing something up another permanent member's ass?"

Stalin and Molotov cracked up, Kolya. A bunch of the advisers moved toward them as though it was a signal. I spotted Vyshinsky's dead-rat-colored pants among them.

"Maybe you won't believe me, Mr. President," said Stalin, "but any of our political leaders here will tell you that there's never been any propaganda against your great regime among the Soviet people. As for the expression you heard, well—Russia's a nation of poets —sometimes it makes my feet—I mean ears—ring just hearing them. Besides, everyone knows that 'through reason Russia can't be known.' In any case, Russians have a tendency to mysticism. Maybe the expression you were surprised by just shows that we'll all end up that way, even the Great Powers with all their colonies and dominions, all of us, even you and me, Mr. President. Let alone Mr. Churchill. Only Lenin lives forever. Anyway, an idiom's an idiom. After the war, I'm interested in doing some work on linguistics. With the help of our agencies, maybe, I might get to the bottom of the origin of some of these expressions. But now, please, gentlemen, let's start the conference."

Churchill came up and said to Stalin, "Let me tell you, Marshal, Colonel Down is not a member of our secret service. But—just in theory, you know—one of your men could very well turn up in my entourage."

"Abakumov, what have you got to say about that?" Stalin said sharply. "Tell me. Mr. Churchill and I don't have any secrets from each other. All they hear over there are stories about our agency's atrocities. So tell us the truth."

There's a pair of boots walking up to Stalin, Kolya. Gorgeous—but there's no creases in the uppers, they don't look as if there's a foot inside them. They look like someone poured lead into them and let it solidify. Now it'll stay that way till the lead melts in hellfire. The boots make their report.

"It's still difficult to put together a total picture of the conspiracy, Comrade Stalin. Even in England it takes more than a day to investigate these very complex cases. But Colonel Goregliad has already given us a lot of valuable evidence. He may be Schirmach and Fillonen as well as Down. He's a very agile, cunning, versatile suspect. He's trying to discredit the Ministry of Health, obviously to revenge himself on Professor Kadomtsev for unmasking him."

"Sly move," Stalin interrupted. "We have to get on, gentlemen. Keep the doctors under observation, and they can keep our health under observation. That way we might catch *someone*—they can't always get away with it. You can arrest that one in bedroom slippers for a start. You can see he's an aristocrat."

"Stalin's an asshole and a fool and a miserable piece of shit! Soon you'll breathe your last and die! You've blown your life completely. Your son's a lush and your daughter can't stand the sight of you! You poor lonely turd!"

"Don't forget the Chinese thing, Vyacheslav. You'll answer to me with your head on that one. It's the number-one priority. I'll show you, I'll make you dance, sweethearts." Stalin rubbed his hands just thinking about the realignment of forces in the world arena and the ruckus in the world communist movement when China sets its sights on Russian and other territories. "I'll cook you up something you'll lick your fingers over. We're going to finish off Germany. We're going to finish off Japan. It's time we helped Mao toss Roosevelt in the Pacific Ocean. Get Kurchatov moving or I'll make Beria president of the Academy of Sciences. I'll show you bunch of hoods what happens when you try to hire my foot. Stalin's a brilliant strategist, and he still has something to live for!"

Those were the last words I could hear, Kolya. Everything went quiet and they started the conference. Major Kolobkov relieved the guard. He got the men down out of the trees and shrubbery, saw they were hopping with impatience, and commanded: "Back to base, on the double, quick—march! Stand up, or you go straight to the front line, shitheads!"

The soldiers tramped by me. I'd been spared death from starvation by an unbelievable miracle, Kolya. The evening before, they'd been getting a little banquet together, and suddenly, presto, something dropped right through the trellised wisteria and grapevines in front of my grating. Before I even reached my hand through the bars, I knew what the bird was that had fallen out of the sky—a goose. A goose, Kolya! But this was a goose roasted for Comrade Stalin—you couldn't describe the taste of that goose in words, Kolya. You had to be there. The devil knows how it got down to me. Maybe the waiter tripped, maybe Stalin thought it looked so gorgeous it had to be poisoned and threw it out the window himself to save his precious life. And Stalin had more than ever to live for, right, Kolya? He left us with a powerful China, and who knows what will happen to our Russia now? It isn't given to us to get a look at the future, Kolya. We're not mountain eagles, you and me, just a couple of regular guys. Hey, how about another drink? No, old buddy, we've drunk to the zeks—the elephants, lions, monkeys, storks, boa constrictors. Let's drink to the guys who look after them! Yes! To the monkey and hippopotamus and bird keepers. Let's hope they don't take away the tigers' and wolverines' meat and the squirrels' nuts and the tomtits' sunflower seeds and the orangutans' bananas and the seals' fresh fish. And let's hope the keepers don't beat up the animals in their cages or tease them or jeer at them.

Down the hatch, Kolya. Now let's get back to the human zoo—back to that stinking camp.

*S*UDDENLY, in the rathouse where we worked, Chernyshevsky yelled at the top of his voice, "Comrades, danger on the left! Chains at the ready! Battle stations!"

I forgot to tell you we were shackled, Kolya. They weren't very heavy, but the shackles weighed on our souls like iron despair. We went to work on the rats and got about eight of them, overfulfilling our plan by two rats. So we rattled our chains and everyone perked up some. We horsed around a little and laid out the rats on stones and gave them names: Martov, Axelrod, Berdyaev, Bogdanov, Fedotov, Mach, Florensky, Avenarius, Nadson. We called the fattest one Vyshinsky. Chernyshevsky proposed we work overtime in honor of Teachers' Day and finish off Jean-Paul Sartre, the uncatchable male boss of the camp rats, in time for Stalin's birthday. The zeks had told me endless stories about this rat. He was huge and sneaky and attacked noiselessly. He only went for the ankles and liked to lash you with his long cold tail when he made his getaway. He could see perfectly in pitch-darkness, although they said he had a cataract in one eye.

You see what kind of punishment Beria fixed up for the Old Bolsheviks. They had to fight rats from morning till night, and there were thousands of them—and besides they had to do it in total darkness. Where did they come from? There were legends about that, too. Let me tell you, there was an infirmary near our camp with a graveyard alongside it—no, a scrap heap for old zeks. The rats stuffed their faces there, and then came down some underground tunnel to our slaughterhouse, just to get themselves some fun. A pretty risky game, right? But the rats just loved it. Makes you think even in nature you can't get by without games. In fact, I think there's some theory based on that. I just kept kicking myself for asking to be sent here. Okay, yeah, a sentence is a sentence, but it's your job to get yourself through it okay, right? What distinguishes us from the pythons and hippos in the zoo? Knowing exactly how long we have to stay inside—although we didn't even know that much till they brought back the "Leninist norms of legality."

I started off by learning how to see in the dark. It was pretty easy. You know I've always liked reading on trains—well, I read somewhere that in the wonderful prehistoric period people had a third eye. Somewhere between the brain and the spinal column, it might have been right on the back of the neck. The total darkness—actually, the *blackness* of the dark—was just torture, and the cold on top of it really got me down. Oh, sure you get used to it, you can feel your way around to kill the time, shoot the breeze, smash up a few rats—there's nothing else to do—but it's just boring. Unbelievably boring. So I said to myself, "You've got to beat the darkness of the moment *and* historical necessity, Fan Fanych, or it'll grab hold of your fate just like the devil!" That's what I said. So I concentrated my mind and all the skill I had in my hands, and started to resurrect my third eye, blind for generations. Beria wouldn't let the veterans of the revolution have matches or get hold of fire in any other ways, however primitive, or let the rays of the sun or moon or stars into the darkness, so I figured Fan Fanych had the right to break the rules, even if he was pretty likely to end up in that cemetery with the rats for good. Yes, sir!

I started by massaging my forehead. No luck. I think maybe my ears itched a little, but I couldn't see any better. I massaged the dent in the back of my neck and had a terrible thought. I got the dent by being hit with a rifle butt back in 1920. Maybe the Red Army rifleman fixed my third peeper for all time without knowing it? What could I do then? That got me very blue. But I worked at it for four months. I found out later that was how long it took Andrei Sakharov to invent the hydrogen bomb as a present for all people of good will, and all this time I'm straining away at my third headlight. I'm not getting anywhere—and then I remembered Toscanini, the conductor. I bet he had a third eye to look at the concert hall with.

In the end I decided to forget about every part of my skull except a little lump like a hillock just under the dent in the back of my neck. I rub it, stroke it, and stroke it again clockwise (you should do everything important clockwise, even pissing and taking back empty bottles). That foul bitch Niurka, the one who sells beer on our street corner in summer? She collects the empty bottles in winter, and if you don't give them back to her clockwise, she either rips you off fifty kopecks or just won't take half your bottles. What did I ever do to her, for chrissake? You know I could care less about fifty kopecks, and I can get Danish beer in cans from the foreign-currency store, but what's the *point* of this petty profiting from the clockwise rule?

To cut a long story short, I worked on that bump under the dent on the back of my neck for twenty-one days, and the hillock began to itch almost like a real eye that was still half asleep. The itching and tickling felt good, and it even got a little damp and dripped a tear. But still zero visibility. It was as dark as ever in the slaughterhouse. Chernyshevsky went on debating whether it had been a mistake to bring in collectivization and dump NEP or not, and I just kept rubbing, rubbing, rubbing at my third eye, blind from temporary disuse. My little sunshine, remember what you used to do for me in the caverns of eternal night, remember! Then suddenly I took my hands off my skull and I could see Dziuba, the boss guard, just a couple of steps behind me in a kind of gray half-dark. Of course I act like nothing's happened. You'd lose an illegal sight organ quicker than a razor when they're frisking you. The great thing about this third eye was that it looked behind me, not straight ahead. Looking sideways was pretty hard at the beginning. But there was Dziuba, and nobody but me could see him. There was something wrong with his face, though, it wasn't like him. There was something normal about it, kind of like the face of some poor dope coming to have a tooth pulled, out of his mind with fear and pain. It was as if inside Dziuba's body, under the Sam Browne and the epaulettes, his sick soul was groaning and groaning and couldn't understand why anyone would want to hurt it so much. I take in the stormers of the Winter Palace with my third eye too. And I could see the same expression in their faces, especially their eyes, as I saw in the face and eyes of Dziuba, People's Jailer of the RSFSR and Jailer Emeritus of the Soviet Republic of Kazakhstan. It was a real nightmare, that expression, Kolya. A kind of final, dumb, teary prayer: Take our souls away! Tear them out! It hurts, for chrissake, it hurts! Isn't it ever going to end? In a word, pain strips a lot of superfluous stuff from a man.

Fan Fanych couldn't stand the sight of this anymore. He wiped a tear from his third eye, shut it, and said, "Look out! It smells of roasted sunflower seeds, borscht, and pork drippings in here!"

"You said it. You can sniff out a Chekist, can't you, snakes? I've got some nice news for you. Nikos Beloyannis the freedom fighter has been shoved in the slammer by world reaction. Don't get too excited. The people are going to rise in his defense. Get out there for the meeting! Line up, and don't lose your chains! Capito, assholes?"

"Hands off Angela Davis!" Chernyshevsky says. "Hands off Nazim Hikmet! We're with you, Corvalán!"

"Shut up, you bunch of cynics! You get three days in the cooler for irony, Chernyshevsky," Dziuba answered.

"Oh, no! Never in the history of the world has anyone been so misunderstood by his political allies! But I'll do the three days in the cooler because you say so, sir. Discipline's discipline, even here. Party discipline's a must!" Chernyshevsky kept on muttering to himself about this on the way to the meeting.

I walk through the camp and look behind me at the zeks, the barracks, the fences, the barbed wire, the watchtowers. My third eye's having a hard time getting used to the landscape here that I know so well. Chernyshevsky says, "Why are you holding your head up like that, Comrade Tarkington? You suddenly have the air of a leader—and you keep looking around you in that strange way."

The dummy was right on the nose. My third eye's field of vision was totally different from the other two. I had to raise my head and turn it around slowly. Of course, when I did this, I couldn't see anything in front of me except the sky and sad gray autumn clouds. It dawned on me that guys who get to be big-shot leaders have a partly open third eye, because they either turn their heads importantly or else they've got very flexible necks, and lean their heads way back and stare at the herd behind them. They screw up their front eyes because who needs them for leading the herd? But what the herd thinks is that the leader can see miles and miles ahead in the distance and has glimpses of things that ordinary mortals can never see—things that are so wonderful, such a glorious life, that they don't grudge sacrificing their lives and their children's, they can stand anything to make their grandchildren and great-grandchildren happy. Poor little things, they'll have all the fruit of our labors, they'll reap the harvest from the ground we watered with the blood of workers, peasants, intellectuals, and soldiers. *They'll* have full bellies!

So the leaders raise their heads to stare at the sad route their people have to take, the people they want to save. But they can't see the abysses yawning in front of them. And they can forget about any glorious future. O Lord, just let our grandchildren have some air to breathe, give them a mug of water and their daily bread, help us to stop turning our beautiful earth, one of your countless creations, into a condemned cell where men suck every crumb of bread and last drop of water from a tin mug before the last moment of life!

To cut it short, Kolya, if your third eye opened one day, if you could see how the executioners and their victims are in torment, and—this is just between you and me, Kolya—you knew you really cared about all of them, then you'd be a normal guy. At a moment like that, it's a good idea to say a prayer for all the poor bastards. But say what you felt was a passionate urge to save everything and everybody, say you just shook with hate and fury, say you thought you'd discovered the real reason for these hellish, inhuman tortures, so you had to change the world and rebuild it so that on the debris of the old life, on some barricade, Nobody became Somebody, Somebody, Somebody—hang on, boys, hang on—then you'd be a Leader, Kolya! Oh, for chrissake, I don't mean *you*, Kolya. You'll never be a leader. Just hang on, boys, hang on, and stock up with aspirin. Now there's a new leader who wants to save you. Move it, bastards! We're hauling you to heaven by the nose and you still drag your feet, you want to be petted as well? Forget it! Go on, move it, jerks! Mush, you dogs, on to the glorious future! Hands off Corvalán!

They took us outside the camp. Stood us next to ordinary free people and warned us we'd be taken care of on the spot if we tried to escape, of course. Then we got the speeches. First some kind of chauffeur scrambled onto the podium. He was so pie-eyed he could barely stand up.

"If there was a real Iron Curtain we never would have found out that those Greek cops had busted Nikos Beloyannis," he said. "Listen, Messrs. Freedom-fighter-murderers, that curtain may look like iron to you, but it's fucking transparent to us! Like glass! Truth doesn't need travel permits or visas, or whatever you call 'em. Get your hands off the Greek people and their eldest son, Nikos, while the going's good, or I'll unload two shifts of zeks on you and put 'em to work. I'll *screw* you!"

His wife yanked him off the podium and swatted him in the mouth a couple of times. "So now where am I going to get your damn paycheck from if they fire you? Help me with this bastard Pashka, good progressive people. He's soaked to his shameless gills again! Hands off women and children!"

They hauled them both off. Chernyshevsky whispered, "Now do you see the dimensions of the task we're faced with, internal and external?"

I said I did and I'd pass everything on to Gallagher.

After the chauffeur, the cute young chief of our camp section got up to say his piece. Oh, he was so pissed about our class enemy's latest move his voice cracked. "Where's your conscience, where's the honor of Hellas? Remember Homer, gentlemen, remember Byron, who gave his life for you! Aren't you ashamed? How could you raise your hand against Nikos Beloyannis and send him to the Tower? Wake up! This is the freedom and democracy you're always bragging about? Freedom to throw the nation's favorite sons behind bars! Listen, comrade . . ." Here Dziuba muttered something to his chief that had him bothered. Beloyannis might be a Greek, but he was also a zek. The chief didn't know what to do and got totally mixed up. First he called Beloyannis "comrade," then "citizen"—that must have been what Dziuba told him to do—and then "comrade" again, so the Greek MGB came out of it all looking terrible.

"Look out for Zeus' anger! Summon Aphrodite to help you! Don't bring shame on the land where fire was born, have mercy on poor sick Prometheus' entrails! Hands off Manolis Davis!"

My poor zeks were yelling along with the free guys and the guards, "Hands off! Hands off Hellas!" Then the head of the women's section of the camp got up on the podium. She also used to sing the bloody little tunes Dzerzhinsky and Yezhov composed, like Dziuba. She said, "Dear comrades, and not-dear-to-any-of-us citizen enemies of the people! I can see Anna Ivanovna Ashkina there in the front row, president of the party regional executive committee—and I say to myself, Where else could a cook run the government? In England? No! The U.S.? No! Guatemala? No! And take me. My husband died at his post in 1939. He used his trusty revolver so much, doing in the worst enemies of the people, that it just blew up in his face one day. So I buried Semyon Semyonych and took his place. My comrades never bugged me once. They backed me up and taught me how to shoot straight. And everything worked out just fine. But what would have happened to me and my kids in America? What do you think? No jobs. I would've croaked right under the Statue of Liberty! You think anyone there would trust a woman with a rotten revolver, comrades and citizens, let alone an electric chair? So I'm adding my voice to the protest. We are with you, Nikos Beloyannis!"

This creep got down off the podium, choking with sobs. "And who's going to bring the poor dear his care packages?" she wailed to the whole meeting. Dziuba signaled to Chernyshevsky. He hustled up to the podium, rattling his chains. He quickly swallowed the lump in his throat and was off and running.

"World reaction has just gone too far! It's time to grab it by the throat. Where else could guards and prisoners stand shoulder to shoulder like this and merge our voices in one angry chorus: 'Hands off Beloyannis!' You tell me, where else! We request that our monthly sugar ration be sent to all the Butyrki prisons in Africa, and that we start an All-Union collection to feed Comrade Beloyannis and help him escape to the Soviet Union!"

Dziuba suddenly interrupted loudly to explain that zeks didn't have the right to call Beloyannis and the carnation in his buttonhole "comrades." To us, he says, he's a citizen.

"We are with you, Citizen Nikos, you are not alone! We are all with you in jail!" Chernyshevsky declared. "Once again the relentless question arises: *What Is to Be Done?* Fight! Fight for the harvest, fight to lower the number of escapes per person from our camps, and for a corresponding increase in escapes per person from reactionary dungeons. Fight for unity in our ranks, and fight against rats of every stripe and the desire to avoid historical necessity. Long live"—here Dziuba yanked at Chernyshevsky's chain—"Long live Citizen Stalin, the torchbearer of our struggle! Hands off Arismendi Angela Beloyannis! Free Corvalán! Death to Solzhenitsyn and Academician-enemy Sakharov! Shame on the murderers!"

"Now, comrade-friends and citizen-enemies," said Dziuba, "we're going to hear a speech by the most reactionary obscurantist asshole who ever existed, who worked as Maxim Gorky's chef and spat in Gorky's fucking soup, as well as his main course and coffee, every day. He spat in them secretly, day after day, and might even have contributed something along the lines of urine and feces, but our agents couldn't make him admit it. Okay, Maryskin, get up here and answer to Comrade Beloyannis. If you can't confess to us, confess to him at least, go on, break down, sing, tell who put you up to the idea of that sickening spittle! Get up on our high podium, snake! Move it, or we'll chase you up there with a rifle butt!"

I saw this little guy move out of the crowd. I hadn't noticed him, since he was a highly unremarkable individual, the kind of guy who always looks like he's trying to hide from somebody, or just sink into the earth. A skinny little guy, the type that looks so pitiful you could hate him just for making you feel sorry for him. And gray as his pea jacket all over. A really gray, hopeless face. No life in him at all—not even his chains rattled when he got up on the podium. He couldn't stop coughing for a long time and then he hawked up, but Dziuba told him he better not spit anywhere up on the podium, this wasn't Gorky's fish soup with piroshki, followed by chicken Kiev. In the end, Maryskin spat on his sleeve. You could have knocked me over with a feather when he came out with this, Kolya:

"Friends! I don't have very long to live. I don't have

to be modest—I'm a fantastic cook. My great-grandfather and my grandfather and my father were cooks. I didn't work for Gorky, I was head cook at the Irtysh, right next to the Lubyanka. One day some investigator found a black lace from an unknown shoe in his macaroni navy-style. They arrested me and I admitted under torture—my lungs are ruined—that I spat in Maxim Gorky's dinner. It's not true! I didn't do it! Never! I'm a cook, good people! And no one's going to blacken my name! Hands off Maryskin! Free Maryskin! I've got a wife and kids in Moscow!"

Dziuba punched him in the mouth, but the little guy just spat out the blood and went on screaming, "Hands off Maryskin! Hands off! Freedom for an innocent man!"

Well, all hell let loose. That scumbag Chernyshevsky was screaming about this double-dealer's unbelievable nerve, putting his personal interests before the interests of the party. Dziuba was yelling at Maryskin to call for hands off Beloyannis, not himself, or he'd bust all his teeth for him and then pour vinegar in his mouth so it'd hurt even worse. But Maryskin just kept right on hollering, "Hands off Maryskin!"

The free guys and the guards dragged him off the podium and mob justice took over. They kicked him again and again in the mouth and on the lips to make that innocent little guy swallow his miserable request just to be left alone and set free. They kicked him and kicked him and kicked him, Kolya, and while they kicked, those pigs—sorry, pigs, I mean people—screamed fit to bust, "Hands off Beloyannis Corvalán! Free Dimitrov and Thälmann!"

But the little guy they were pounding into the autumn

mud said, in a clear, pure voice—Christ knows where he found the strength—"Hands off Maryskin! Free Maryskin!"

Dziuba yelled at us, "Back to camp, bastards! And don't lose your chains!"

Maryskin's lips were a mass of bloody blisters. He kept trying to bury his face in his knees, trying to leave life the way he'd come into it, curled up in a ball in his mother's belly. He'd gotten tangled up in his chains, poor little guy, but he still kept on shouting, "Hands off Maryskin! Free Maryskin!"

We were almost back in camp. It was forbidden to look around when we were marching, so I kept staring and staring with my third eye at Maryskin's little body, which the free guys and the guards were stomping on, mad as hell because they couldn't totally destroy the free man in Maryskin however hard they tried. My third eye wept happy tears—cross my heart and hope to die hanging upside down if I'm lying—because Fan Fanych never met anyone in any country in the world, or in any of its lousy jails, who was as much his own man as Maryskin, who croaked in the autumn mud that day. Glory to him forever and ever!

Make a meal of that one, Kolya, as our internal and external enemies say.

*L*IFE IN our rat slaughterhouse was a whole lot easier for me with my third eye, Kolya. Dziuba took us over there the morning after the meeting and said we had to overfulfill our quota by five rats or we'd work on Sunday too. I took my ax, checked out all the rats' entrances and exits, and barricaded them. As soon as one of the bastards showed its face, I sliced its head right between the ears with the ax. Chernyshevsky made me a Shockworker of Communist Labor. He wanted me to fulfill the quota for the whole year, but I finally got the sucker to realize Dziuba would just up the daily quota of dead rats if we did that and then we'd really be up shit creek. And even if we did finish off all the rats that fast, who knows what kind of creepy-crawlies we'd have to go after then. I'm a terrible chicken when it comes to bats, spiders, wood lice, and other icky things that never did me any harm anyway. Or else Dziuba would send us a bunch of ants, and they're even harder to fight than rats.

Well, I finally got my comrades to see the light, but they still branded me a trade unionist, a pragmatist, a kulak, a petty bourgeois, and White Guardist garbage.

All because I wouldn't try to beat the world record for political-prison rat extermination. So I just took care of the rats quietly every shift. But their boss, the one they called Jean-Paul Sartre, don't ask me why, never showed his cataract and his long cold tail. He was probably urging the rat masses to attack and sending them to the last decisive battle while keeping an eye on our skirmishes from his lair or some other cranny.

I killed the rats because they would have bitten off our legs if I hadn't, and also they make me sick. I took care of them and that made my comrades happy. Fan Fanych did all the work and thanks to him they could sit around for the whole shift discussing the alignment of powers in the international arena, the tragedies of Portugal, Spain, and Yugoslavia, Ilyich's modesty and simplicity, Dzerzhinsky's kind heart, Stalin's iron logic, and the liberation of the whole world when communism comes. Chernyshevsky worked out all the details of an ultimatum to Britain. He gave them a week to exhume Karpo Marx's skeleton from Highgate Cemetery and fly it to Red Square in the true motherland of socialism, where it would be dressed in a suit and beard and placed in the tomb next to his greatest disciple. If those bastards in Britain refused to hand over the skeletal genius, we would have to break off diplomatic relations with them immediately and hold the embassy staff as hostages until the furious British people said "No!" to the Queen and her obedient slave, Parliament. They decided to give Dziuba the ultimatum to pass on to Churchill. If he wouldn't, and pretended he had too much to do in his vegetable garden and his wife was pregnant, Chernyshevsky proposed we all pull out our gold fillings and bribe Pashka the chauffeur. He could mail the envelope, and we'd just have to wait for the House of Commons to go for the House of Lords' throat.

Chernyshevsky also wanted to know how I managed to ax every rat, without fail and with completely unexpected 180-degree turns. "How do you do it, Tarkington?"

I said it was because I looked behind me, not in front, like some people, and I could see perfectly in the pitch-dark.

"Your English comrades should be proud of you, Tarkington!"

I decided to have a little fun, Kolya. Fan Fanych wouldn't be playing any more games once he was tucked up in the damp ground in his wooden overcoat and his last pair of slippers. But while he was still alive he was definitely going to gladden his poor unhappy heart with some magical laughter, whatever blows fate dealt him. So what did I do? I found a sharp stone and scratched some words on a rock with it. I blew the dust off to make it seem as if it was at least a hundred years old and said to my camp colleagues, "I've found an inscription on this stone. We've got to decipher it. Who wants to try?"

Chernyshevsky started reading it by touch, whispering it to himself. I heard him gulp when he said, "Comrades! This is unbelievable—it seems to be a tactile hallucination! Listen to this! It's written in prerevolutionary script: THE SOONER YOU GET IN, THE SOONER YOU GET OUT. KÜCHELBECKER, 1829. Comrades! This is more than just a historical or paleographical discovery! It boldly surpasses all bounds! It proves that under the conditions of tsarist penal servitude—which, as we now see, were the objective catalyst for his thought processes —the great Decembrist's russified mind had left that

235

idealist Hegel's unwieldy and multivolume dialectical system far behind. The dialectic of Küchelbecker, this spiritual leader of all political prisoners, is utterly simple: the sooner he got in, the sooner he got out. More than once we've bitterly regretted not being in the famous rebellion on Senate Square. But that's not the point. It goes way beyond our friendly party envy of our long-since liberated comrades. The point is, our Küchelbecker discovered the theory of relativity long before Mr. Einstein. 'Sooner' is the time category, and 'getting in' and 'getting out' represent the space category. We can see Wilhelm's immortal aphorism as a universal formula that explains all the laws governing the sociopolitical processes in the life of the Russian state and nation. Quite apart from the fact that a verbal formula's always better than a mathematical one, not being light-years too complex for the broad masses. Or for any of us. Now do you realize I was right? Now you understand Stalin's iron logic, his historical rightness and courage when he reluctantly began mass repression much earlier than Bukharin and that bunch told him to, and engulfed the first socialist state's entire territory in the repressions. That's what I call a Marxist understanding of the relativity of time and space! Trotsky and Kamenev and Zinoviev and company wanted the party to put us inside a lot later. But the party said 'No!' and because of that we'll get out much sooner, comrades. The enemy's played his hand—can he have any trumps left at all? Long live Küchelbecker, the great dialectician of Russia and her revolutionary process! Hey! Get Sartre! What's your problem, Tarkington? Get Sartre! It's him! He's biting me! Ouch!"

I missed Sartre that time, Kolya. I got his tail, though.

Hey, old buddy, did you notice I haven't toasted any caged animals since I started yakking about the rat slaughterhouse and all the fun and games there? I thought so. What do you say we drink to rats? Zoos aren't interested in them, they mostly keep them in labs for experiments. But, however sickening and disgusting they seem to us, they feel pain from life and wounds and hunger too, and if we could compare how I feel when I burn my hand with a cigarette, like this, and how a rat feels if its foot gets burned, believe me, Kolya—I can see you believe me by your sad eyes—you couldn't tell the two kinds of pain apart. No way. Human suffering is no better by a single tear or scream or faint than a butterfly's or a cow's or an eagle's or a rat's. That's the only thing I'm sure of. What a dope—I burned my hand for nothing. Now let's drink to every living thing, and hope that no creature ever feels any pain at all—I mean, butterflies flit over fields of daisies and die when their time comes, without anyone laying a finger on them—or at least that every living creature should feel as little pain as possible. As little as possible.

You know, it just occurred to me, Kolya—no special reason—animals in zoos have a lot of upheavals in their lives. For better and for worse. One fine day, crash, and they're carting a tiger away, he's in transit. They chase this proud, untamable creature from one cage to another on wheels and drag it off who knows where. Let's just hope the poor animals don't end up in a traveling menagerie. That's perpetual transit, with all its tortures. Better just to end up in another zoo. New atmosphere, maybe a nicer climate—or the opposite, if the citizens of Archangel or Murmansk can't stand life without a tiger anymore. Then the poor thing really freezes his ass off.

Sometimes they take tigers and other beasts to the circus. You can only guess what kind of boss you'll end up with there or if your keeper's honest enough not to rip off half your dinner.

A few zoo animals end up with the Durovs. But that's the biggest special animal camp, for a few lucky bastards. Take elephants, say. They live for ages, and the Durovs only keep one or two. The rest wait their turn for years and years, and just die that way and never make it. Have you noticed actresses have the same problem? They spend their whole lives waiting for some Yablochkina or other to retire or move to the operating theater, which would make a lot of roles available all at once. But it's as if Yablochkina can smell their hopes, she hauls her wreck of a body onto the stage with a crane, she can barely move, her jaw shakes, she stamps on the prompter's tongue to make him mutter a little louder— and they even say they put diapers on her before the really tragic scenes. She won't leave the Kremlin orchard and the cherry chimes and so forth, all just to spite those poor wasted young actresses getting older every minute. You see, it's her ambition to rot down to her skeleton right in front of that Soviet audience, which as everyone knows is the most attentive and demanding in the world. How the hell did I get started on Yablochkina? Sorry, Kolya. I think I was talking about big upheavals in the camp lives of elephants and tigers.

Finally, they let me out. I sure wasn't expecting it. After the hands-off-Beloyannis meeting where they trampled Maryskin to death, Dziuba didn't show up at our barracks anymore. A mute sergeant took us to the rathouse every day instead. The pig heard every word there was to hear, but he never opened his mouth. He took us there and counted us all over again—don't ask me where we could have got to in the meantime, especially since the underground Bolshevik cell had passed a resolution of Chernyshevsky's saying escape was a violation of discipline that couldn't be tolerated in a member of the party. So the mute counts us again, goes out, comes back nine hours later and counts us again, collects the daily quota of dead rats, and back we go to the barracks. Thanks to my third eye I was zapping rats faster than I used to sort cookies at the Bolshevichka factory. A blow between the eyes with the ax, and there's the rat with all four feet in the air. I was the Stakhanovite of rat-killing. Time kept on passing—but I gave up counting the days and weeks, even the months. Just winter and summer, winter and summer. Like that song young people sing today: "Winter's gone, summer's begun. Thank the party for the sun."

We didn't get the tiniest snippet of news of the outside world. A couple of times the wind blew in some torn sheets of *Pravda* or a bit of *Komsomolskaya Pravda* someone had used for wrapping herring. That way my party guys found out something about the Korean War and Stalin's linguistic researches. They chewed that one over for six months, naturally. It led to endless discussions, schisms, reprimands, retractions of reprimands, party conferences, and internal purges, but Chernyshevsky finally had everyone convinced that Stalin was right, as always.

"Everything depends on language. Sometimes the party and the people speak different languages, which holds up the march of the idea toward its goal. Say, for instance, the party says, 'You must!' And the people say, 'We shall!' The party's certain that 'We shall' means the people have promised solemnly to carry out some historic decision or other, even if they die in the process. But actually nothing happens, although this never crosses the poor party's mind, and it goes on peacefully thinking up lots of other historic decisions, so naïve it never suspects the people are stiffing it on the sly—drinking, stealing, just refusing to get rid of capitalism's blemishes, the good-for-nothings. And only after our great agency's investigated it minutely," said Chernyshevsky, "do they suddenly find out that in the people's language 'We shall' means the same as 'We've had it.'" And if he, Chernyshevsky, were still a member of the Central Committee, he would have pointed all this out to the party and the dangerous slogan would have been strangled at birth. "The words 'must' and 'shall' are natural enemies. We need a cruel, merciless campaign to make the people overcome the language barrier!"

They sang the "Internationale," proposed a toast in honor of Stalin's brilliant intuition, and shuffled the counters around on their homemade international arenas. Our lackluster, rat-ridden days and nights went on, just as dumb as ever. My poor little underground Bolsheviks didn't even know Stalin had kicked off and Beria and some of his hoods had been rubbed out. According to Chernyshevsky's calculations, everything suggested there'd been revolutions in France and Italy, and Red Terror was now raging there. The parties there were just snowed under with work, so they had to get the Mafia and the big gangster syndicates to go to work for the Italian and French Chekas. That was problem No. 1. The U.S.A. was one big concentration camp by now. China had liberated the Japanese, and England was just an island full of unemployed people. The final crisis was stalking through the stock exchanges of the great capitalist countries. The workers of the world were just about to unite ecstatically, set fire to Du Pont, Ford, and Rockefeller, and scatter their ashes on the Pacific Ocean. The world was soon going to be the UCSE—the United Classless Society of Earth.

This stuff was what the Bolsheviks started the day with, yakked about every day while I was zapping rats, and then went to bed with. But all of a sudden they started taking them away, one by one, Kolya. And it looked serious. They took them away with their things —so our comrades weren't coming back. The mute sergeant stopped taking us to the rathouse. Were they doing them in or transporting them? I have to tell you, liberation didn't even cross my mind, Kolya. I certainly didn't doubt Soviet power was for real and here to stay. Finally it was just Chernyshevsky and me left. We cooled our heels playing cards all day, with a deck I fixed up out of Stalin's *Short Course*. I cut out stencils of the suits and mixed the soot I got by burning my boot heel with our piss to make India ink. And off we go. At first he got the suits mixed up, but he soon got into it and then he started to beat me. I was losing ten or more hands in a row. Fan Fanych was up to his neck in debt. I made a great picture, sitting on my bunk half naked, wrapped in a camp sheet, trying to work out why he was whipping my ass like this. But I was in too deep to stop. I started playing for a sugar ration every hundred deals —I ended up hocking my ration right up to the fiftieth anniversary of the Revolution. My opponent used his advantage to make me agree to marking time by this kind of date. We played for two months and I kept on losing. It couldn't have been worse if I'd been playing with the devil himself. I handed over my bread ration up to the KGB's fiftieth anniversary, my soup up to Stalin's hundredth birthday, promised to take out the pisspot till Lenin's hundredth birthday and clean the barracks till Soviet power was established in Switzerland, capitalism's greatest sanctuary. Then suddenly it was over. Chernyshevsky stopped. I have to admit he was within his rights. The international crooks would have shuddered to find out how deep I was in. There was nothing left to play for. I was in such despair I said if they let me out I'd get Karpo Marx's skeleton exhumed and brought to Moscow, if he'd just let me win back my bread ration. I told him this big story about my connections among the gravediggers at Highgate, but no dice. Believe me, Kolya, no crook in the history of the world ever went down the way I did. And not a soul around to help me win a penny back. Maybe beat up Chernyshevsky? Not nice. I'm a fair guy, I don't duck out. I said I'd play ten hands for my life against three days' bread ration. I hadn't eaten a thing for four, five days, maybe. Like they say, tea in the a.m., play all day, meetings in the p.m. I'd scarfed all the rusks the vanished Bolsheviks left behind in their night tables. Can you see me poking around on all fours in other people's night tables, Kolya?

"So tell me, are we playing for my life or not, you devil with goat horns?" I said.

He wouldn't go along, the sadist. You see, it wouldn't be a game anymore then, that would make it a duel to the death inside the party, eliminating one of us communists. And that was objectively playing into reactionary hands.

"All right! I'll do in the mute sergeant and attack the

guardhouse. I'll burn down the barracks and shout, 'Marx's teaching is all-powerful, because it's right!' I'll do anything, but please, Nikolai Gavrilych, if your heart isn't made of stone, just give me the chance to win back one little crust of bread!"

"No, Tarkington, I'm sorry. We've played as far as one great historical landmark, the revolution in Switzerland. That's it. Besides, we're communists. We can't bet on terror. It's better if reaction doesn't have any trumps, and we're not going to give them any, right? Excuse me!"

I mean, Kolya, can you see it? I waited for my special case for years and years. I signed up for it. I dragged out the worst months of my whole life in that No. 3 (Deluxe) cell. I was tried at a so-called trial of the future. I got the death sentence. I died once . . . a phony flight in that bogus spaceship . . . I nearly flipped again that time. Saved by a toenail. I died a second time . . . the camp . . . my third eye . . . my shockworker victory over the rats. Now get this. Fan Fanych is five minutes away from kicking off for good, and how? From starvation. All because he let a crazy goat-faced sick monomaniac with a frozen heart and mind take him for everything he had. He played fair, you know, never sneaked an extra card, I'm no sucker. He just had a gigantic run of luck. You don't know how I used to beg him, out loud and mentally, for a crust of bread or a bowl of soup, just one in four days, like you get in solitary. But that old bastard even managed to surprise me with his appetite, slurping up his and my sugar, bread, and soup rations. It was better just to lie there and buy the farm than ask him for anything, though it was a shame to see Fan Fanych slowly giving up the ghost on his bunk in this absurd way, wrapped up in a camp sheet. I was a candle, burning out, guttering quicker than the wick could burn. There was no way out. No making contacts among the staff. Nobody coming in with sandwiches on trays. I'm burning out. For no good reason I suddenly remembered *Lenin in 1918*. He gave half his bread ration—it might have been the whole thing—to some worn-out worker called Vasily. Chernyshevsky seemed to be reading my mind. He said, "All the same, I always felt closer to Stalin. The other guy was decisive off and on, but basically he was too soft. Just too soft. If he'd started the historically necessary repressions in '23, we would have got out long ago."

I'm burning out, Kolya, burning out. Inevitably. I would have burned out altogether, but suddenly they came and took that prick Chernyshevsky away, with all his things.

"If you ever get out, Tarkington," he said, "tell every communist in the world that our route and experience should be a model for the workers of the world, even if we did make a few mistakes. Victory's coming soon. You can have my bread ration. We communists are humane."

I gobbled the crust down—too far gone for crook's pride. Soon there was soup in the feeding trough, and sugar and hot water in the morning. Fan Fanych was coming back to life—just as well, because one foot had been right there in the grave. I tossed around on my bunk trying to work out what happened. I figured it was the deck of cards that screwed everything up. I thought Chernyshevsky was thinking over every single card real slow. It drove me totally crazy. Of course, what he'd been doing was reading all the bits out of the *Short Course* on the backs of my cards. And on top of it all,

the old prick wouldn't stop humming the "Internationale." I couldn't stand that stupid little tune pretending
to be the most serious song in the whole world, but I
kept my mouth shut, like a gentleman. And tried to
ignore the idiot's way of mumbling "one step forward"
or "two steps back" or "objective reality" or "right-wing
opportunism" or "your left deviationist shall not pass"
or "forward toward armed insurrection," whenever he
played a card. When he played a hand in clubs or
diamonds the louse would giggle, and sing: "But from
the taiga to the British seas, the Red Guard is strongest!"

In other words, there's no doubt that the devil is
equally involved in games of chance, especially cards,
and the *Short Course* on party history. And so, thanks to
our game, Chernyshevsky became Somebody and I just
missed being Nobody at all. Thank the Lord they took
him away.

as long as there's something wrong with his uniform. Like his wife forgot to sew his collar on. After six hours' discussion he'll let you have a smoke. And in solitary, mind you.

"Well, bud, I'd say you've been snoozing like a fireman at the Reichstag. Forty-eight hours straight," said the cop. "C'mon, on your feet. You've just got time for a hair of the dog before the train comes."

"Excuse me, but . . . uh . . . am I, uh, free?"

"Hey, c'mon, bud. Don't play games. I don't like it, not even in my slippers. On your feet!"

"Did I really get loaded yesterday?" I asked the cop. I still couldn't figure out what was going on.

"If you hadn't gotten loaded you would have slept with Zinka the switch girl, not Karpo Marx. She takes care of all you rehabs. On your feet, bud, on your feet!"

I walked about twenty steps away from that fantastic flower bed and took a bird's-eye view of it. The cop was right. I'd been snoring right on Karpo Marx's beard—they'd grown it out of white pansies. It was a little crushed right now, and so were his red tie and blue jacket. Poor old Karpo Marx—there's just no getting away from him—I'd made him look like some old wino with a tremendous hangover who just blew all his capital and surplus value.

"Hmm," I say. "I was pretty far gone, huh?"

"Just thank your lucky stars you didn't pass out on You-know-who over there, or I would've fined you a hundred rubles. Well, pull yourself together and get back where you belong."

"Who's You-know-who?" I said, gawking at the other flower bed.

"Lenin."

"Where's Stalin?"

"In the mausoleum."

"Hey, wait a minute. Did they kick Lenin out, or something?"

"No, they're in there together. But if you ask me, ol' Mustache won't last long. Nikita really pulled him to pieces at the Congress. Exposed him right down to his underpants."

"I get it, I get it," I said. I was catching on finally. "What flowers did you use to make the bald part of Lenin's head?"

"He's wearing a cap—made of black pansies. A zek did them. They knocked fifteen years off his sentence for it."

I felt around in my pocket. I found an official release notice, a ticket to Moscow, and cash—around a thousand. Free at last, Kolya, free at last! The winos can sense what time it is. They're starting to make their way toward the beer stand across the empty, hot, dusty, crummy square. A little old bus brought some tattered peasants and their wooden suitcases to the train. It was as if nothing had happened to me all those years; no one had anything to do with my jail sentence and no one had anything to do with Fan Fanych's liberation. But what the fuck! It *was* liberation! I stood there wondering why the hell I wasn't getting a bigger kick out of it. Maybe the guards did snuff all the life out of me after all? That's what the bastards wanted. But the real taste of freedom's like prewar vodka or a really good old brandy. You don't feel it right away. When you do, though . . . I had an hour and a half before the train came. I talked to Zinka the switch girl and caught up on the new chapters I'd missed in the *Short Course* since I'd been away.

———

Finally Freedom started bubbling in my veins, penetrating my whole soul and pervading Accursed Time and Unhappy Space all around me. Fan Fanych was drunk on freedom, like a rooster on a fermented cherry! I wandered over to the beer stand. A few depressed derelicts were standing around.

"Hi, Beria dragon-slayers! What's your problem?"

"Stepanych won't give us credit. It'll kill us for sure."

"Don't worry, folks," I say. "You're not going to die while Fan Fanych's still alive! I'll fix you up, you history-makers!"

I felt so bad for those poor winos I reminded myself Fan Fanych had hypnotized worse assholes than Stepanych. I didn't care for his face. He'd probably ripped off more than a million. I transfixed the bloodsucker with my crook's eyes till *his* eyes glazed over and his shoulders sagged. And then we partied—boy, did we ever. Stepanych started popping champagne corks and slicing cans open with an ax so as not to waste time, right in front of the amazed winos, who felt just as if they were in a fairy tale. Under my influence Stepanych, on his knees, brought each of them a half-liter mug of brandy and champagne. Then he gave everyone a wad of dough for suits, watches, umbrellas, and teddy bears for the kids. He got up on the counter to sing the "Hymn to Democratic Youth" and "Suliko," and tore up all their IOUs. I hadn't talked to an ordinary guy in so long I was just dying to hear about everything, life and the domestic and international situations, and I got good and loaded, happy as a clam. Finally I suggested to Stepanych he'd better not water the vodka or dampen the sugar or suck people's blood anymore.

Well, here I was in Moscow's Yaroslavsky station, not

a cent to my name, but an official release notice in my pocket. I looked pretty terrible, but that didn't bother me. "Mud on my boots/ On my pants and jacket grime/ But jail's behind me—I've done my time . . ."

I stood in line at a phone booth humming to myself, clutching five kopecks in my hand for the magic call. The ladies near me turned up their noses. They didn't care much for my cheap boots and my ugly old gray canvas jacket. I dialed a number even Kidalla couldn't make me forget.

"Hello, Stalnoi," I said. "Still lying around reading comic books? Well, get up, on your feet, shake off the fleas. I'll be over in half an hour. *Adieu!*"

The cabdriver didn't want to take me, just sat on the running board sneering. Take a louse like you? What for? I told him: "Get behind that wheel, pervert! Take me to the Lubyanka, Gate 3, and make it snappy! You want to wreck our whole operation, asshole? I'll bust your axle!"

The cabdriver—they're a low, petty, cowardly bunch—dived into his seat like a tank commander on red alert, grabbed the steering wheel, and screeched off under the bridge, across Domnikovka Street and Ulansky Boulevard onto Sretenka.

"Make a left at the red light. Honk four times and stop shaking, jerk!"

He put his foot down and swerved onto Sretenka right in front of a tram, tires screaming. When he heard the honking, the guard saluted me, just in case, and the driver almost crashed into the gates under the sign KGB RECEPTION. I grabbed his log and wrote on it that the cab had been requisitioned for operational purposes and the driver had to give anyone a ride who asked, without griping, from beggars to counterespionage officers. Step up your educational work, comrades. Don't place cabs above the state. Signed, Major Pronin.

The driver read the note. His jaw dropped and he tore out of the gates. I walked over to Stalnoi's pad.

He was my antiquarian consultant. I went into his house-museum, and just stood around for a while admiring the Impressionists, the Chinese bronzes, the chandeliers, and Robespierre's escritoire. Then I changed my clothes. All this without a word from Stalnoi, who was playing with his engraved stones. I took fifty thousand out of a Dürer commode and said, finally, "So, tell me, Stalnoi, what kind of chair was Louis XVI sitting on after they pronounced his death sentence?"

Stalnoi spread his hands.

"A wet one," I said. He was an intelligent adventurer, he could appreciate my grim little joke. And he knew it had something to do with my own—unkingly, thank God—fate.

We sat around awhile, brewed coffee in Tamerlane's own pot, and shot the breeze about some of our deals. I just didn't want to go one little bit. Was there anywhere more comfortable or dignified to savor life in than this warm house-museum, surrounded by wood, glass, canvas, cloth, and metal things that never forgot for a second the love their makers had created them with, which guaranteed them an endless, almost cloudless old age? I pushed off in the end, just hoping none of his glorious or shabby things would ever end up on the barricades, nor we the people on the rack or in death ovens.

I HEAD HOME. Everything was just the same on the streets. "Glory to the CPSU." "Glory to Labor." "The Printed Word Is the Strongest Weapon." "The Party and the People Are One." "Long Live Our Beloved Government!" "Forward to Communism!" "We'll Catch Up and Overtake Them!"

This stuff is hard for an ordinary guy to understand. I never saw any slogans like "Glory to the Labour Party!" or "Long Live Our Beloved Conservative Government!" in England, or in France or America either. Well, maybe for stuff like Senate elections. When they throw dough around over there, it's for advertising—and at least they get something back for the money. Anyway, all those Glories and Forwards are just blinding me on my way home—they got me thinking how there's nothing to advertise in our country except the party and labor and immortal Ilyich—but I still couldn't figure out who got anything out of it. But yeah, sure I can. Every day our leaders go off to work at the Kremlin or the Lubyanka or Old Square and squint out of their car windows at all this crap and say, "That's right, that's the way it ought to be. Long live us. You can see we're doing a great job. The people don't praise us for nothing. Long live us!"

Well, to hell with them, Kolya.

The apartment door was open when I got home. There was an unbelievable stink. Some woman in a gas mask was spraying the baseboard, a sofa, end tables, easy chairs. Right there in our communal foyer. I yelled at her—I guessed it was Zoika. She didn't hear me. I held my nose, rushed in, and nudged her. She turned around and collapsed on the sofa. I took off her gas mask. It was Zoika, sure enough. She'd just gotten a little fatter.

"When I saw you, I thought the insecticide was making me crazy or the gas mask wasn't working right. Look, I'm trying to get rid of the bedbugs and cockroaches. Those bedbugs are just impossible," said Zoika.

"Where'd the bedbugs come from?"

"After you went, they just started breeding. We never had them in the apartment before!"

Then I remembered how I felt sorry for the bedbug and pushed it under Zoika's door before my trip to the Lubyanka. "Go on, live," I said then. "After all, bedbug, you were meant to live five hundred years." So he found himself a girlfriend, or she found him, and they had a lot of little bedbugs and pestered Zoika. And life had gone on here without me.

I took my key out of its hidey-hole and went into my den. It smelled okay—I'd left the vent window open. Let the lightning get in if it wants, I thought when I left. But then I heard a piercing chirp. A couple of sparrows with butterflies in their beaks flew into the room, saw me, and flew out again. They didn't dare come in and flapped around outside the window. There was one nest on the sideboard, another behind the picture of "Me in Venice," and a third in my top hat. There were hungry little baby birds opening their beaks wide in every nest, stretching their little necks, skinny as an old camp veteran's. The floor's covered with droppings and there's a six-year-old bottle of brandy on the table, both of them spattered all over. The bottle looks like it's been gathering dust in the Duke of Orléans' cellar for years. How many generations of sparrows were born and grew up here while I cooled my heels?

"Let's get rid of them, too," said Zoika. "Like the bedbugs."

"I'm not getting rid of any of them," I said. "They'll fly away by themselves in a month or two. Maybe sooner."

"How are you going to live with a bunch of sparrows?"

"I'll manage. If you saw the people I've put up with, you wouldn't worry about a few birds."

I went over to the window and opened it so the mamas and papas would have an easier time getting in with their catch. Right there on the sidewalk opposite—that's fate!—was the same dear little girl from six years ago, running into the bakery in high-heeled shoes, carrying a purse! I couldn't be wrong, Kolya. When I was saying goodbye to freedom, counting off my last moments, I looked out of the window and saw her in her brown dress and white pinafore. I guess she was about fifteen then. I said firmly to my old buddy Cupid the sniper, "I'll take the rap as usual, okay?" So Cupid let off a long automatic salvo straight to my heart, and I shouted out the window, "Hey, miss! Miss!"

She stopped. She thought the shouting must be for someone else. I hollered again. She turned her little face up and said, smiling, "Do you mean me?"

I yelled, "You come right up to apartment 7!"

She shrugged her shoulders, but I waved very urgently and she crossed the street. I could hardly believe it.

I plunged out of the insecticide stink onto the landing. Onward and upward, Kolya!

"Excuse me," I said. "I'm a very intuitive guy. I had this feeling from a distance that you know something about biology."

"That's right—I'm studying biology at the university. You've guessed it—if you really didn't know anything about me before, I mean."

"I couldn't have known," I said. "By the way, don't worry about the smell—we're exterminating bedbugs. Hold your nose, please, and come right in. I want to show you something cute."

I said I'd noticed her watching the sparrows sympathetically—well, I hadn't exactly been in a position to notice any such thing. The kid's name was Galya. I took her into my big nest and told her how it got that way. Galya started catching flies and dropping them in the nestlings' beaks. I told her a few of my stories and she cheerfully cursed Stalin out. He'd done in two of her aunts, her cousin, and an incredible number of her neighbors. She asked me if I'd read Pasternak's poetry in camp, and finally we uncorked the bottle I'd left waiting for me. The sparrows decided to brave the danger—they couldn't let their kids go hungry—so they were flying in and out cheekily. If you don't mind, Kolya, I'll jump ahead a little here and move the story along. Galya went home. She was back again in a couple of days, bringing grubs for the nestlings and begging me to tell her everything I'm now telling you. When I got to the trial, she burst out crying, kissed me on the cheek, and said, "I ought to become a woman if I'm going to hear all this, Fan Fanych . . . excuse me . . ."

You better believe it, Kolya. We didn't leave the nest for several days. And then it was only to buy something to eat. *L'amour*, old buddy, *l'amour*. Then the sparrows flew away. They got their feathers and off they went. I had to clean the whole place up. Sorry, I'm running ahead again. Galya and I had a little talk and she went home. I was just pie-eyed from Freedom. Let's pray I don't do anything really dumb, I thought. My head was spinning. I should have just stretched out on that guano-covered sofa, had forty winks, and slept off this crazy feeling. Not a chance. Fan Fanych just can't sit still. I started by cleaning the droppings off the Marie Antoinette table Stalnoi offered me a fortune for. All I said was *"Jamais!"* I cleaned it up, walked around it to admire it, went out for a bottle of vodka from the grocery store, and stopped on the corner where the beer stand was.

I said to that awful bitch Niurka, "Half a liter," and gave her a coin. Niurka held back the beer, so it came gushing out, mixed with gas, like oil out of a new well, so full of foam you could put out the fire in the Reichstag with it. Niurka gave me the change with her other hand. Finally, she looked up, and she recognized me all right. Her puce-colored face swelled up so much she couldn't open her trap. Only her sneaky, bovine, piggy eyes kept on flapping open and shut. Wolf Messing himself couldn't have hypnotized Niurka into pouring more beer after the foam had settled. I waited with my usual aplomb. There were a couple of other guys waiting too. But Niurka was frozen to the spot. The beer—well, the foam—was already running over the rim. Suddenly Niurka, in her white coat, turned blue and crumpled up behind her counter. She crashed to the floor. Fan Fanych had to wrench off the padlocked door, drag Niurka out by her blue legs into the fresh air, splash beer on her horrible face, and shout in her ear, "The inspector! The inspector!" Believe me, Kolya, she came to right away, and I gave the clamoring winos their beer, pouring it out ever so carefully. I had a couple of mugfuls myself, munched on a pretzel, and said to Niurka, "I think you'd better spend a year inside. You'll slim down, and then maybe you won't die of a stroke. Besides, the sooner you get in, the sooner you get out."

I left Niurka thinking hard, Kolya, though not even Sherlock Holmes could have detected any trace of thought on her face. Then Fan Fanych jumped in a cab. "The Lubyanka. Wait for me outside Reception."

When we got there, the cabdriver asked if he'd have to wait long. I said very solemnly I'd be somewhere between twenty minutes and ten years. Just stay cool! I went up to the window.

"I have to see your prosecutor for special cases—he must be a colonel by now—Comrade Kidalla," I said with an English accent.

They told me to wait. In about five minutes a middle-aged cop in civvies came into the waiting room.

"Good morning. May I see your papers?"

"Here's my release notice."

He took me to a little room somewhere. There was a

dark square next to Lenin's picture where Stalin had been, and a bronze bust of Dzerzhinsky on the desk. I explained I wanted to find out about Kidalla's state of health. I could talk to him on the phone, but I wouldn't mind getting together. Don't worry—no emotional outbursts, revenge, liberal hysterics, et cetera. I just felt a spiritual, historical necessity to hear or see Comrade Kidalla. For one thing, I wanted to thank him for fate's bringing us together in so many ways. If it hadn't, I never would have gotten to know the most beautiful girl in the world, who was running to the bakery in her brown dress and white pinafore on the black day when they put me inside. So could I see him? I have to tell the cabdriver something.

"You've had a couple of drinks—you're a little excited. Don't send the cab away, because you're not going to hear or see any Kidalla."

"What happened? Did they bust him? I mean, they threw him out of the agency?" I said, extremely surprised.

"There's never been any citizen by the name of Kidalla working in the agency," said the cop in civvies.

"Come on, buddy, don't give me that crap. Just take a look in my dossier. I'm not just anybody, I'm Fan Fanych. I'm a sweet guy, but I've stood up to prisons in the New World and the old one. Kidalla's the bozo who investigated my case and cooked up the trial of the future. I'm Cariton Ustinych Newton Tarkington, who viciously raped and murdered Gemma the kangaroo on a night between July 14, 1789, and January 9, 1905! I've done my time, and now you give me this shit about Kidalla never working in the agency."

"I think you'd better go straight to the psychiatric

clinic, Fan Fanych. It was ex-Major Mokhnatov who investigated your case, not some Kidalla. He's an ex-major because they purged the agency of guys like Mokhnatov when the party brought back the Leninist norms of socialist legality. And quit running yourself down this way. You never raped or murdered anybody. You were arrested and falsely accused of attempting to assassinate Kaganovich and Beria. You're going to be rehabilitated and you'll get a free trip to the writers' colony in Peredelkino. Goodbye."

"Excuse me, but why the hell should I want to go to some writers' colony?" I said like a dope. I was pretty flabbergasted.

"There are many writers who didn't go through your experiences who need labor-camp material urgently. You can tell them a few horror stories about Beria when you're shooting the breeze at mealtimes, or around the pool table. Then they can write it all down. It's useful. Now, goodbye."

"Goodbye. You can tell the president of your committee, General Serov, that I can respect total loss of memory. And say hi to Kidalla, if you haven't disposed of him altogether. And tell Serov something else—Fan Fanych is no sucker. He's not signing himself into the loony bin. *Adieu*. You can go off to the writers' colony instead of me."

Well, what do you think of that, Kolya? Nice, huh? After all I've been through, they say I need a cure! Those barefaced assholes—they're really some new breed. What a world! My poor cabdriver was going out of his mind. When he saw me, he wagged his tail, squealed with joy, and practically licked my face.

"Where to, sir?" he said.

"The zoo, kiddo, the zoo. Don't you know that criminals always want to go back to the scene of the crime?"

"You mean the amnestied zeks and the rehabs?"

"You got it," I said. "You're a bright kid, Vasya."

I TOLD HIM to drop me off at the service entrance on Bolshaya Gruzinskaya and thanked him for waiting outside the KGB, a pretty nerve-racking business. Then I repeated everything I'd done in the movie at my own trial. I looked shiftily around and made like I was going to sneak in the back door, without really knowing why I was doing it.

"Citizen! Citizen! Your pass!" I heard what hack writers call a strangely familiar voice. I went on walking as if I hadn't heard a word. "I'm telling you, stop!"

I turned around and there was Rybkin the watchman, large as life and twice as natural, maybe a little older, with his Stalingrad medal pinned to his decrepit jacket.

"Hey, it's the actor! Hello!" said Rybkin, as if we saw each other all the time. I rushed over, threw my arms around him, shook him by the shoulders, and kissed him. The old lush powdered his nose so his bosses wouldn't see how purple it was, but he still stank of beer and port wine. Somehow I felt a kind of kinship with the old guy.

"Hello, Rybkin, old buddy!"

"They don't let up, you know. You have to play the cop from morning till night," said Rybkin. "Well, you just have to take it. My relief man had two sables and a big beaver ripped off yesterday. You know how much that's worth in foreign currency? Let's step into my shack," said Rybkin, staring at my bulging breast pocket.

We knocked a few back. I kept telling him I was just old Fan Fanych and no kind of actor, but he thought it was a big joke and said I ought to get myself back on Antabuse at the clinic, or the DTs would get me, like what happened to some black man from one of the African embassies. He drove up to the zoo one night in a cream-colored Ford and climbed over the fence. A cleaning lady found him in the crocodile pool the next morning. He was sitting in the water, crying, while the terrified crocodile was crouching in a corner somewhere. When he sobered up a little, he told the agency he boozed because he was so homesick for Africa, and he'd already sneaked in more than once to spend the night in the elephant or antelope or monkey house. They threw him out of the country less than twenty-four hours later—didn't even let him have a hair of the dog.

"Can you imagine what it must have been like getting on a plane without one single drink?"

"I sure can," I said. I'm not going to be able to convince Rybkin I'm me. He and the phony Fan Fanych acted, drank, got paid, and ate lunch at the Actors Union together. Whenever I tried to explain, he just said, "Let's have another—and stop the bullshit, okay? Turn it off for a while."

"Okay," I said, after I'd run out for another bottle, "did they kill the kangaroo or not?"

"Sure they killed it. Or else there wouldn't have been any movie. It was all just like it really happened."

At this point, I dropped my head in my hands. My buzz was gone. I don't know how long I sat there like that, but Rybkin must have thought I'd passed out. He left and shut the door quietly. Why hadn't I picked an attempted assassination of Malenkov, Kaganovich, Molotov, Bulganin, and their sidekick, Shepilov, instead of raping Gemma? What would it have mattered? Nobody ever really thought of killing those dummies—I mean, you might try assassinating a real *personality*, but shitheads like them are just a dime a dozen. I wouldn't have spent any more time inside, and the poor beast would still be alive and well. I'm no good. Besides, Nikita would have given me the Medal for Valor, if he was in the mood maybe even made me a Hero of the Soviet Union, like General Nasser. And what about the private apartment and the dacha? Here's to you, Kolya! Let's drink to the memory of poor innocent Gemma . . .

"Rybkin," I shouted. "Rybkin!" But he didn't come back. I went over to the window and saw him frisking some architecture students and checking their blueprint tubes.

"Well," I said when he came back. "Did they kidnap any cobras? An otter, maybe?"

"Kids nowadays! There's no souls inside 'em, only tapeworms," said Rybkin. "Feeling better?"

"When did you see me last?" I said.

"I guess a month or two before the Generalissimo died. Then you vanished. Well, I thought, he was fed up. Picked up and went off on tour."

"Oh, yeah? So they got him out of the way, huh?"

"Who?"

"Me."

"Well, so what did they do with you—uh, the other guy?" Rybkin asked. Sometimes ordinary people just love talking to types who they think are total loonies.

"They locked me up in a rat slaughterhouse. It was pitch-dark—like before the Creation. Let's have another, Rybkin."

"Ha, ha! So what did you do in this, uh, slaughterhouse?"

"I clobbered rats between the ears with an ax. I had to fulfill a quota."

"Well, I've got you now, actor! How the hell could you have hit these rats at all, let alone between the ears, if it was pitch-dark? Come on! You're not crazy, you're just a little confused. Get ahold of yourself! You know, I see rats too, around ten minutes before the DTs start. Sometimes it's black geese wearing white felt boots and carrying Mother-Heroine medals in their beaks."

"Here's looking at you, Rybkin. But I swear I was killing rats."

"Okay. Suppose you were. How did you see 'em?"

"This third eye opened up in me. It's right here on the back of my neck. Feel it. Don't be scared."

Rybkin approached my head as if it was the plague.

"Liar! I've got a bump just like that on the back of my neck."

Jesus, I get so pissed at all the people who can't believe in a higher reality, who deny our tragic, joyful existence, even if they're basically decent types. I told Rybkin I'd bet him a bottle and go stand with my face to the wall. We made the bet. I stood in a corner and pulled out the radio plug to shut up Yuri Levitan and his hundred thousandth ton of iron ore produced by Norilsk cottonpickers. I stood there and massaged my third eye. I could see every move Rybkin made, no sweat. First he stuck his tongue out at me. Then he made a rude gesture with his finger, pulled a face, silently poured out half a glass of vodka, and gulped it down. He stood his rifle on the floor, barrel down, wondering what to do next. Weird—he couldn't think of anything. Deep thought. He buttoned his fly, moved the picture of Krupskaya noiselessly from one wall to another, made a face again, contorted his mouth to keep himself from laughing, took off his boots, sniffed his foot rags, put the boots back on, saluted ten times, rubbed his medal on his sleeve, checked some people's passes, stuck his tongue out at me again good-naturedly, went to open gates for the camel and tiger in their cages, came back, stared sadly at the bottle, and sighed. My guess is he was ashamed of swigging that half glass without me.

Essentially, Rybkin acted like he didn't believe for a moment that I could be looking at him, but deep down he was still scared out of his mind. What if my third eye really was working, and he, Rybkin, was making all these faces and rude gestures, and saluting some invisible guy—he had to look like some kind of loony himself. I just stood there. Not saying a word. The old guy couldn't take it anymore. He powdered his purple nose, took another silent swig and a bite of cheese. He didn't even smack his lips that loud. He was so terrified that he might actually be being watched, it did a lot for his manners. He wasn't making faces now, just goggling at my back with a warm, friendly, kind look on his face—and a tinge of guilt.

"Okay, okay, that's enough crap. Turn around, actor."

"You lose," I said. "But don't worry about the bottle. I'll get it myself. You're a great guy, Rybkin."

He blew his lid, just went out of his mind, called me every name in the book, said I was a lousy actor with DTs and nothing better to do than make fun of an old soldier, and on top of that I had no intention of paying back the thirty rubles I'd borrowed while they were making the movie.

"Go get that bottle, or you'll get a taste of my rifle butt that'll clear your head pretty fast!"

When he'd finished, I told Rybkin everything he'd done in detail, except the crummy part where he drank the vodka without me—you could forgive the guy a real human weakness. He frisked me—thought I was looking in a mirror. It took all that to make him give in. But then he really gave in.

"Wish I had a third eye like that," he said. "I could do both shifts here. These two could sleep and the other one could watch, and then the other way around."

I went out again for another bottle. We shot the breeze a while longer, but there was no way I could convince Rybkin I was Fan Fanych, not some actor. He wouldn't even look at my release notice. He said only real screwballs had stuff like third eyes. He told me a couple of stories, one about his wife buying salt pork at Tishinsky market to make cabbage soup. Well, somebody'd just kidnapped a young South American boar from its pen in the zoo. The cops came with a German shepherd dog. It headed straight for Rybkin, so he figured the boar had been done in and sold at Tishinsky and he smelled of boar meat, a kilo of which cost about five rubles in gold. Luckily, he had an alibi—he'd been sleeping it off down at the drunk tank. Then he told me how one time a colonel rolled up in a black car and showed the director of the zoo some kind of paper. The director went off and caught a peacock for him personally. It was stuffed in the car trunk. Rybkin knew for sure they'd taken the peacock to the Kremlin and let it out in the great big office where Stalin had been trying to persuade Marshal Tito not to screw around with the international workers' movement, for five days straight. The peacock paced up and down the room for two days, worrying. So did Stalin. Tito just sat there gloomily on his chair without a word. Finally the peacock displayed itself in all its glory, and Stalin said to Tito, "So what's your problem, buddy, puffing yourself up like this peacock?"

"Your mother . . ." was apparently what that no-good bragging marshal said.

Stalin called in Malenkov and said, "Take him away."

"Which one, Joseph Vissarionovich?" asked Malenkov.

Stalin paces up and down the room for two more days without a break, puffing on his pipe, while Malenkov stood to attention, no lunch, no dinner, waiting for him to say which one to take away. Tito must have been struggling to keep from dumping in his pants. Finally Stalin said, "Take the peacock away." A moment later he said, "They still say he's the best and most beautiful bird in the so-called free world. Unlike some former eagles."

Apparently Tito gave a big sigh of relief and asked to go outside. He went out and didn't come back.

It was Rybkin who took the peacock out of the trunk of the same black car with his own hands when they brought it back. It had been off its rocker ever since and never spread its tail anymore. Now Nikita and Marshal Tito were drinking buddies. They stuck to triple-distilled vodka—it doesn't give you a hangover.

"I'm sorry, actor. I did something terrible. I had a drink without you when you were standing in the corner," Rybkin said suddenly. He burst into tears.

"Hey, old-timer," I told him. "I just thank God I fell for a gorgeous chick and met a great guy like you today. Thank the Lord! So what? So—you drank it. Big deal."

"It was bad. I thought you couldn't see me. It was real bad! I'm sorry. Only for chrissake stop giving me this crap about meeting me for the first time today."

"Okay," I said. "Here's what I owe you. But you loaned me three thousand when the producers paid us, not thirty. Remember?"

I had a hell of a time convincing Rybkin he'd gotten five thousand old rubles, not two—I said I took three to buy a TV and so's he wouldn't drink the lot.

When we said goodbye, Rybkin said to me, "I guess sometimes you don't think a guy's crazy and he really is. And sometimes I guess it's the other way around. Take care, and don't go visiting the kangaroos. You'll get the blues again and go right off the rails. I mean, I still have to work here, you know."

Well, I was pretty far gone, Kolya—I hadn't been doing much hard drinking all those years—but I still found my way to the kangaroo. I went up to the fence feeling just like I was going to meet a girl. My heart was thumping. It might just have been the vodka. It's more like arsenic every day. You think they're doing it on purpose? Everything looked just the way it did in the movie, but no kangaroo in sight. Hey, that was where I raped her, poor Gemma, just over there, and there's where I kept stabbing her with the knife, and that's where I finished her off. Suddenly a kangaroo come loping awkwardly out from behind a green shed. I looked at the sign: Kangaroo, "Gemma." Born 1950. She was the double of the one they killed!

"Gemma!" I cried. "Gemma!" She comes up to the fence. "Hello, baby." I threw her a French roll. "So it was you I was going to blow up, you and your mommy, when I put a hand grenade in her pouch? And you were saved!" I said. "Haven't you gotten big. And pretty. Eat, baby!" I stuck my hand through the bars. Gemma breathed warmly on it and poked her quivering nose into my palm. Only a computer could think Fan Fanych was capable of screwing and murdering some poor foreign animal. We're still better than machines and Kidallas think.

"Eat up, baby, eat. I'm going to bring you packages every week. I'll get you corn and wheat, I'll swipe greens for you in the botanical gardens. If you were in the Hamburg Zoo, I'd buy you out and put you on a boat for Australia with an official release notice, but here . . . I'm sorry, all power belongs to the soviets, and there's nobody we can ask what to do. What can we do, Gemma? What's going to become of us? Do you have any idea how many years of my life—eat up now—I left behind in that terrible experiment? No? And why me, do you know that? I don't either. But I think I

270

don't know because my soul is stupid and imperfect. Tasty? I love bread, too. I've fallen for a girl, Gemma. Listen to me—she's life itself! You've got Fan Fanych for a faithful friend now, you poor little orphan."

"Citizen!" It's a cop, Kolya. "Are you feeling all right?"

"Fine. Terrific. *Toujours* terrific, *monsieur l'agent.*"

"You shouldn't be talking to the animals in an intoxicated condition," he said. A young guy. Replacing Beria's thugs. Polite. "Did you just come to Moscow?"

"You said it," I say. "Wanna drink?"

"Where from?"

"The other day," I said, "I woke up free in the middle of a heap of daisies, objectively speaking in Karpo Marx's beard. Re-hab-bi-bi-bi-li-li-li . . ."

He escorted me to the exit. I took his arm and hollered fit to bust, "Free Gemma! Free the ocelot! Free the feline family and the suborder Artiodactyla! Hands off hyenas and jackals! We are with you, polar bears! Free the elephants and tapirs! Hands off the antelopes and gorillas! Hands off chimpanzees and sea lions! You can't crush our friendship, you can't kill it, you can't kill it, you can't!"

I got home in my cab without any more trouble. But when I walked into the building, I heard the unmistakable voice of a professional colleague behind me. "Signor Fanfani!"

"Sì, sì!" I said. We talked in Italian. He said he'd been sent to find me by Don Pasta, the capo of a small Chicago-based gang. He was pretty amazed when he heard I'd only been outside for five days. We went upstairs. The nestlings were cheeping. I had a little brandy left in the bottle and we slugged it back. He acted cool and collected, even when he got some sparrow poop on his shoulder. He didn't seem like a wop.

"So how's Don Pasta doing?" I said.

Don Pasta wasn't doing too well—in fact, it looked like he wouldn't be doing anything at all pretty soon. So he'd been thinking over who he might choose to carry on his good work, and he'd picked me. I had the experience of working in rough sociopolitical conditions, I had a spotless reputation and was devoted to the cause. I didn't have much Italian blood, but it was enough to come down hard on any mafioso who'd gone too far. What did I think? He'd like an answer in two days, since the trip home might present a few problems.

"Then how did you . . . uh, get here?"

"Truth travels without visas," said tl.e emissary in broken Russian, grinning like a bandito. I didn't beat around the bush. I just told him I couldn't accept Don Pasta's flattering proposal. I had a hell of a lot to do at home. The biggest financial operation in history. Hundreds of billions of rubles. The Italian's eyes were popping out. I explained a little. The government, and Nikita Sergeevich personally, was really pissed at the people. It turned out the government was in debt from handing out stacks of bonds in return for stacks of loans for years and years. The people had gotten pretty used to all the drawing and cashing-in, and their appetites had gotten bigger and bigger. The government kept on having to give them back huge amounts practically every month. After all, it all started when the people kept pushing the government to borrow money off them to get agriculture set up and developed. It led to an abnormal situation, with the government bled white by

272

its own vampirish, usurious people. The party said, "Enough!" Nikita told them to put a stop to this disgusting state of affairs. "Hands off the official loan repayment schedule!" "We say no to our greedy people!"

"You see, *signore*," I said, "I really have a lot of work to do here."

"Your boss Khrushchev is one great mafioso!" the *signore* enthused.

"He inherited our glorious mafia from Stalin and had to get it out of the mess it was in. What can you do? You've got to have your finances in order," I said. "So *ciao, amico, ciao*."

"Is that your last word?"

"Signor Fanfani doesn't throw his last words around lightly. Say hello to Don Pasta and tell him to get well soon. And a big hello to Maestro Toscanini too. *Ciao!*"

I saw him out and went by Zoika's to watch TV. Some big-deal conference. I wasn't too surprised when I pointed to the screen and told Zoika the third guy on Nikita's right was Chernyshevsky. We were inside together and I lost all my clothes and my sugar and bread rations to him playing cards.

"Our oldest party member, one of Ilyich's comrades-in-arms, one of the men who helped storm and capture the Winter Palace, Nikolai Gavrilovich Chernyshevsky, will now take the floor . . ."

I went off to bed. I lay down on the sofa, but I couldn't sleep. I'd totally sobered up. I thought about my girl, the way a boy does. The quiet in my soul was warm and dark, the only sounds in the world came from the sparrows rustling their wings and the blind nestlings squeaking in their nests. I thanked the Creator for revealing this vision of Freedom to me and bit my lips,

terrified, remembering the epileptic Bolsheviks screaming from their bunks in the night, and how I had to
sort out that bellowing, shrieking human mess. Thank
God that was all over.

Oh, Kolya, my little girl Galya should be getting back
from the Crimea any minute. Let's take the empties
out to the yard and not cash them in for once. Look
how many we went through! Pretty good, guys! We'll
get rid of them, clean up my little chick's nest some, and
go by the Beriozka, that glorious store commemorating
the October Revolution and Stalin's constitution. Let me
tell you how I got hold of the foreign-currency coupons.
One day the international legal bureau calls me in and
says:

"In accordance with the last will and testament of
the Australian millionaire James Clark, you are to receive an inheritance of £200,000 sterling."

"Did this guy get the wrong address?" I asked.

"No. There has been no mistake. The inheritance has
been waiting for you for seventy-six years. It was willed
to the first man of any nationality to rape and viciously
murder a kangaroo, stabbing it with a knife fourteen
times. So everything tallies. Sign here."

"Hey, wait a minute," I said. "The agency has no
memory of that. Now they say I was sentenced for attempting to do in an anti-party cell while Stalin was still
alive. They said the kangaroo story was just delirium
and camp paranoia and stuff like that."

"You're no dope. You have to realize we're talking
about a huge amount here. Foreign currency. The
country needs it. If we waste any time, the news will
travel all around the world, and there'll be mass mur-
ders and rapes of kangaroos all over the place by

false pretenders to the inheritance. The party considers you to be Clark's only lawful legatee. Sign here."

I wasn't in a hurry. I ask, "Was he maybe a little nuts, your guy?"

"Kangaroos made frequent raids on his fields, ravaging them, and toward the end of his life Clark developed a grave form of kangaroophobia. He jumped around on all fours and carried a pouch full of gold on his stomach. When he died, he left the strange will you see here. The cultural attaché at the Australian embassy heard about you from the leaks about your crime and court case, and the deal was set in motion, with Nikita Sergeevich's approval. Sign here, please, for the amount of 221 rubles 86 kopecks."

"What do you mean, 221 rubles 86 kopecks?" I said. "What do you take me for, you rip-off artists? Just fork over that £200,000 sterling right now and convert it into coupons, no haggling. The late Mr. Clark's wishes have suddenly become sacred to me. I want to abide by the will."

A very smooth-looking big shot came out of the inner office. Hair parted down the middle. Gold-rimmed glasses. Chic cuff links. A suit straight out of the Forty Years of the Soviet Union exhibition. Holding a cigar. "Come in, Fan Fanych, please." We went into his office. On an elegant low table were scotch, bananas, Coca-Cola, seltzer, sandwiches, and Japanese beer crackers. The beer itself had the honor of being on ice.

"So shoot, Comrade International Jurist. This international crook's listening," I said. "But no fibbing. I'm not wet behind the ears, you know."

To cut a long story short, Kolya, after I suggested we raise a glass in the eccentric old Aussie's memory, he told me how they'd got to the sum they were offering me. There was some law or instruction or something that said they had to pinch seventy-five percent of my pounds right away. Then I was supposed to transfer some huge amount out of what was left to the peace fund. Then there were deductions for childlessness, income tax, not being a party member, vacations—and *then* they stuck me with guess what, Kolya? Yep, you got it. These pigs had the nerve to ask me to pay out an incredible amount in gold rubles for dead Gemma, and child support for the artificial feeding and upkeep in the young animals' enclosure of her little orphaned kangaroo baby. Well, I had to take the whole thing with a big pinch of salt and laugh it off, Kolya. If I'd tried to take it seriously I would have gone out of my mind with hate and anger.

"*Jamais,*" I said. "You can take your two hundred and shove 'em. I don't want it. I'm calling Australia tomorrow. Hands off Mr. Clark's will!"

The smooth guy laughed and said, "Take my advice, Fan Fanych. Sign it. You'll get your dough. We'll see you get a couple of hundred more—we'll forget about the deductions for vacations and we won't charge you for the cost of the court proceedings and the filming."

"*Jamais. Adieu.*" I got up to go.

The smooth guy roared with laughter again. He appreciated the humor of the situation more than I did, needless to say. "Sign it, Fan Fanych. There's still a lot left—enough for three years' shopping in Beriozkas. I have to tell you, Nikita Sergeevich was very insistent. If you don't accept the will, I'm afraid you're undermining the nation's foreign-currency supply. You know what that means, right? It's not my idea, believe me."

"That's really great," I said. "Us poor old crooks and jailbirds have to be taught how to carve up someone else's dough. I'm really impressed. Well, don't let me get in your way. But you have to knock off the per diem and room deductions, for malnutrition reasons—and pay me for killing 570 rats at current rates."

"Okay, okay," the smooth guy said. "I like a business-like attitude. And I can also let you have the defense attorney's fee and the cost of the beer and sandwich. Total: 2,701 rubles even. Sign here."

Those bastards had even tried to rip me off for the beer I wanted in the intermission between court sessions, and my pre-death salami sandwich. Bastards.

Don't think it was Nikita's threats that made me see the light, oh, no. I was fed up with trying to get the cooks who run our country to play by the rules. And what was the point of being greedy? Take the money and run, and hope to God they don't catch up with you —that's my motto. Greed has finished off more than one crook, you know. It even did in a crook on the level of Adolf Hitler. And one day it's going to do in Soviet power—sucking people's blood just for laughs, destroying innocent souls, wearing out their strength and keeping the human spirit humiliated for half a century.

So I signed, Kolya. I could hardly believe all of fate's twists and turns and how little we know about the chain of events. That's why you can always count on a decent bottle of vodka from the Beriozka, or a sausage that tastes the way a sausage used to taste, or jeans and a fur coat for Vlada Yurevna, and all the other trash you can buy on every street corner for ordinary cash in regular countries. Beriozkas, Kolya, Beriozkas! Was it really worth massacring sixty million guys just to open those stores? It's crazy! I'm running on ahead again. I never finished telling you about that first day back in Moscow, how I finally dropped off and called you after I woke up. Well, what's to tell, when we know the rest? I called you. We went out to Vnukovo airport to a bar under the roaring planes. Do you remember the toast I proposed, Kolya? Nope? I do.

"To you and me," I said. "Here's looking at you, Kolya! God grant it won't be our last. Let's drink to Freedom, old buddy!"